Poets of Modern Ireland

Poets of Modern Ireland

TEXT, CONTEXT, INTERTEXT

NEIL CORCORAN

UNIVERSITY OF WALES PRESS
CARDIFF
1999

© Neil Corcoran, 1999

British Library Cataloguing-in-Publication Data.
A catalogue record for this book is available from the British Library.

ISBN 0–7083–1513–5

The right of Neil Corcoran to be identified as author of this work has been
asserted by him in accordance with the Copyright, Designs and Patents Act
1988.

Typeset at University of Wales Press
Printed in Great Britain by Dinefwr Press, Llandybïe

For Daniel John Corcoran

Contents

Preface

This book collects a number of essays on modern Irish poetry, some of which were written for specific occasions and in response to specific invitations. I have, however, revised these, in many cases extensively, and I hope that they combine with the newly written essays to tell one interesting story about their subject. Although I want them to tell this story in the form of individual but related entities, it may provide a useful initial orientation for the reader if I review some of the preoccupations of this volume, which are also, obviously, the reasons for my continued interest in, and enthusiasm for, this work over the years.

Modern Irish poetry is the subject of a great deal of critical contention. In the argument between varieties of 'post-colonial' criticism – which some consider to be 'nationalist' criticism under a new name – and a range of 'revisionist' positions, much of this poetry has been given an intense scrutiny, which has issued in some highly charged polemic and debate. This argument surfaces for consideration at various points in these essays, and it is itself inevitably part of the structure of reception in which any individual critic now reads this poetry. It surfaces as a political issue even in the matter of nomenclature. Some of these essays, for instance, refer to an entity I call 'the poetry of Northern Ireland', even while discussing the work of some poets – Seamus Heaney, Derek Mahon – who have explicitly repudiated the label in the interests of a commitment to an all-Ireland understanding of the island's literary culture. In my introduction to a collection of essays by various hands published in 1992, *The Chosen Ground: Essays on the Contemporary Poetry of Northern Ireland*, I justify the nomenclature of my sub-title by urging that this poetry has its own distinct history and context, which makes it meaningful to treat it as a separate body of work shaped by a specific and analysable set of political and cultural circumstances. This seems to me still to be the case, but in this regard there may well be a distinction to be drawn between the work of poets who continue to live in Northern Ireland, and that of those who have long since left. Since usage of the phrase may, in some quarters, also appear to imply ease with the continued separate existence of the place in its current political arrangements, I should probably emphasize here that, in this book, 'the poetry of Northern Ireland' means a poetry which refers specifically to some of the political events that have occurred there since 1969, or to their cultural contexts; it in no way refuses assent to the impulses behind the repudiations of Heaney and Mahon.

With regard to Austin Clarke and Padraic Fallon, the poets of the Republic of a previous generation whom I discuss, the critical arguments outside Ireland have been relatively muted – and, indeed, in Fallon's case, within Ireland too, since his work, with its odd publishing history, has been very little known. I am attracted to their solitude and singularity, to their prickly or unaligned and in many ways heroic fortitude and patience, and to the resilience of their negotiation with Yeats, as members of the generation that followed him who had to find a way of standing – rather than kneeling – in his enormous shadow. In this respect, I hope that these opening essays effect both a useful introduction to, and a continuity with, the others, since in the work of contemporary Irish poets too Yeats continues to be complexly and sometimes surprisingly negotiated. The manner in which he is written into the scripts of the poets who have succeeded him may itself be regarded as a prelude to (and is conceivably one reason for) the many relationships of cross-reference or intertextuality among contemporary poets themselves, and between their poetry and the work and figure of Louis MacNeice. Indeed, this poetry sometimes seems a theatre of internal citation, a polyphony of resourceful or cunning echo and answer; and in some of these essays I attempt to listen in on these exchanges and to offer an account of their significance. The process in fact begins in my opening essay on Yeats himself – the Yeats of *The Winding Stair* – in which I locate, and develop an argument about, a significant intertext for the volume in a poem by the Irish-language poet Anthony Raftery; in which I contest Yeats's summoning to his symbolic tower of a number of exemplary presences in the poem 'Blood and the Moon'; and in which I offer interpretations of subsequent encounters between the Yeats whose profile may be derived from this volume and MacNeice and T. S. Eliot. In MacNeice's criticism, and in a haunting moment of Eliot's poetry, Yeats figures as a crucial element of self-understanding and self-definition. The moment in Eliot, in the 'Little Gidding' section of *Four Quartets*, is also, as I indicate in another essay, of considerable relevance to the representation of the poet in debate with the ghosts of his personal and cultural life in Seamus Heaney's sequence 'Station Island'.

The concept of the 'exemplary' in Heaney's earlier critical writing has relevance to all of this, but it extends too beyond any merely local application. Indeed, one of Heaney's exemplars is the American poet Robert Lowell; and in my essay on Derek Mahon I show how Lowell is also, although in a very different way, a crucial influence on this poet. I also examine there Mahon's subtle and corrective exploration of the Irish trope of exile. America provides a significant elsewhere in the work of Paul Muldoon, too, whose '7, Middagh Street' locates Louis MacNeice and W. H. Auden there, in debate with Yeats and with each other. Ireland and America supply the poles of one instance of what Heaney has called 'place and displacement' in this poetry; and the whole idea of place – Yeats's Anglo-Irish Coole Park and Ballylee, Clarke's dilapidated and repressed early and mid-century Dublin, Fallon's Athenry, Heaney's South Derry, Ciaran Carson's collapsing and endlessly altering Belfast – and what might undermine it, provide another centre of critical enquiry in these essays, and one of the primary contexts I attempt to chart and probe.

Place in this poetry has strong political connotations too, however, since the places of Ireland have been, or continue to be, fought over; hence I examine central instances of the intermeshing of a topography and a politics, and also of this poetry's own scrutiny of the possible relationships between poetic form and political subject-matter, emotion, instinct or, indeed, prejudice. I also give attention to the fascinating, and much revisited, trope in which a politics is bound together with sexuality, in a poetry which is, in any case, frequently the scene of a rich textualization of the sexual and the erotic, from Yeats's Crazy Jane poems to Michael Longley's poems of botanical species. If this possibly has its roots in a reaction against illiberal or repressive religious structures – both Catholic and Protestant – that may be one of several reminders to us that in this poetry, too, religious impulse, or at least the ghost of religious feeling, persists much more clearly than it does in most recent poetry in English. There is ample testimony in this writing to the survival of energies which some (including at times these poets themselves, it

would appear) regard as profitably long since abandoned by the
sophisticated sceptical intelligence; but the poetry is sufficiently
sophisticated – and sometimes sufficiently sceptical about its own
scepticism – to recognize and explore, even while at times detaching
itself from, such deep, if residual, Irish structures of feeling.

One further persistence figures frequently in this poetry: that of
the Irish language itself, sometimes in acts of translation, sometimes
in referential gesture or imitative form, sometimes as a more remote
or approximate nod of recognition. The presence of Raftery in
Yeats's 'Coole and Ballylee, 1931' may, in this regard, be considered
paradigmatic: the almost exhausted remnant of the Gaelic tradition
rises to a sudden, newly disturbing kind of life. The closeness of this
other language to the consciousness, and linguistic consciousness, of
some of these poets, and the political exacerbations or sorrows of its
current desuetude, are therefore registered in some of their work.
The fact of the Irish language, however, and its persistence in the
forms of English spoken in Ireland, are reasons why some of these
poets retain it as an aim to register, with authoritative force, the
individuality of an Irish accent or timbre in the language of English
poetry – that aim which surfaced long since with Yeats and the
Literary Revival. This characteristically pushes this poetry towards
original, experimental and occasionally subversive structures and
forms, and often results also in a thematizing of language; in a more
than usual instinct for the energies of etymology; and even, at times,
in a foregrounding of textuality itself which has affinities with, and
may be usefully interpreted in relation to, some kinds of postmodern literary and cultural theory: hence, in particular, my
importation of Jacques Derrida to focus an issue in Ciaran Carson.

These, then, are some of the contexts and intertexts within which
I situate or site this poetry. I conclude my essay on Michael Longley
with a brief reading of his poem 'The Ghost Orchid', which opens,
self-referentially, 'Added to its few remaining sites will be the stanza /
I compose . . .'. The poem, that is to say, is itself situated here as the
place where what would otherwise vanish forever from the world
might be preserved; and the poems I discuss in this book are the
remaining sites of complex, intelligible, sensitive, graceful and
exceptionally articulate movements of the consciousness as it
defines and confronts its personal and cultural history. I also like,
though, in Longley's lines, the idea of the stanza as a 'site' of
potential permanence, since the word 'site', so prominent in literary

criticism and theory at present as the definition of the place where 'contestation' might occur, is here redirected towards composure. Many of the poems I discuss are, of course, written from, or about, sites which are the scene of violent contest; but the poems themselves, at their best, offer testimony to the effort at integration, the will to accord, which alone can inflect contest towards composure.

St Andrews, 1998   Neil Corcoran

Acknowledgements

Some of these chapters, or sections of them, first appeared, usually in substantially different form, in the following journals and books: *Agenda*; *Irish University Review*; *Princeton University Library Chronicle*; *Thumbscrew*; *Yearbook of English Studies*; *The Chosen Ground: Essays on the Contemporary Poetry of Northern Ireland*, ed. Neil Corcoran (Seren Books, 1992); *Irish Writing: Exile and Subversion*, ed. Paul Hyland and Neil Sammells (Macmillan, 1992); *Louis MacNeice and his Influence*, ed. Kathleen Devine and Alan J. Peacock (Colin Smythe, 1997). I am grateful to the editors and publishers for permission to reprint revised versions. An earlier version of Chapter 1 was first presented as a lecture at the Thirty-ninth Yeats International Summer School in Sligo in 1998.

I want to thank all those who commissioned essays or conference papers from me, and would like to remark particularly on the several Ulster Symposia run by the University of Ulster at Coleraine in collaboration with Colin Smythe which I have attended; they have been occasions of great good cheer and intellectual stimulation.

'The Briefcase' from *Madoc* by Paul Muldoon is quoted by permission of Faber & Faber Ltd. and Farrar, Straus & Giroux, Inc.

'Bog Cotton' and 'The Linen Industry' from *The Echo Gate* by Michael Longley are quoted by permission of Michael Longley.

'The Ice-Cream Man' from *Gorse Fires* by Michael Longley (Secker & Warburg) is quoted by permission of Random House UK Ltd.

Architectures of Yeats: perspectives on *The Winding Stair*

I

The title of the volume *The Winding Stair and Other Poems* (1933) advances an idea of continuity with that of its predecessor volume, *The Tower* (1928), even as it suggests a disjunction from it. The continuity is, of course, the architectural conception itself, in which the titles of both *The Tower* and *The Winding Stair* gesture directively towards the various architectonics to be read out of both volumes. There is the literal architecture, first of all, primarily that of the Norman tower, Thoor Ballylee, in which Yeats intermittently lived, and of the Big House, especially Lady Gregory's Coole Park. This literal architecture is redolent of the Anglo-Irish, notably in what Yeats considered the cultural high point of their eighteenth century, and of the modern Irish nation, attempting to find a shape on the other side of a civil war. There is in the volume, too, as there is to some degree in *The Tower* (notably in 'Among School Children'), an architecture of the self or, indeed, the body, in which a set of symbolic or emblematic correspondences is arranged by the poet's emphatically fore-grounded and self-aware utterance. There is a figurative architecture of psychology and sexuality in which, notably, the crucial choice of perfection of the life or of the work in the poem 'The Choice' is imagined as the abandonment of a 'heavenly mansion' for a condition of 'raging in the dark', and in which, in the Crazy Jane poems, 'Love has pitched his mansion in / The place of excrement'. And there is, finally, an architecture of the utterance itself, which is primarily but not exclusively to be recognized in those well-dressed stanzaic patterns of *ottava rima* in such central works as the Coole Park poems, sections II and III of 'Vacillation', and the extraordinary poem 'Her Vision in the Wood' from the sequence 'A Woman Young and Old'. The architectural command of these stanzas is the product of the merging of an almost theat-rical representation of extreme emotion and an almost glazed polish or finish. They are stanzas which inflect exacerbation towards composure, but in gestures whose effect of compensation still carries with it the effortfulness of the will imposed. The poems are therefore manifestly yet a further phase in the endless quarrel with oneself; which is, of course, poetry.

Yet, as I say, if these kinds of architecture maintain continuity with the preceding volume, the title *The Winding Stair* gives notice of a disjunction too. It signals a move from exterior to interior, from unyielding straightness and assurance to anxious circuitousness; from, it may be, phallic authoritativeness to a tempered or even shaken insecurity. The disjunction is enforced by the way the later book occasionally makes explicit reference to the earlier: when, for instance, the new poem 'Byzantium' calls back to 'Sailing to Byzantium'; when the sequence 'Blood and the Moon' offers correspondences with the sequence 'The Tower' itself; and when 'A Woman Young and Old' matches the earlier sequence 'A Man Young and Old'. This move has, also, its gendered dimension; and, although C. L. Innes is perhaps too assured in her claim that 'while the tower is a phallic symbol of masculine power and intellect, the winding stair is a symbol of female sexuality', it is certainly true that women figure extensively in the volume.[1] The book opens with a poem 'In Memory of Eva Gore-Booth and Con Markiewicz' and closes with an evocation of Antigone consigned alive to the 'loveless dust' because of her anti-patriarchal rejection of the will of her father, Creon. Between these poems, the book includes a hauntingly metonymic representation of Lady Gregory in old age in the poem 'Coole Park, 1929', further revisitings of the permanent Yeatsian poetic site that is Maud Gonne, notably in 'Quarrel in Old Age', and, in the sequences 'Words for Music Perhaps' and 'A Woman Young and Old', some poems in which William Butler Yeats, Nobel Prize winner and Irish senator, who has, in *The Tower*, described himself as 'a sixty-year-old smiling public man', speaks as a woman.

I am emphasizing the relationship between the titles of the two volumes partly because its significance is manifestly deliberated by Yeats, since there is in fact no poem in the book actually called 'The Winding Stair', despite the fact that the volume's eventual title on its 1933 publication was *The Winding Stair and Other Poems*.[2] The deliberation alerts us to the psychology and aesthetic actually at work in the book. I want to look, then, at the two places in which the title figures: lines spoken by the soul at the opening of 'A Dialogue of Self and Soul', and lines from the second section of 'Blood and the Moon':

> I summon to the winding ancient stair;
> Set all your mind upon the steep ascent,
> Upon the broken, crumbling battlement,
> Upon the breathless starlit air,
> Upon the star that marks the hidden pole;
> Fix every wandering thought upon
> That quarter where all thought is done:
> Who can distinguish darkness from the soul?
> ('A Dialogue of Self and Soul', 1–8)

The material of *A Vision*, which Yeats first published privately in 1925, lies behind this poem, as it does behind many poems in the volume, with its masks, antinomies and gyres, and the support-structure of interrelationship can be sensed in these lines. Yet they also present, as many other poems in the volume do too, some-thing more nakedly unsupported or unaccommodated: that is, the poet making a reckoning in advancing age, and indeed after the very recent experience of a life-threatening illness.

The reckoning is in fact figured less as a dialogue than as a judicial process and review, and the winding stair is the symbolic site of that process. As such, it promises the opportunity of ascent at the same moment in which it registers the reality of slow progress and disintegration; and what obtains psychologically is the effortfulness of self-recognition and the extreme effortfulness, at this point, of attempted self-renewal. The stair is the place where an instruction in concentration is given, but ambivalently directed towards another place where 'all thought is done', which possibly puns on 'undertaken' and 'over' or 'finished': a place, that is, which might offer genuine renewal – psychological, emotional or imaginative – but which may, equally, insist on the termination of all such capacity in this ageing 'Self'. This pun on 'done', if it is that, would be in harmony with what I also take to be a pun in the Self's subsequent definition of the phase of human maturity as 'the finished man among his enemies', where 'finished' suggests both 'polished' or 'perfected' and 'exhausted' or 'terminated'. When the poem subsequently attempts an evocation of the circumstances of reincarnation as a willingness 'to pitch / Into the frog-spawn of a blind man's ditch', it is surely permissible for the non-believer in reincarnation to read the lines as a fiction of heroic self-renewal at the very extreme of effort. The adequate symbol for this element in the volume would be not Sato's Japanese sword itself as it figures in 'A Dialogue of Self and Soul', that sword which the writer keeps beside his pen, but the ragged embroidery in which it is wrapped which 'Can, tattered, still protect, faded adorn'; and the lyric forms Yeats is brilliantly inventing in such poems as these manifest the mind in all the convolutions – even, indeed, the convulsions – of intensely difficult self-definition.

If this is a matter of aesthetics – the poet shaping a form in the teeth of an urge to formlessness or disintegration – it is also, clearly and redeemingly in the volume as whole, a matter of confessional psychology. This poem, for instance, culminates in the speaker joyfully casting out remorse, that emotion which, it may be thought, has no place in the apparently deterministic cycles of Yeatsian character and history. However, as more than one commentator on these lines has urged, it is not for Yeats (or for anyone else) to cast out remorse, but to seek forgiveness. And yet later in *The Winding Stair*, in the fifth section of 'Vacillation', he appears to say something remarkably like this himself:

> Things said or done long years ago,
> Or things I did not do or say
> But thought that I might say or do,
> Weigh me down, and not a day
> But something is recalled,
> My conscience or my vanity appalled.

These are the lines that T. S. Eliot makes over into his own verse in that section of 'Little Gidding' devoted to the partly Yeatsian figure of the 'familiar compound ghost'; and Eliot's dialogue with the lines, and indeed with the figure of the Yeats of *The Winding Stair* in the *Quartets*, may be taken as testimony to his recognition of something I think palpable in the volume as a whole: the fact that, as Terry Eagleton has said in another context, there remains something in Yeats 'which cannot be simply flattened out as dialectical'.[3] The poems 'A Dialogue of Self and Soul' and 'Vacillation' are dialectical, and the sequence 'Vacillation', as its title declares, is itself internally dialectical; and critics, from Louis MacNeice in the 1940s to recent employers of the Bakhtinian and Kristevan models of carnivalesque and polyphony in relation to Yeats, are of course right to emphasize the lack of a unitary self, the idea of subjectivity as fracture, display and drama in the poems. But the dialectics propose an apprehensible synthesis too, in which the bundle of accident and incoherence is much closer to the surface of the intended, complete thing than Yeats's theory would allow. The synthesis, that is, lies in the visible and audible effort these poems make to turn the one into the other, an effort which registers as strain in the very fabric and texture of the verse. *The Winding Stair* is a title that alerts us to this, and presents us with a poet, in the words of Thom Gunn's finely Yeatsian poem 'In Santa Maria del Populo', 'resisting, by embracing, nothingness'. Louis MacNeice was well attuned to this element of the work when, in his critical study of Yeats, he entitled his chapter on the later poetry with a phrase taken over from T. E. Lawrence: 'the ash of poetry'.[4]

I say that this element figures 'redeemingly' in the volume as a whole because I think there are things that require some kind of redemption in some of the attitudes to death on display in the book. The poem simply called 'Death' is prominently positioned as the volume's second poem:

> Nor dread nor hope attend
> A dying animal;
> A man awaits his end
> Dreading and hoping all;
> Many times he died,
> Many times rose again.
> A great man in his pride
> Confronting murderous men
> Casts derision upon
> Supersession of breath;
> He knows death to the bone –
> Man has created death.

W. J. McCormack has written persuasively on the ways in which attitudes to death and reincarnation are deeply complicit with an authoritarian politics in Yeats; and this poem was occasioned by the assassination of Kevin O'Higgins, the Irish Minister for Justice responsible for the judicial murder of over seventy republicans after the founding of the Free State in the 1920s.[5] Widely known as 'the Irish Mussolini', O'Higgins attracted Yeats's approval. The derision cast by the O'Higgins figure on death in this poem, however, clearly implicates Yeats too, and it seems to me that nothing in the rest of the poem – not even the mordant, almost Beckettian pun of its penultimate line – prepares us for its final statement. I take it that the line 'Man has created death' means more than merely that humans, unlike animals, fear death because they are self-conscious. If the line meant only this, the poem would reduce to an extended tautology since this is, of course, explicitly the thought of its opening lines. Louis MacNeice struggles to interpret the line and eventually decides that what Yeats means is: 'I, W. B. Yeats, am old and soon shall die. But only because I choose to. Death is one of my inventions and I choose to try it out.' MacNeice is forgiving enough about this, reading it as one element of Yeats's late paradoxical vitality – the vitality, he wonderfully says, 'of Cleopatra waiting for the asp'.[6]

But surely, with its attendant belief in reincarnation, this is so far from the way most of us think about death – or, rather, have thoughts of death thrust upon us – as to have really very little to tell us. Further, it turns the largest metaphysical question into a kind of empty theatre and a grandly rhetorical bravura; and it is of interest that when Seamus Heaney writes very positively about attitudes to death in Yeats, compared to those in Philip Larkin, in the essay 'Joy or Night: Last Things in the Poetry of W. B. Yeats and Philip Larkin', he ignores the poem actually called 'Death'.[7] This poem almost demands, that is to say, the complement or antinomy of the more humbled and chastened consideration the matter receives elsewhere in *The Winding Stair*, in the poem 'At Algeciras – A Meditation upon Death', where this coldly forbidding theatre is replaced by the far more arresting and distressing shapes of self-examination and self-rebuke. That poem's final stanza stages another judgemental encounter, now between the poem's speaker and the minatory figure of 'the Great Questioner':

> Greater glory in the sun,
> An evening chill upon the air,
> Bid imagination run
> Much on the Great Questioner;

> What he can question, what if questioned I
> Can with a fitting confidence reply.

The line 'Man has created death' in 'Death' is uttered with an apparently great confidence, whether fitting or not; but here, antithetically, the speaker is put in a position of anxiety about how answers may be found with 'a fitting confidence'. The implication clearly is that there may be no confidence at all fitting to this occasion, and the poem is estimable and sympathetic because of its vulnerability, in a way that points forward to one of the greatest of all Yeats's poems, 'The Man and the Echo', written shortly before his death, where any vestige of final confidence is put in jeopardy by the only answer the human questioner himself now receives, the scathingly undermining one of the echo itself. Indeed, it could even be argued that 'At Algeciras' casts its retrospective shadow on the poem 'Death' by making its last line appear less a firmly held belief than a desperate desire; less an insistence, against all the evidence, that this poet, W. B. Yeats, will not really die, than a defiant outcry against the imposition of death that 'Man' must assuredly suffer but has most certainly not 'created'.

Thinking further about the title *The Winding Stair*, I turn now to the lines in which the phrase recurs in 'Blood and the Moon', a poem once more proposing a set of symbolic and emblematic associations for the tower, Thoor Ballylee:

> I declare this tower is my symbol; I declare
> This winding, gyring, spiring treadmill of a stair is my
>   ancestral stair;
> That Goldsmith and the Dean, Berkeley and Burke
>   have travelled there.

This mimes what the philosopher J. L. Austin, in *How to Do Things with Words*, calls a 'performative' – a speech act in which 'the issuing of the utterance is the performing of an action'.[8] It wills something into being by the very act of announcing it; and the catalogue of names takes its place in the extensive onomastics that is Yeats's whole poetic corpus. Here, the names of those whom Yeats considered the flower of the Anglo-Irish eighteenth century are called upon to establish a tradition for the poet and his poetry in the face of what he elsewhere calls 'the filthy modern tide'. This harmonizes with a rhetoric characteristic of certain aspects of the Modernist endeavour and is, in Yeats, given sanction by the ideas of *A Vision*, in which the modern period occurs at gyre's end; it is also given epigrammatic expression in very short poems in this volume such as 'The Nineteenth Century and After' and 'Three Movements', where the aristocratic tradition of the epigram receives a further jolt of disdain and *hauteur* in modern poetry in English.

Critics such as Deane and McCormack have argued for the absurdity of Yeats's conception of a unitary Anglo-Irish tradition here; and the strain shows up as an over-insistence in the lines.[9] The performative declaration demands a repetition which, far from seeming authoritative, appears merely vulnerable, and vulnerable furthermore to the charge that, in asserting this unlikely inhabitation of his tower, Yeats is in the throes of self-delusion or self-aggrandisement. 'You were silly like us,' said W. H. Auden in his famous elegy for Yeats; but this is surely to be silly in a way quite unlike the majority of 'us'. Not so much resisting nothingness by embracing it now, indeed, as attempting to raise an architecture with no foundations whatever. Yet if the winding stair here represents the circuitous route of Yeats's supplying himself with good connections, it is also, in these lines, the site of a self-confessedly extreme difficulty – a 'winding, gyring, spiring treadmill'. The metaphor of the treadmill both puts the poet into a kind of prison and sets him on an unlovely path of monotonous routine, the kind of activity that Yeats elsewhere calls 'our stitching and unstitching'. The weariness of such confined effort produces, in this very poem, some of Yeats's most beautiful concluding lines; but the reader must take the effortfulness with the ease, the spiring with the irreducible simplicity of 'the moon / When it has looked in glory from a cloud'; and this seems to me the meaning of the title *The Winding Stair* too. It evokes readerly response as well as writerly effort.

II

I want to pursue one or two of these significant kinds of spiral now in relation to some of the poems in the volume in which architectures of various kinds are the explicit material. I shall begin with its poems of the Big House, since that is of course where the volume itself begins. 'In Memory of Eva Gore-Booth and Con Marciewicz', 'Coole Park, 1929' and 'Coole and Ballylee, 1931' all summon their memorable and gorgeous imagery of the houses Lissadell and Coole in contexts of loss, diminishment or depredation. In the explicit elegy for Gore-Booth and Markiewicz this is a contrast between youth and age, one enforced by an imagery not merely of physical decay but also of political corruption, as Yeats reads it: 'Two girls in silk kimonos, both / Beautiful, one a gazelle' become, 'When withered old and skeleton-gaunt,/ An image of such politics'. The image of the girls in kimonos is perfect and iconically static in the poem's four introductory lines, which lack a verb, and the stasis is emphasized by the repetition of the image at the end of the opening stanza or section. Its charged but poised eroticism is powerfully reinforced by the lapsingly beautiful, and utterly unexpected, rhyme of 'Lissadell' and 'gazelle' at the start, and then made mnemonically insistent by the pararhyming of 'recall' and 'gazelle' at the end. The aesthetic perfectionism of this verbal *japanoiserie* is perhaps intended to deflect attention from the savage prejudice of the poem's politics, which indulge a long literary and political tradition of hostility to the revolutionary woman. Here, the particularities of these women's complex and lifelong political engagements are reduced to 'conspiring among the ignorant' in one case, and in the other to the even vaguer 'I know not what the younger dreams – / Some vague Utopia', which is one of those disingenuously dismissive statements, calculated for rhetorical effect, not uncommon in Yeats's poetry or prose. The prejudice makes Markiewicz and Gore-Booth almost stereotypical Madame Defarges, unindividualized and bereft of actual personality, and in fact, apart from the poem's title, bereft of name – only 'two girls', 'the older' and 'the younger'; which is a telling lapse in, as I have already said, a poet of much nominative bravura elsewhere. The political outrage virtually expunges the elegiac origin and, after repeating the opening image, the poem swerves or winds altogether elsewhere:

> Dear shadows, now you know it all,
> All the folly of a fight
> With a common wrong or right.

> The innocent and the beautiful
> Have no enemy but time;
> Arise and bid me strike a match
> And strike another till time catch;
> Should the conflagration climb,
> Run till all the sages know.
> We the great gazebo built,
> They convicted us of guilt;
> Bid me strike a match and blow.

Originating in elegy and ending in apocalypse, this poem seems an image, indeed, of *Yeatsian* politics in the 1920s and 1930s. The figuring of fiery conflagration may well accord with one of the images from *Anima Mundi*, as Daniel Albright tells us,[10] but it is also congruent with the realities of the revolutionary and civil-war period of Ireland's history a few years earlier, when hundreds of the big houses of the Anglo-Irish gentry were torched by incendiaries; and the magnificent edifice of Lissadell, a house which actually evaded the torch, dwindles in the poem into that of a gazebo, a garden folly. The Anglo-Irish house Lissadell, which may be read as metonymic of the Protestant Ascendancy itself, is therefore evoked here, almost despite Yeats's best intentions, as subject to irreversible decline, rather than as the heroic emblem of resistance. Even so, the evocation is made in terms of the savage indignation implicit in one of the idiomatic Irish inflections of the word 'gazebo', which can mean 'the whole thing': the lines therefore imply that at least 'we' – the Anglo-Irish – having made it all in the first place, are now at liberty to raze it all to the ground too.[11] Straining in opposite directions, therefore, and perhaps inheriting in a more than usually exacerbated form the element of satire often inhering in the genre of elegy, this is itself a winding, gyring, spiring stair of a poem.

The Coole Park poems do not offer themselves officially as elegies, but elegies, nevertheless, they are. Daniel Harris, in his excellent book *Yeats, Coole Park and Ballylee* (1974), offers a reading of these poems, and others of Yeats's Big House poems, as both developing, and also distinguishing themselves, from the Jonsonian tradition of the English country-house poem. Their marks of distinction all inhere in the extent to which Yeats figures the termination of these houses in a way quite the opposite of

Jonson's evocation of an eternally harmonious reciprocity between house and environment and house and history in 'To Penshurst'. 'Coole Park, 1929' includes the richly seductive imagery of romantic ruin, 'When all those rooms and passages are gone, / When nettles wave upon a shapeless mound / And saplings root among the broken stone', and is also, as Harris points out, proleptic of the death of Lady Gregory, an anticipatory elegy which, using the word 'shapeless', takes an edge from all the alternative kinds of shaping that go on in Yeats's poems and prose. And 'Coole and Ballylee, 1931' concludes with one of Yeats's most memorable and perfectly cadenced stanzas of *ottava rima*, writing the end of the house as the end of an imagined tradition of Anglo-Irish accomplishment:

> We were the last romantics – chose for theme
> Traditional sanctity and loveliness;
> Whatever's written in what poets name
> The book of the people; whatever most can bless
> The mind of man or elevate a rhyme;
> But all is changed, that high horse riderless,
> Though mounted in that saddle Homer rode
> Where the swan drifts upon a darkening flood.

Harris's account of these poems is more politically innocent than Deane's in his influential (but, when he writes of an Irish novelistic tradition, quite wrong) essay 'The Literary Myths of the Revival'; and Deane is persuasive when he tells us that Yeats's work as a whole gives 'dignity and coherence to the Irish Protestant Ascendancy tradition'.[12] In the Coole Park poems, however, the elegiac quality, or what Harris calls their quality of 'embattled defence',[13] serves precisely to call into question any such ideas of dignity or coherence – or, rather, to undermine such ideas with a sense of extreme unavailingness. Lissadell cedes its place to a gazebo; Coole collapses into a mound of rubble. These are poems compelled to admit not the dignity and coherence of an ideal social arrangement, but the extent to which any such ideal is tarnished by its inability to translate itself into a future. This is a dignity only of retrospect, which is a peculiarly self-cancelling one. Stan Smith, indeed, in his reading of the ending of 'Coole and Ballylee, 1931', suggests that the phrase 'high horse' is ambivalently phrased for both Pegasus and a presumptuousness or false pride. 'Is Yeats', he asks, 'saying that it was right to get down from that high horse, right to abandon the pretensions of "traditional sanctity and loveliness"? Is there more than a hint of dismissal in that opening proposition: we were hopelessly romantic, like Pound's E.P., out of key with our time?'[14]

This reading against the apparent grain may exaggerate an effect of the lines. Nevertheless, the poem does manifest an uncertainty about, or a destabilization of, the ground upon which Yeats would desperately wish to stand more firmly or – his word – 'foundedly'. There is something both poignant and shameful in the spectacle of the fiction that opens 'Coole and Ballylee, 1931' with a topography invented to suit a putative social ideal when Yeats links his own tower at Ballylee to the big house at Coole by a non-existent underground stream which, he feels compelled to tell us, includes ' "dark" Raftery's "cellar" drop'. This is, the footnotes usually say, the 'strong cellar' of a line of the blind poet Raftery, which Yeats understood as referring to a hole where the river sank underground. Anthony Raftery, however, was the last, nineteenth-century remnant of a long tradition of Irish-language poetry and, therefore, of Gaelic literary and social organization. Yeats's fiction here is thus one in which he attaches himself more closely to Lady Gregory's architecture of Anglo-Irishness than the actual topography of Sligo did – by means of the fictional underground stream – while, in the same gesture, pausing to include, with a combination of honesty and guilt, what the social and political arrangements of the Anglo-Irish had occluded or destroyed: the cultural products of a different language. Raftery's is a cellar, therefore, which the social architecture behind this very poem, 'Coole and Ballylee, 1931', might well drop into, since the great houses of the Anglo-Irish await their fate in the political arrangements of the new Ireland which the book was entering on its publication in 1933. This was in fact an Ireland which showed scant respect for such houses, many of which were allowed to fall into ruin or to be destroyed; and it was also an Ireland which, in an ultimately doomed piece of social and cultural engineering, made the Irish language an educational and professional requirement in the attempt to reconnect with the tradition to which Raftery was heir. In fact, congruent with all this, 'Coole Park and Ballylee, 1931' finds its image for contemporary depredation in yet a further architecture, although this time an extremely insecure one: 'Man shifts about – all that great glory spent – / Like some poor Arab tribesman and his tent.' 'They came like swallows and like swallows went,' says 'Coole Park, 1929' of the house's visiting writers and enthusiasts, attempting both a metaphorizing of culture in terms of nature and a tribute to the taming or focusing power of Lady Gregory's cultural authority; and yet, in the context of domestic and architectural instability and insecurity evoked by these poems, the image seems redolent rather of mere transience than of eternal recurrence. What begins in veneration in the poems of Coole Park, which is a register of belonging, ends in self-disinheritance and abjection. These architectures appear, in the end, only very temporary or false refuges, and what survives the poems is less an idea of dignity than an imagination of despair.

III

And what survives the Crazy Jane poems? I observed earlier that the best-known of them, 'Crazy Jane Talks with the Bishop', includes a kind of architecture too, and so it does, another 'mansion' in a book which features what it names as an 'old Georgian mansion' in 'In Memory of Eva Gore-Booth and Con Markiewicz'. This is the poem, voiced of course for the eponymous Jane:

> I met the Bishop on the road
> And much said he and I.
> 'Those breasts are flat and fallen now,
> Those veins must soon be dry;
> Live in a heavenly mansion,
> Not in some foul sty.'
>
> 'Fair and foul are near of kin,
> And fair needs foul,' I cried.
> 'My friends are gone, but that's a truth
> Nor grave nor bed denied,
> Learned in bodily lowliness
> And in the heart's pride.

'A woman can be proud and stiff
When on love intent;
But Love has pitched his mansion in
The place of excrement;
For nothing can be sole or whole
That has not been rent.'

Elizabeth Cullingford sets the Crazy Jane poems in the context of Yeats's last year as an Irish senator, 1928, which saw the introduction by the new state of the draconian Censorship of Publications Bill, an attempt – and, as it was to prove, a successful one – to seal the Irish literary and cultural frontiers, and one enthusiastically prosecuted by the Catholic Church. She reads Crazy Jane as a fusion of carnivalesque grotesque and 'low', socially orientated and once-anonymous ballad poetics, a construction aimed like a weapon at the monologic identity of the Irish Church and State.[15] This is a useful and probably accurate way of historicizing these poems and it notably relates their excremental imagery to contemporaneous cultural debates, or propaganda, which made use of such terms as the 'literary cesspool', and so on. In this context, Cullingford reads Crazy Jane as another Molly Bloom, a persona in which the imagery of female sexuality that has been appropriated by a masculinist literary tradition (running from St Augustine to Georges Bataille) is made over into a positive term. Historically suggestive and alert as it is, however, this reading nevertheless makes the Crazy Jane poems seem a little more decently intended than I find them. For instance, another turn of this historicizing screw might plunge the lines back into Yeats's despair about the fate of the Protestant Ascendancy: since, opposing the legal measures of the new, increasingly Catholicized state, he is conceivably poeticizing the same kinds of political emotion or class interest nakedly manifest in his senatorial speech against the new divorce laws ('We against whom you have done this thing are no petty people'). Crazy Jane would then become the other side of the Anglo-Irish coin, the gentry now outside, rather than above, the petty law of their social inferiors, the wild Irish girl in a newly vehement metamorphosis. There is a quality of anarchistic outrage in these poems, something incommensurable, which seems not only socially uncontainable but socially un-directed; and this is the way I read the architectural figure here.

The Bishop is intrusive, presumptuous and sententious in his directing Jane to live 'in a heavenly mansion, / Not in some foul sty', but in doing so he is of course employing Christ's own figure from St John's Gospel: 'In my father's house are many mansions'. Jane's riposte to this ecclesiastical disapproval and aggression, 'Fair and foul are near of kin', is phrased in an allusion to *Macbeth* which identifies her with the witches of that play; and it is a witchlike perversity, as far as orthodoxy is concerned – although it is also a Blakean one – to suggest the identification of fair and foul, innocence and experience, grace and sin. The poem's third stanza, however, even given the querulous unorthodoxy already uttered by Jane, is unpredictably explosive. There is a sexual ambivalence about the word 'stiff', since it is more usually applied to men than to women when engaged in the act of love; and when the word 'love' moves, as it does, from lower case in the second line to upper case in the third, it carries suggestions of a move from sexual or secular love to divine love since, as the Bishop will know, 'God is Love', and the lines therefore have a certain blasphemous charge. When the following lines move the mansion from an opposition to the 'foul sty' of the opening stanza to an identification with it, they do so in a way that insists, of course, on the contiguity of the genital and excremental functions. Harold Bloom says of the lines that 'Love has the audacity to pitch its mansion where it lacks priority',[16] but this makes it seem that Love is admirable for so doing. Surely one implication of the notorious punning on the word 'pitch' is that Love can anticipate an only very temporary stay here: you 'pitch' a tent (like an Arab tribesman), not a mansion. And the further obscene punning on 'pitch' and 'whole' is scathingly reductive of Love's audacities or expectations. The true horror of the lines is that they insist that, in the end, the place of love and the place of excrement will be not merely contiguous but one and the same, since this is the reality of death and decay, when the whole body will become a place of excrement. All of which, I have to say, seems far enough away from a satiric engagement with the Censorship Bill, even if the explicit literary expression of such things in Ireland would, of necessity, demand the bill's failure. 'Nothing can be sole or whole / That has not been rent': a uniqueness and an integrity may, for the Yeats of *The Winding Stair*, be derived only from this kind of fracturing and self-dividing knowledge, the suffering of a pain of rending.

IV

These lines, then, in the extremity of their figuring of a mansion pitched in a place of excrement, harmonize grimly with the Georgian mansions pitched in the place of apocalypse or absence earlier in the volume; and they may also propose a reason why the word 'rending' occurs to Eliot at the climax of the encounter in 'Little Gidding', where the compound ghost offers his compoundedly desolate imagining of 'the gifts reserved for age' in words alluding, as I have already said, to 'Vacillation':

> And last, the rending pain of re-enactment
> Of all that you have done, and been; the shame
> Of motives late revealed, and the awareness
> Of things ill done and done to others' harm
> Which once you took for exercise of virtue.

Eliot's inclusion of Yeats here is – uncharacteristically, it may be – appreciative and generous, particularly since, of course, the aesthetics and metaphysics of the two poets are so totally at variance, Eliot's tending to simplification and evacuation, Yeats's to complication and repletion; although Eliot is also possibly, in choosing the Yeats of 'Vacillation' as his intertext, critically locating a moment of extreme self-doubt in the older poet, and also slyly insinuating that there is more than a shared belief in the miraculous preservation of saints' bodies to ally Yeats and the Catholic von Hügel to whom he says his fond farewells in the last line of 'Vacillation': 'So get you gone, von Hügel, though with blessings on your head'. Eliot may well be recognizing that counter-movement in *The Winding Stair* which twists assurance into doubt, celebration into lament, vaunt into recrimination, architecture into rubble.

Louis MacNeice tells us that, with his poetic ear finely attuned to Eliot, he was initially incapable of responding to Yeats, who appeared 'too mannered; like a figure from a fancy-dress party he looked wrong in the daylight'.[17] In *The Winding Stair*, I think – and this is conceivably what the Eliot of the *Quartets* was recognizing – he moves far enough forward into a kind of daylight, and in dishevelled costume, to be fully recognizable as our contemporary. Which is why I want to conclude by quoting the final stanza of 'Byzantium', a ferociously difficult work, which I take to be a poem about its own possibility, in the accepted symbolist manner, but one which nevertheless appears so exacerbated and so pitched at the level of conflict as to be equally readable as a poem about its own impossibility. It is also – conveniently for my purposes of peroration here – a poem initiated by reference to one further architecture in this architecturally entitled volume, that of the cathedral of Hagia Sophia in the Byzantium of the poem's title. The cathedral dome in the poem's first stanza 'disdains / All that man is, / All mere complexities, / The fury and the mire of human veins', but 'Byzantium' subsequently plots a trajectory which, like that of the book itself in my view, and of other individual poems within it, saves itself from disdain by the register of an incapacity to control which is one of the great glories of an art that nevertheless everywhere appears to desire control. When the 'mere complexities' of the human surface again at the end of 'Byzantium', they are an instruction in the way the art of this poet survives not in self-mastery, but in fitful and endless surrender to its own mystery:

> Astraddle on the dolphin's mire and blood,
> Spirit after spirit! The smithies break the flood,
> The golden smithies of the Emperor!
> Marbles of the dancing floor
> Break bitter furies of complexity,
> Those images that yet
> Fresh images beget,
> That dolphin-torn, that gong-tormented sea.

2

The blessings of Onan: Austin Clarke's 'Mnemosyne Lay in Dust'

I

Austin Clarke's reputation has, to a large extent, remained a coterie one, and that it should be so is almost self-consciously programmed into the work itself by some of its strategies, tactics and stances. In a first attempt to overcome what had been an original slavish indebtedness to Yeats and some of his programmes for the Revival, Clarke, partly under the influence of his tutor, Thomas MacDonagh, returned to the assonantal metres of Irish poetry and attempted to reproduce, or at least in some way to imitate, them in English. The result has always seemed to some awkward, factitious or even puerile: evidence of an immature phase of the culture as well as of the individual poet. Between 1938 and 1955 he published no poetry, concentrating instead on a series of verse dramas which seem now to have very little vitality or viability; and this long absence inevitably made him difficult or impossible to assimilate or place on his return. These factors were then instrumental in his failure to find an audience; and, in combination with other pressing reasons for disaffection, this was responsible for a poetry of increasing bitterness, in which venomous social satire meets a deeply distressed self-disgust and self-rebuke. Where the satirical modes of the earlier poetry hit their (usually clerical) targets with memorable accuracy, as in the superbly concentrated quatrain 'Penal Law', which has the final subversive word on the draconian censorship laws of the Irish Free State, the later ones often miss in a flurry of bile and inconsequence, and they also tend to slip uninterpretably under the feet of the reader who cannot recognize the intensely specific causes of their anger. In many of them Clarke became, and continues, what he feared he would become: a 'local complainer'. There are undoubtedly poems in which an almost heroic loneliness becomes its own reward in a resourcefulness of pained address, but there are many others in which it becomes a self-defeating and desperate incarceration, flailing and jejune.

For all these reasons, Denis Donoghue is unfortunately to be believed when he says that 'there is no evidence of a sustained relation between Clarke's mind and modern poetry in any of the forms in which it has continued to be audible'.[1] To aid audibility, therefore, Clarke is much better read in selection than in bulk, and he has been lucky – in this, if in little else – in the devoted punctiliousness of his editors: first in Thomas Kinsella, and latterly in Hugh Maxton's excellently introduced and annotated edition for the Lilliput Press (subsequently published by Penguin Books).[2] Read in selection, the work has the proper opportunity to make itself heard; but nevertheless the critic who does pick up the Clarke frequency in such a way that it continues to haunt the ear as a viable possibility – infuriating at times, certainly, but also entrancing, and indisputably there, present and firmly registered in the range of modern possibilities, and registered as a feature of a fully charged modernity, not as nostalgia or antiquarianism – is more than usually called upon to justify the estimate. The late poem 'Mmemosyne Lay in Dust' focuses many of the issues in ways that make it a test case, a paradigm and an alertly self-reflexive work, even if it is, characteristically, an almost febrilely unsettling and demanding one.

First published in 1966, 'Mnemosyne Lay in Dust' takes as its basic material Clarke's own experience of insanity and incarceration in a mental hospital – St Patrick's, 'The Mansion of Forgetfulness / Swift gave us for a jest' – almost fifty years previously, in 1919. This poem about loss of memory, about Mnemosyne consigned to the dust, is itself dependent on a very long memory indeed. Clarke never directly admits to this devastating event from his early life in his previous poetry, and it is glossed over in a paragraph or two even in his later autobiographical prose, although in 1988 his son published a section from a memoir written shortly after his release, which does more directly confront it.[3] The lengthy period of repression and blockage before the poem's dark matter could be manipulated into the light of articulation finds its odd biographical correlative in the long poetic silence between 1938 and 1955 to which I have already referred. Thomas Kinsella has suggested that this silence – which he thinks had a peculiar appropriateness in an Ireland 'depressed so thoroughly that one scarcely noticed it' – had something to do with 'difficulties encountered in the writing of a long personal poem'; he observes that 'Summer Lightning', which appeared as the penultimate poem in the harrowing volume *Night and Morning*, the last book before the withdrawal, eventually resurfaces as Part VIII of 'Mnemosyne'.[4] If we note too that the long and apparently effortless volume *Flight to Africa* (1963) contains, in 'Fragaria', a rehearsal for Part XII of 'Mnemosyne', then it is not difficult to imagine Clarke incubating the poem until the schooled intricacies of the later manner, in which an energy of vituperation is knotted together with a kind of melancholy exasperation, provided the only form that could contain the anguish and assuage the sorrow. Given the date of the poem, we may also be casually inclined to think that Robert Lowell's *Life Studies* and John Berryman's *Dream Songs* provided Clarke, in the early 1960s, with some sense of how the thing might actually be done. Clarke's scathing review of Lowell's *Poems 1938–1949* in the *Irish Times* discourages much speculation in that direction; although the evocations of the other inmates and the imitations of their speech in Part XV of 'Mnemosyne' are bound, now, to seem 'Lowellian'.[5] And the opening of Part VI – 'One night he heard heart-breaking sound. / It was a sigh unworlding its sorrow' – has the plangency that is to be heard again and again in Berryman, although both may have an origin in the melancholy vowel music of Tennyson, which Berryman manages, extraordinarily, to transport from Victorianism into a thoroughgoing function of poetic modernity.

To bring these American mid-century poets into the orbit of 'Mnemosyne' is, however, to become immediately aware of the need for discrimination. The paradox of their work is that they seem never so much themselves – articulate, masterful, persuasive – as when charting the process of their dissolutions. In Lowell's poems about madness, there is frequently a graceful and even mournfully humorous self-deprecation: the insistence of the poems is that, however bad things have been, there is, in the moment of articulating them, still a 'self' to deprecate, and that the ironic play may be therapeutic ('Is getting well ever an art, / or art a way to get well?'). In *The Dream Songs* too, however worryingly and perversely, the desperation is stubbornly buoyant; the ventriloquism and slapstick are a performance of the self, a self-display. In Clarke, however, the fear of madness is articulated, precisely, as the loss of self. The self, which maintains its perilous autonomy within the accretions of history and experience that we call memory, dissolves when memory suffers attrition. On its first American publication, Clarke actually 'translated' the mythologizing gesture of his more familiar title and named the poem *The Loss of Memory*.[6] His protagonist, Maurice Devane, cannot remember who or what he is; and the absence of personality, the absence of a secure or stable identity, is the hollow or vortex at the centre of this very long poem. The loss of memory is also the loss of creative power, and therefore an explanation of both Clarke's psycho-biographical writing-block and of this poem's title since, in classical mythology, Mnemosyne is the mother of the Muses, and therefore the mediatrix of poetic resource.

The process of 'unselfing', which is initiated in a brutally catalogued series of physical deprivations and humiliations, is charted early in the poem and provides the work with much of its immediate, and raw, emotional power. Maurice is removed from any recognizable social or natural world and placed within the constrictions of prison bars, strait-jackets and the manhandling indecencies of at best uncomprehending doctors and warders; their sometimes inhumane punishments for the body's uncontrollable rebellions are the focus of Clarke's sustained revelation of the ethical disease of this typical state institution. The early parts of 'Mnemosyne' are sodden with bodily voidances, with involuntary urinations, excretions, vomitings; the poem maintaining a rhetoric of disgust in which Maurice's human body is transformed into the warders' 'Dogsbody'.[7] Within the context of this rhetoric, the ultimate 'unselfing' created by the loss of memory is quietly but powerfully insisted upon:

> Often he stared into the mirror
> Beside the window, hand-drawn by fear.
> He seemed to know that bearded face
> In it, the young man, tired and pale,
> Half smiling. Gold-capped tooth in front
> Vaguely reminded him of someone.
> Who was it? Nothing came to him.
> He saw that smile again. Gold dot
> Still gleamed. The bearded face was drawn
> With sufferings he had forgotten.

To be physically scarred by sufferings which the mind knows nothing of, and to have attention called to this in a mirror – the mirror looked into, beside the window not looked out of – is to be torn apart within one's own being; and the accompanying disintegrative and minatory emotions – of anxiety, fear and guilt – are oppressively conveyed within the texture of the poem's language and form. Clarke's varied intricacies of metrical and stanzaic patterning, and his assonantal devices, which are elsewhere in the work frequently a form of play, are here all turned towards the expression of depletion (when 'mirror' and 'fear', 'drawn' and 'forgotten', for instance, tremble awkwardly and charmlessly against each other); they construct at the heart of 'Mnemosyne', where human personality is missing, a density and pressure of unease. This afflicts the reader with a burden of alienation powerfully indicative of Maurice's condition. The absence of personality is, so to say, tangibly actualized within the tensions and obliquities of the poetry itself, so that, just as 'Nothing came to' Maurice, nothing comes to the reader by means of poetic forms which render nothingness with chilling economy and thereby manifest the poem's plot as one in which Maurice himself may indeed come to nothing.

The true distinction of Clarke's achievement in 'Mnemosyne', however, is the way in which this very loss of self-identity, the loss of anything that may be distinguished as individual personality – what the poem actually describes as 'burial alive' – is rendered an exceptionally full absence at the centre of this text. Perhaps because of Clarke's lengthy meditation on the poem's root-experiences, and its own lengthy gestation, the 'darkness' created by Maurice Devane's loss of self becomes radiant with implication. 'Mnemosyne Lay in Dust' is a poem of self-enclosure which locates within its confinements and constrictions an implicit judgement on the world beyond the self – its politics, its theology, its sexuality – as cauterizing as the poems of *Night and Morning*; and it goes beyond that volume, too, by enacting and implicitly justifying the poetics to which Clarke – in the face of hostility, incomprehension and neglect – gave his allegiance in all his most significant work.

II

Although – as we have already seen – a great many substances visibly flow from his body in the early parts of the poem, one substance is permanently blocked and checked in Maurice's memory. The scrap of memory in which this blockage is announced comes to him in a padded cell, inside its 'wall of inward-outness':

> Lo! in memory yet,
> Margaret came in a frail night-dress,
> Feet bare, her heavy plaits let down
> Between her knees, his pale protectress.
> Nightly restraint, unwanted semen
> Had ended their romantic dream.

'Semen' here resolutely refuses to flow. Indeed, it cannot flow in a 'romantic dream', since romantic dreams transcribed into poems use only the exhausted locutions of what Eliot called a 'worn-out poetical fashion'. 'Lo!' as an exclamation, and woman as a 'pale protectress', may be possible in the 1890s modes of, say, Arthur Symons's *Silhouettes* or *London Nights*, but they cannot keep their countenance when 'semen' is about. In this stanza, however, they set the tone, as it were, since they are foregrounded by their archaism; and semen, 'unwanted', is checked in its flow, pulled up sharply, abrupted, by the blocked rhyme of 'dream'. This is a prime instance, in fact, in which Clarke's substitution of assonance for rhyme acts functionally and expressively. The refusal of 'semen' to rhyme with 'dream' is a poetic *coitus interruptus*; and what we may regard here as not so much assonantal rhyming as a deliberately atrophied or failed rhyme implies that the inability to discharge semen is inevitably the discharging of all romantic 'dreaming' by one, or both, of the lovers.

When semen does flow later in the poem, in Part x, it flows in a stanza that relaxes and gently releases into articulation, simultaneously, a burden of contained emotional energy and a trope which has implications for the whole procedure of 'Mnemosyne Lay in Dust':

> Often in priestly robe on a
> Night of full moon, out of the waste,
> A solitary figure, self-wasted,
> Stole from the encampments – Onan,
> Consoler of the young, the timid,

The captive. Administering, he passed down
The ward. Balsam was in his hand.
The self-sufficer, the anonym.

The masturbatory evocation is clearly a figuring of Maurice's
intense isolation, of his solipsistic withdrawal from any more
satisfactory outward flow; although it is certainly worth remarking that his solipsism here is a kind of communal solipsism, in that
Onan's benediction is administered indiscriminately to the entire
ward. The figure is, however, much more inclusive than this. It is
perhaps not necessary to have read Clarke's account, in the
autobiographical *Twice Round the Black Church* (1962), of an
appalling childhood confession in which he was forced to admit,
in terror, to a 'sin' which he had barely imagined, let alone committed, to realize that Onan's priestly garb is an ironic comment
on the sexual fixations and obsessions of Irish clericalism; an
irony of understatement, it must be said, not common in Clarke's
many variations on the theme. This priest of the religion of Onan
brings, as consolation and balm, what the Irish Jansenists of
Clarke's childhood and early manhood would forbid as, literally,
damnable, since they would have classified masturbation as a
mortal sin; indeed, the lines have their blasphemous element
because the 'balsam' carried in, and administered by, the hand of
an actual Catholic priest would, of course, be that of the sacra-
ment of the Eucharist. Beyond that blasphemy, Clarke is also undoubtedly making a sly point about the inevitable connection
between clerical celibacy and masturbation, and therefore about
the consequences for social, sexual and marital life of a system in
which a Church profoundly influential on the State and all its
institutions makes clerical celibacy mandatory. In this context, it is
worth remembering that a large part of Clarke's fascination with
the period of the Celtic-Romanesque, which he makes the imaginary location of much of his earlier work, is that, in his view, it
joined together sexuality and the Christian religion in a humanly
satisfying way: it was a period when, he said, 'we almost had a
religion of our own'.[8]

This whole nexus of revulsion, critique and attachment, as it
may be read out of the priestly figure of Onan in the Irish-
assonantal English of 'Mnemosyne Lay in Dust', is placed in a
new perspective, and a new perspective of the culture, as it were,

by the Irish-language poet Nuala Ní Dhomnaill's 'Féar Suaithin-seach' which Seamus Heaney has translated as 'Miraculous Grass' in *Pharaoh's Daughter* (1990). The ironies of this translation are multiple: they include Heaney's male voice speaking in female persona in a poem by an Irish woman; his own frequent correlations in his critical writing, and occasional correlations in his poems, of the poetic and the priestly, the aesthetic and the theological; his collocation of the liturgical and the erotic in 'The Chasuble' in *Station Island*; the hostile criticism he has attracted from some feminist critics; and Ní Dhomnaill's managing, in the Irish language, a subversive kind of poem far more fundamentally in tune with Clarke's spirited licentiousness than with the ortho-dox expectations of the repressive, Irish-language-promoting State with which Clarke himself had to struggle. 'Miraculous Grass' makes the balsam of the Communion wafer a sexual and political blessing too, as its female persona registers a priest's sexual attrac-tion to her (the Communion wafer falls out of his hands when he sets eyes on her at Mass). Taking to her bed with an unspecifiable, incurable illness, she imagines how he will come and heal her, but only after 'the whole straggle and mess / that infests my green unfortunate field' has been uprooted. The poem's concluding lines bring another priest with balsam in his hand into modern Irish literature, in a gesture that might be regarded as redeeming, while erasing, Clarke's Onan, and also making the Irish language once more vibrate with a correctively subversive sensuality that Clarke would have admired. In Heaney's translation this reads:

> And there where the sacred wafer fell
> you will discover
> in the middle of the shooting weeds
> a clump of miraculous grass.
> The priest will have to come then
> with his delicate fingers, and lift the host
> and bring it to me and put it on my tongue.
> Where it will melt, and I will rise in the bed
> as fit and well as the youngster I used to be.[9]

Onan is important in 'Mnemosyne Lay in Dust', however, not only in an ethical-theological context, implicated in Irish Catholic sexuality, but also in that the specific comfort he brings is offered as mollification for the hurts and ravages of Irish political violence. In the 'encampments' from which Onan steals, Maurice has, in a feverishly visionary way, imagined his hospital warders transformed into a battalion of soldiers 'after the long rout' who

> lie, in the dark,
> Watching the fire, on the edge
> Of a storybook jungle: they watch
> The high boots of the colonists.

Routed, in defeat, colonized, the warder-soldiers become part of a history which seems almost a textbook case of what post-colonial theorizing has to say about the way nationalism mirrors or repeats the imperial or colonial forms it replaces. In this passage, which prominently figures a 'storybook' (that is, a narrative of interpretation), the terrifying and torturing warder-gaolers of this Dublin mental asylum in the 1920s 'watch' those fascistic high boots in that attitude of eager pupillage which precedes emulation.[10] Watching high boots, the implication must be, is only a step away from licking high boots; and the warders, in turn, have already been revealed in the poem expecting that the patients of this hospital should, in turn, lick their high boots. This vision or nightmare of the poem's protagonist connects with other images of battle and violence. In Part v, Maurice becomes, explicitly, the 'Daring Republican of hillside farm-yards' and imagines that, presumably in a civil war, he has committed 'parricide'; and, here in Part x, there is the altogether surreal manifestation of a severed head on a pillow near him in the ward, and the appearance on his own bed of 'a terrible Twangman', a ghastly nursery-rhyme horror, who calls for his hanging. These are all phantasmagorically transformed versions of the history Maurice has lived through beyond the hospital walls; and, since they figure so prominently now in the dreams and hallucinations of his incarceration, they are implicitly as responsible for his mental condition as the sexual miseries which also feature there. In fact, there is urgent biographical pressure behind these moments in the poem, since Clarke's tutor, Thomas MacDonagh, was one of the executed leaders of the Easter Rebellion in 1916, and Clarke was subsequently appointed to his post at University College Dublin. The guilt and self-rebuke of the involved non-combatant may well, therefore, fuel the poem's distresses.

In Onan's appearance in the poem, then, the religious, the sexual and the political are knotted together as the root of the diminishment Maurice suffers and endures. The absence at the poem's centre, that of personality, is filled with the presence of the conditioning circumstances that have provoked and produced that absence: the impossibility of a true sexual relation; the anxiety induced by a religion which makes impossible, contradictory and deeply inhibiting demands; and the terror of living through a period of violent political upheaval. Maurice, like Onan, is a self-sufficer, an anonym; but, implicitly in Clarke's poem, the anonymity is given its name. What makes for distressed, disintegrating self-sufficiency is a recognizable and definable shape or mis-shapenness of the culture, even if it has taken this poet fifty years to articulate that shape in the formal shape of his own poem, so great is the distress that it once shaped in him. It is against all of this, out of his hand and 'out of the waste' – which is, punningly, both the desert of his existence and the 'waist' below which sexual activity occurs – that Onan offers his benediction and 'balsam'.

III

The balsam Onan offers in fact completes his nature as presiding genius of the poem; for it establishes his relation to the oscillating approach to, and retreat from, the mythopoeic in 'Mnemosyne'. In an essay on Clarke, in which he is compared to Padraic Fallon, Donald Davie insists that he is 'further from mythopoeia than any poet one might think of';[11] but although this manifestly holds good for the rest of his work, it does not – quite – for this poem. Onan is, of course, himself a mythopoeic flourish (deriving from the Genesis myth or narrative of the Onan who spilt his seed on the ground and thus gave his name to the word 'onanism') in a way that allows Clarke the opportunity for both rhetorical heightening and euphemistic obliquity. The balsam he administers to the patients of the asylum involves Onan further too, however, in the mythopoeic tendency of Maurice Devane's imagination as Clarke traces it. In Part IX, Maurice attempts to construct, out of his misery and incoherence, the possibility of some kind of alternative. He has heard the warders talking of a gate, a garden and a fountain encountered on a climb to 'the Robbers' Cave / Beyond

Kilmainham', where the place-name, of course, recalls the Irish gaol in which the leaders of the 1916 Rising were incarcerated and executed. As he falls asleep, the three words 'gate', 'garden' and 'fountain' become infused with Maurice's aspiration, charged with possibilities of release from these psychological, social and political constrictions:

> The words became mysterious
> With balsam, fragrance, banyan trees.
> Forgetting the ancient law of tears,
> He dreamed in the desert, a league from Eden.
> How could he pass the Gate, the sworded
> Seraphim, find the primal Garden,
> The Fountain? He had but three words
> And all the summer maze was guarded.

This mythopoeic construction of Gate, Garden and Fountain subsequently recurs throughout the remainder of the poem. That it is shaped specifically as erotic consolation is made apparent by the fact that it is set 'a league from Eden'; for, in Part IV of 'Mnemosyne', one of his earliest visions or hallucinations describes an eroticism at once satyric and tender in just such an Edenic landscape. At first Maurice – 'mere prick beneath those vast erections' – is 'a tiny satyr' in a forest of 'the holy ictyphalli'; but then

> Joyously, through a gateway, came a running
> Of little Jewish boys, their faces pale
> As ivory or jasmine, from Lebanon
> To Eden. Garlanded, caressing,
> Little girls ran with skip and leap. They hurried,
> Moon-pointing, beyond the gate. They passed a pale
> Of sacred laurel, flowers of the future. Love
> Fathered him with their happiness.

The shimmer of erotic delight here is also a familial delight: Maurice, who, as we have seen, thinks of himself as a 'parricide', is here, for the only time in the poem, aware of a potential paternity and a potential future. Both exist, however, only in the imagination's visionary constructions; in the reality Maurice must still actually inhabit, the guarded maze restrains him from any real bodily satisfaction, erotic or paternal. Or, indeed, poetic or artistic, since the essential lack here is figured as the lack of words – Maurice has 'but three' – and since the image of the maze inevitably brings with it associations from that other partially mythopoeic Irish text figuring Catholic sexual repression, priesthood, artistic striving and the mythical maze of Daedalus and Icarus, Joyce's *A Portrait of the Artist as a Young Man*.[12] Once again, in the first of the stanzas above, technique in Clarke is therefore expressive: the assonantal rhyme of 'sworded', 'words' and 'guarded' entwines in the verse a register of creative incapacity all the more forceful and distressing because the word 'sworded' guards within its own verbal form the word 'word(s)'. Words are indeed warding swords for those who have lost the capacity to use them; and the edgy, tiptoe reticence of the versestructure is a way of expressing this while also both acknowledging and accommodating the pain of it.

In fact, in keeping with Clarke's more customary poetic as it is rightly described by Donald Davie, the apparent resolution of 'Mnemosyne Lay in Dust' – which is also, it would seem, the relieving of Maurice's psychological distress – comes not at the level of mythopoeia, but as a benediction from the natural world. Maurice is in danger of dying because he does not eat; in fact, at one point this is described as a 'hunger-strike' in a way that again parallels contemporary Irish political circumstance.[13] His mother, however, inspired by a personified 'Nature / Remembering a young believer', brings him strawberries:

> In June, upon the little table
> Between the beds, he saw a dish
> Of strawberries. As they lay
> There, so ripe, ruddy, delicious,
> For an hour he played with his delay
>   Then in delight
> Put out two fingers towards the wished-for,
> Ate for the first time.

These strawberries have as much exuberant presence in the poem as William Carlos Williams's plums have in 'This is Just to Say' (those famous plums – 'they were delicious / so sweet / and so cold' – may, indeed, be recalled in Clarke's fourth line), but they also act as a later, and admittedly very much reduced, version of the meal not eaten by the lovers in Keats's 'The Eve of St. Agnes'. Not that Maurice has anyone to share his meal with; but when he 'plays' with his 'delay' for an hour before turning it, assonantally, into his 'delight', he is doing so in something of the same spirit in which Madeline and Porphyro delay the eating of their meal. They delay it so long, in fact, that it is never eaten, and its delight culminates instead in the 'solution sweet' of an implicit act of love. Maurice's delay is, similarly, a kind of tantalizing erotic-degustatory foreplay which continues beyond the end of the penultimate line of the stanza, when the epithet 'wished-for' is gerundively made to contain, or delay, without ever releasing, its possible noun. The benediction of the season and the fruit – which reverses the earlier curse of disgorgement – may be the blessing of a personified 'Nature'; but it is nevertheless recorded in a language which sets it in rich consonance with the eroticism that also prompted Maurice's mythopoeic constructions.

I have referred to this moment as the poem's 'apparent resolution'. It does seem to be so, in the general economy of the poem's structure. It occurs, however, in Part xi of a poem which goes on for another seven sections. It is impossible, in these sections, to trace any process or progress of further resolution, any gradual growth towards the light, in Maurice; and, eventually, his becoming 'Rememorised' in the final part is bound to seem abrupt and perfunctory, especially as the rhythms of the concluding lines are casual to the point of the headlong, as they slip, tumble and gabble flatly down the page:

> Rememorised, Maurice Devane
> Went out, his future in every vein.
> The Gate had opened. Down Steeven's Lane
> The high wall of the Garden, to right
> Of him, the Fountain with a horse-trough.
> Illusions had become a story.
> There was the departmental storey
> Of Guinness's, God-given right
> Of goodness in every barrel, tun,
> They averaged. Upon that site
> Of shares and dividends in sight
> Of Watling Street and the Cornmarket,

At Number One in Thomas Street
Shone in the days of the ballad-sheet,
The house in which his mother was born.

The point of these lines is, however, precisely that they should seem casual; for what happens in them is that the mythopoeic turns back into the literal and the quotidian. 'Story', through the agency of one of Clarke's favourite devices, *rime riche*, and once again expressively, becomes 'storey': the fictions Maurice has constructed, those hieratic or priestly potentialities of the imagination, the symbolist transformations of the real, tumble back into the sights, sounds and smells, and into the advertising slogans, economic exigencies and disappearing local topographies of contemporary Dublin life. The implication is that there is no resolution of Maurice's conflict in symbolist visions of transcendence, since they too are a 'romantic dream'. The Gate, despite its initial capital, opens on to no 'primal Garden': it is only the gate of the asylum which gives on to its garden in Steeven's Lane; and the Fountain, which has previously been evoked imaginatively as transcendently 'self-poised' – an adjective with a Yeatsian inflection which relates it to other such symbolist fountains – is only a common fountain with a horse-trough, the site of the routine transport necessities of an early twentieth-century city.

Maurice's 'rememorization' is dependent on the implicit acknowledgement of such actualities: he moves from 'the house where he was got' in the poem's first line to 'The house in which his mother was born' in its last; and the movement is, emotionally, from the archaizing self-dramatization of the disgusted monosyllable, 'got', to the unheroic, unassertive, plain report of that final 'born'.[14] There is a house for the fiction and a house for the truth; and, if the latter is plainer and duller, it is also necessary for sanity. Leaving the Gate, the Garden and the Fountain, Maurice goes out into the sub-harmonies and half-rhymes, the *rimes riches* and assonantal chimes, of contingent social and economic realities in the ordinary urban world of early twentieth-century Ireland. 'I am alone, now,' says Maurice to himself in Part vi, 'Lost in myself in a mysterious / Darkness, the victim in a story.' When the 'story' has become the 'storey' of Guinness's brewery, Maurice has been emboldened to leave his darkness, to become other than 'victim'; and the structural oddity of 'Mnemosyne Lay in Dust', in which the genuine resolution comes early, and the climax abruptly, is a formal insistence on the untidy incompleteness of any such willed resolution or climax when the will at work in the poem is one with the will that must operate also in the life of which the poem is part. For it is at this point that the fiction that separates 'Maurice Devane' from Austin Clarke is itself exploded. We know, of course, from the autobiographies, as I have already noted, that Clarke did himself suffer a breakdown and consequent hospital-ization of the kind also endured by Maurice; and some of the poem's visions, hallucinations and fantasies are ascribed in the autobiographies to Clarke himself. We also know of the disaster of Clarke's first marriage, which lies behind the lines on 'Margaret' in Part vi, although Hugh Maxton informs us that 'marriage to "Margaret" followed, and did not prompt, Clarke/ Devane's release from St. Patrick's Hospital'.[15] The name of the poem's protagonist is a confessionally transparent disguise, in any case, for someone who published reviews under the name 'Maurice Devane'. Yet the fiction, however tenuous, is a mask necessary to Clarke in order for him to be able finally to articulate what had been entirely unsayable for such an extremely long time.

'Maurice' collapses as a mask in the poem not at the level of autobiographical material, not at some inchoate stage of pre-verbalized disjunction, therefore, but at, precisely, the point of most intense articulation: at, that is, the point where the poet is enacting a paradigm of his poetic procedure, and a defence of it. For it is the critical task in any consideration of Austin Clarke to account for a poetry that so resolutely refuses to transcend the quotidian contingencies of its composition. Characteristically, large gesture is restrained by local reference; satire is collapsed in journalistic invective; rhyme becomes uncertain, tentative, edgy and attenuated in assonance and acronym. 'Mnemosyne Lay in Dust', by summoning the large mythopoeic alternatives to this manner of proceeding, identifies them as the 'illusions' which become an untrustworthy 'story'. Martin Dodsworth has excel-lently said that 'a force of passion is countered by a force of judgement' in the poem.[16] But it is not just Maurice Devane's psychological predicament that is on trial in this work; also in the courts of judgement are the possible ways of coming to terms with this predicament in poetry. The polished, the finished, the perfectly adjusted are all implicitly rejected when the mythopoeic orientation of Devane's psychological life and therefore, presumably, of at least a part of the poet Austin Clarke's own attachments and sympathies, is reined in – articulately, if not explicitly – during the course of the poem itself, and subjected to the other, paradoxical authority of what Thomas Kinsella has described in the late manner, in terms appropriately redolent of the ache of modernity, as 'rupture, truncation, displacement, fusion and confusion under pressure'.[17]

In an important sense, this is the movement of Clarke's entire career. From his early handling of the 'matter of Ireland', through his re-making of a rich personal world out of the Celtic-Romanesque, to the late enterprising nakedness of the satires and self-explorations, his work represents a growing suspicion of the transcendent, a radical re-examination of the mythical and mythopoeic. If this procedure is, essentially, a strategic and life-giving swerve from Yeats, it is also revealed in 'Mnemosyne Lay in Dust' as fundamentally written into Clarke's sensibility. What makes this poem exceptional in his work is that in it the inscription is itself painfully scrutinized. Examining its shape and contours, the poem discovers there a theology of despair and desuetude, a politics of violence and unfulfilment, a sexuality of lack and diminishment. These are not susceptible to the histrionics of transcendence, the aesthetics of the mythopoeic; they need, primarily, not to be transformed or transcended as symbols or systems for poetry, but to be challenged and confronted where the discourse of poetry can be made to meet the discourses of the journals, advertisements and 'ballad-sheets': not by the Gate, the Garden and the Fountain, but 'At Number One in Thomas Street'. 'Mnemosyne Lay in Dust' implicitly defends the necessity for such a poetic while itself making over into form the tensions and disjunctions, the self-divisions and blockages, that are the reason in history, as they are the product in language, of such a put-upon poetic.

3

Makeshift monologue:
the poetry of Padraic Fallon

I

Padraic Fallon has been described by Declan Kiberd as 'chrono-logically displaced':[1] publishing only in journals and anthologies during his lifetime (1906–74), his first book was the elegant Dolmen *Poems* of 1974, the year of his death; and – a kind of Janáček of Irish poetry – he produced some of his finest work in the last fourteen years of his life. Kiberd makes this observation when he opens his introduction to the section of the *Field Day Anthology* devoted to contemporary Irish poetry with an account of Fallon which makes him appear a more central and determining figure in modern Irish poetry than any other such historical overview has ever given him credit for. Kiberd remarks in particular on his inheritance of an 'ecumenism' from the Revival, in which he is thought to combine, without rancour, both Gaelic and Anglo-Irish elements. Returning Fallon to critical visibility in this influential place, Kiberd bizarrely renders him invisible again, however, when his subsequent book on modern Irish writing, *Inventing Ireland* (1995), fails even to mention him;[2] and there is still so little critical literature on this poet that, nearly twenty-five years after his death, anyone writing about him must feel the need for introductory remarks of the kind I am making here. However, the publishing visibility of Fallon was aided when, following the Dolmen edition, Carcanet and Raven Arts Press published *Poems and Versions* in 1983, and when Carcanet and Gallery Press published a *Collected Poems*, edited by the poet's son, Brian Fallon, in 1990.

That edition contained a generous, if carefully discriminating, and self-referential, introduction by Seamus Heaney, who encount-ered Fallon properly for the first time, he tells us, in the early 1970s while, presumably, he was writing the poems which eventually formed *Wintering Out* in 1972. Although Heaney does not say precisely that Fallon influenced him then, he does cite the opening of the poem 'Gurteen' and remarks that it was 'a discovery and a resource, a manifestation of kindred spirit'.³ Anyone coming on it for the first time – it is published as the first of the three poems forming the sequence 'Three Houses' in the *Collected Poems* – could be forgiven for thinking that Seamus Heaney has invented Padraic Fallon:

> I had no gift for it.
> It hung out in the welter of the moor;
> A black-faced country staring in
>
> All day. Never did the sun
> Explode with flowers in the dark vases
> Of the windows. The fall was wrong
>
> And there was uplifted the striking north
> Before the door.
> We lived in the flintlights of a cavern floor.

Heaney writes of this that 'the natural pitch of voice in his lines managed to embody a recognizably indigenous note and yet remained at ease within the decorum of the English tradition. Here was a voice that had somehow freed itself of the slightly too colourful diction and too animated address which were the legacy of the Revival to the poets of Fallon's generation; and yet it had retained its original Irish accent'.⁴ Fallon, that is to say, appeared to Heaney to have solved in his work, and long since, the problem of the relationship between Irish experience and the English literary tradition which he himself addresses in his well-known early and ingenious, but possibly to some degree fanciful, conception of 'Irish' vowels and 'English' consonants combining to form 'vocables adequate to my whole experience'.⁵

In Heaney's view the Irish–English relation figures differently, but also naturally, casually and convincingly, and in a more straight-forward political form, in Fallon's late poem 'Dardanelles, 1916', which explores a subject-matter common in Irish history but uncommon in its literature: the presence in Ireland of Irishmen wearing British army uniform during the First World War, prior to their deaths overseas. Heaney is himself the poet of a further exploration of exactly that theme in 'In Memoriam Francis Ledwidge' in *Field Work* (1979). Again, in 'Painting of My Father', in which Fallon – now living briefly, at the end of his life, in Cornwall – observes the weather of St Michael's Mount 'taking over/The whole south of England at a blow', Heaney discovers in the lines 'a passage towards new poetic conditions; they are at ease and posthumous to the old cultural, linguistic and historical anxieties'.[6] Heaney is therefore, over the course of a significant part of his own career, reading into Fallon a congruence with his own efforts to discover a way of allying, in a definitely, even definitively, post-Revival spirit, an Irish and an English poetic, and to bring into a poetry that is ungainsayably Irish, even though written in English, material of a kind that neither the literary politics of the Irish Revival nor the cultural politics of the Irish nationalist tradition would leave any space for, even though such material reflects the actual experience of numerous Irish people. Kiberd's *Field Day* essay and Heaney's introduction, then, set the aesthetic, cultural and political parameters of what ought to be Fallon's current new visibility, or audibility; although, as I have already noted, he has not yet been at all adequately absorbed into, or assimilated by, the traditions to which these critiques attach him. What I offer here is one further attempt at integration.

II

In attempting a genuinely post-Revival Irish voice in English, even though he had begun as a poet at the time of the tail-end of the Revival itself, Fallon, of necessity, had to lay a Yeatsian ghost to rest; and he did so by taking on the Yeatsian challenge in his own work. Donald Davie, an admirer of the spirited but also inevitably anxious enterprise, observed that Fallon's 'direct and unabashed dialogue with that overbearing predecessor is strikingly at odds with Austin Clarke's evasive obliquities';[7] and certainly, if Clarke evinces throughout his career a wariness which is also, in the end, a weariness with the Yeatsian heritage, Fallon's acknowledgements of it offer appreciation and awe as also the site of deviation and self-definition. The 'dialogue' with Yeats is a contestation too and may be read as almost a textbook demonstration of a Bloomian poetic oedipality, except that in Fallon it is more self-conscious and will-driven than the Bloomian conception of poetic anxiety as the sublimation of aggression would normally allow. Various poems make reference to Yeats or to his associations and affiliations (Lady Gregory, Maud Gonne, the poets of the nineties); but four in particular constitute what might be considered a sequence of interrogation and self-interrogation, a circling of the matter with a view to getting it right and getting it rightly expressed: 'Yeats's Tower at Ballylee', 'Fin de Siècle', 'Yeats at Athenry, Perhaps' and 'Stop on the Road to Ballylee'.

The image of Yeats projected in these poems is that of a mastery and authority before which Fallon is adulatory without being abject. Indeed, the images of power associated with Yeats are also connected with a steadying, resolve or empathy in the younger poet who is their witness, even as the poems accumulate a residue of Yeatsian quotation. In 'Yeats's Tower at Ballylee' – written, as an editorial note informs us, after Fallon had visited the tower, then in a state of decrepitude, in 1950 – Yeats is 'a man in whom man cried with a great wound'. His cyclical vision of history, as it responds to the Irish civil war of the 1920s, and his theory of self and anti-self, which has scope for both violence and sanctity, are still, and newly, relevant to this poet as he himself responds to the Korean War (and its threatened apocalypticism in a Third World War): 'O the higher we climb up the wider our despair'. In 'Fin de Siècle' Yeats is caught in that early phase of his protracted poetic immaturity when the first literary stars of the nineties are being destroyed by alcohol, drug-dependency and suicide. The poem's appropriate and pointed mixing of mythologies conceives of them as at once both Pegasuses and Icaruses, while Yeats waits his moment in dedicated preparation ('out on the periphery he put in the time'). The poem's final lines render the long-since triumphant Yeats in the continued self-assertiveness of old age; and they do so in a suitably immoderate image which turns the Pegasus of poetry into a hungrier animal altogether (perhaps with an implicit nod in the direction of Yeats's sexuality in age, and also with due acknowledgement to the horses of Yeats's own poems):

> A bit unsound in wind, heavy of limb,
> He rises from his years to find
> A great carnivorous creature under him.

For Fallon, who put in his own time on the periphery for so long, and whose later work came into possession of new capacities and tonalities, there is presumably an element of self-identification in this Yeatsian conception. The poem knows in its bones what a hunger for mastery is like, and it celebrates here not only triumphal self-assertion but fortitude, resolution and patience.

If these poems figure forth authority, however, they also emblematize what might, initially, be taken for insecurity. In 'Yeats's Tower at Ballylee' the idea of making what the opening line calls a 'pilgrimage' to the Yeatsian shrine is apparently ironically undercut by the fact that this poet-protagonist arrives 'in a Ford car / At the Tower talking of markets and wool'; and the poem concludes by coming full circle, when the poet hears two countrymen 'talk of cattle and the price of wool'. This might be said to frame the empathetic understanding of Yeats's poems and theories evident in this poem's twelve stanzas – whose solidity of architectural shape recalls the great stanzaic patternings of Yeats after the mid-point of his career – with an abiding image of the poet as countryman or even 'paudeen', that figure of Yeatsian derision. Even more, in 'Yeats at Athenry, Perhaps', an image of Yeats is offered in contradistinction to that of the young poet, 'The jerseyed fellow driving out the cows'. The poem's title, with its defensively conjectural or conditional adverb 'perhaps', is the measure of an apparent insecurity culminating in resentment: the poem imagines how the young Fallon might have encountered Yeats as he changed trains for Gort, since Fallon was brought up in Athenry in Co. Galway, only a short distance from Lady Gregory's Coole Park estate; but it concludes with a possibly almost envious question about Yeats's presumed motivation which insists on the way a shared topography need not imply the sharing of anything else, even when those who share it are both poets: 'Why muddy a feathered foot when a great house waited?'

'Yeats at Athenry, Perhaps' therefore marks the distance between the two poets as that between Anglo-Ireland and 'Irish Ireland'. Resentment, however, if it forms part of the poem's motive, is itself challenged by a more robust response too which takes its place in what might be thought a series of displacements or disruptions of the Yeatsian image in these poems. Fallon imagines Yeats disapproving of the architecture of Athenry, including its 'weathered Famine chapel'; and he aborts the thought that Yeats might nevertheless have been attracted to its still relatively pagan maytime rituals by the opposing thought that he would also have disapproved of its Catholic icon of the Virgin, finding it not heroic but Italianate-pathetic. Yeats's disapproval, however, is met by a finely-toned confidence in Fallon's own attachment to the Gaelic history of Athenry. Ghosted by the battle there in 1319 in which the last Gaelic king of Connaught was defeated, 'Yeats at Athenry, Perhaps' implies that, even had Yeats ever actually been in Athenry, he would have had no access to this alternative, still imaginatively viable history; the poem begins, indeed, with an assertion of distinction which is caught between pride and vulnerability: 'We had our towers too'. If, in the act of making its claim for poetically defensible difference, this has still its Yeatsian cadence ('I too had pretty plumage once'), it nevertheless challenges Yeats on the ground of imaginative sympathy. Where the poet of 'Yeats's Tower at Ballylee' is sympathetically inward with, and appreciative of, Yeats's apocalyptic conception of history, the poet here views Yeats as disdainfully and limitingly shut off from the history and religion which form the deepest imaginative structures of the lives most people in fact lead in the west of Ireland. Resentment is also, therefore, an act of defiance. Similarly, we may think, the images of the poet as countryman, paudeen and driver of a car in 'Yeats's Tower at Ballylee' insist on the contemporary realities of the agricultural Irish state which succeeded the civil war. The figure of the poet in his Ford car may be thought implicitly to rebuke the anachronistic or histrionic epitaph Yeats wrote for himself ('Horseman, pass by', when most of those doing so would be in automobiles, not on horseback, as the poet must have known perfectly well). The poems therefore imply that driving a car rather than walking on pilgrimage, and talking of markets and the price of cattle, are no bar to sharing with the would-be aristocratic Yeats, at least in part, an aesthetic and a historiography. Fallon, that is to say, finds in these poems a self-image as poet which allows him to withstand the Yeatsian *hauteur*; the poems give him a way of acknowledging Yeats without being false to himself or the rural Irish Catholic people he comes from. Yeats is prominently included in Fallon's work, but he is also judged and found wanting there; and the mode of inclusion is therefore also a mode of survival.[8]

This is the burden too of the complex, ambitious and not quite satisfactorily resolved last poem in what I have identified as this sequence, 'Stop on the Road to Ballylee'. Written in the Poundian manner which Fallon occasionally adopted in his later work, its stop on the road to Yeats's tower is in fact a stop at the mental hospital at Ballinasloe, which appears to have been the building which once housed the school Fallon attended. Again in a brief epitome, as it were, of a Poundian system of subject rhyming, the poem interweaves Fallon's schooling, and an incident in which some of his schoolfellows were 'sacked' for sexual misconduct, with attitudes to the mental patients in the asylum and allusions to Yeats and to the Horace whom Fallon read at school. The poem's nostalgia, scruple, pain and perhaps paradoxical self-assertion are, in the end, poised on a knife-edge of uncertainty in relation to Yeats and the Yeatsian example: this 'stop on the road to Ballylee' is occasioned by the necessary duty Fallon must do to his own origins and, more, to some of the most pitiful members of his own community, about whom Yeats would have had nothing whatever to say:

> Now joy is difficult (like Beauty), but the big tower would have us
> Make our verse like his, sing
> Jubilant Muses. And these sad quidnuncs
> Sidling by and round some broken thing . . .

Which is why the poem draws to a close in lines which make the necessary obeisances, even as they pose an opposition (and do so in terms which employ what may be read as an ironic or subversive reference to the third section of *Hugh Selwyn Mauberley* – 'What god, man, or hero / Shall I place a tin wreath upon!'):

> Three measures
> Of clay and we're at liberty to leave
> To lay our tin wreathes on more iambic matter
> At the Big Tower (those centenaries)
> In Ballylee, Ballylee.

The sad quidnuncs – those who say 'what now?' – are of course the mental patients in their abjection; but they are also, surely, figures for the poet himself asking what might succeed the Yeatsian model, example or provocation when you know that the Yeatsian sonorities and assumptions can never be your own. The 'more iambic matter' is, of course, the well-dressed Yeatsian stanza itself, which Fallon inherits successfully enough in 'Yeats's Tower at Ballylee' and 'Yeats at Athenry, Perhaps', but which, in this poem, he interrupts decisively in favour of the more floating, almost evanescent tread of the Poundian, essentially dactyllic metres which seem to erase, even as they imprint, their metrical footfalls. The 'broken thing' that is a particular kind of un-Yeatsian Irish historical experience is responsively imitated by a broken Poundian metric, rather than an insistently or even arrogantly Yeatsian one. The stop on the road to Ballylee, therefore, is both a literal halt on the way to a centenary celebration at the Yeatsian tower and a figurative interruption by a successor to the autocratic serenity of a Yeatsian aesthetic imposition. The poem thus renders itself 'at liberty to leave' in more than one sense: it has done its duty by the 'quidnuncs', stopping for them where necessary, and as a matter of ungainsayable obligation; but it has also paused in its approbation of the big tower, undermining Yeatsian unities of Being with the fracturing fragility of 'some broken thing'. The phrase 'big tower' significantly figures in the poem in both lower and upper case, as though Yeats's chosen residence at Ballylee is in a constant process of aspiration to the heights of the 'big houses' his poems celebrate so frequently; and the political charge of this typographical emphasis makes this poem one answer to the anguished question once asked by Elizabeth Bowen, the owner of one such house: 'have they been called "big" with a slight inflection – that of hostility, irony?'[9]

III

Fallon's *oeuvre* challenges Yeats, then, by opposing to his Celtic Revival version of the West of Ireland an actual rural West going about its necessary post-Independence business but still haunted by its Gaelic origins. In this conception, the figure of the blind minstrel poet Raftery runs through the work in a way that is presumably partly intended to offer a variant on the revivalist appropriations of him by Yeats, Hyde and Lady Gregory. More prominently, Athenry itself figures in the poetry as both a realistically realized and a quasi-mythologized location. In poems such as the spaciously associative 'Poem for my Mother' and 'A Visit West', family origins and ties are given their affectionate but discriminating expression; and in such work as the sequence 'Athenry' itself, an autobiographical intrication in historical, political and mythological contingency is rendered in a way that occasionally recalls the similar autobiographical mythologizing of the English poet Geoffrey Hill in his *Mercian Hymns* (1971).[10] This, for instance, is a section which differentiates the intimacy of the poet's knowledge of his place from that of the guidebook:

> Notable for its cattle fairs, says the book.
> Follow me here. I am
> The Antlered boy,
> A wood of horns my home. I move
> Where great beasts in the street rise out of mud:
>
> I go forth in a caul of dung. I
> Am at home in the house of the people,
> Their genuflections are mine,
> Mine the Barbaroi with the green thumbs,
> Cousins on the one dug.

These lines identify the poet with his tribe – the barbarians as opposed, it must be assumed, to the *civilisés* of Yeats's poems – in the same gesture in which they inevitably detach him from it, as the knowledgeable purveyor of Frazerian myth; and they have a political implication ('Their genuflections are mine') which becomes explicit in several poems, notably 'The Young Fenians' and 'Heroes 1916'; the latter maintaining feelingful respect even as it registers disenchantment.

They also have a religious implication which is writ large elsewhere in Fallon, and strikingly identified in 'For Paddy Mac', a poem written at least in part in memory of the poet Patrick MacDonough. Critics of Fallon usually cite some of these lines to suggest the way in which he distinguishes himself from revivalist conceptions of Western identity, and they are right to do so, since this is Fallon at his most engagingly wry; yet the poem also, it seems to me, goes extraordinarily elsewhere as it advances:

> That was my country, beast, sky, and anger:
> For music a mad piper in the mud;
> No poets I knew of; or they mouthed each other's words;
> Such low powered gods
> They died, as they were born, in byres.

Oh, maybe some rags and tatters did sing.
But poetry, for all your talk, is never that simple,
Coming out of a stone ditch in the broadlands
Newborn, or from
The fitful pibroch of a lonely thorn,

Or old saws at winter fires.
Muted the big words. Love was left
To eloping earls or such
Lest the snake creep up, usurping the ancient timber
And some odd bloom come bursting from the Cross.

If these lines agree that a broken poetry of the actual West is – even if only just – possible, they also know the intransigent difficulties ranged against any such thing; they realize the ways in which the pieties of mid-century Irish rural Catholicism may banish poetic resources at the same time as they banish a satisfactory sexuality. When Fallon finds 'Love' lacking in the culture of his own place, his judgement is phrased in an image which appears to indict the religion by offering it scandal or affront. The Biblical 'snake', or serpent, is here transformed into a phallic snake which, usurping the sacred timber of the Crucifixion, blooms and bursts forth as Christ's erection.

Such an eroticized Christ may knowledgeably accord with what Leo Steinberg has more recently catalogued – to my mind, but not to everyone's, persuasively – as the erectile sexuality of many Renaissance Crucifixions and Depositions, a sexuality which he believes has strong (and orthodox) theological connotations.[11] It is also continuous, however, with Fallon's mythologizing of the figure of the Virgin in such poems as 'Virgin', 'Assumption', 'Mater Dei' and 'Magna Mater'; the point here being that if in Fallon 'Their genuflections are mine', they are so only by his in fact varying the piety of genuflection with the heterodoxy of a Catholicism more conformable to, or recuperable by, a post-psychoanalytic sexual sophistication. If the tendency and orientation of this is Fallon's equivalent to Austin Clarke's versions of the Celtic-Romanesque, it is also at one with the anthropological mythologizings of Eliot and, notably, Pound. Fallon is nowhere more thoroughgoing a modernist than when his Virgin is Atlas, vestal, Syrian fertility goddess, object of *amour courtois*, Venus and Diana before she is also, but emphatically, the 'mild lady' of Irish Catholic iconography. The collocation of mythologies, however, also insists on the way the Christian myth desexualizes woman, and man too: for Fallon, it is a myth in which, precisely, there is no 'bloom' on the Cross. The collocation therefore supplies some of his most characteristic and witty ruminations, such as the opening stanza of 'Magna Mater':

> A dove plus an
> Assenting virgin is
> An odd equation; the bird of Venus, the
> Shotsilk woodhaunter and
> A country shawl
> In congress to produce
> The least erotic of the gods.

There is an elegant comedy of discrepancy at work in those lines, in which gently clashing registers – the computational language of algebra and the rich figuration of 'shotsilk woodhaunter' – are humorously expressive of the theological or mythological discrepancy itself, in which God becomes man in an act of intercourse virtually purged of sexuality ('congress' has its sexual, but also its governmental sense). By implication, such an act of congress produces a religion similarly cleansed.

Some of Fallon's mythological poems therefore go on the prowl for more erotic gods. He has versions of classical themes – Orestes, Odysseus, Argos, Penelope as Lady Gregory in 'Kiltartan Legend', and the dismembered Orpheus of the outstanding metamorphic sequence 'The Head' – which give the originals vividly contemporaneous forms, despite the fact that they have all been already much written into modern literature. This is notably the case when 'A Public Appointment' revisits the encounter between Odysseus and Nausicaa, which is, of course, transformed by Joyce in the 'Nausicaa' section of *Ulysses* (with its own prominent association between the Homeric virgin and the Virgin Mary), in order to offer a final image in which 'Love' is returned in a newly eroticized form; a Nausicaa, we might say, as a substitute for the demure Virgin of Catholic iconography:

> Yes, though he died old and slowly
> Into his vineyards, requiring like the sun
> One whole horizon to decline upon,
> The image that remains

Is the haunted man on the main of love, forever
Sailing, and beside him a virgin at the tiller.

'Decline' is richly, and punningly, expressive: this post-Tennysonian,
post-Joycean Odysseus descends towards death even as he is
inflected grammatically, until he fetches up as a figure in numerous
subsequent works of art, a 'whole horizon' of possibility, opportunity and allusive derivation; and the echoing phrase 'the main of love',
which itself half-echoes Shakespeare's 'the main of light' in the
Sonnets, portrays an Odysseus endlessly restless for the new
opportunities of sexual love rather than restless until his heart rests
again in his return to Ithaca (even if the word 'virgin' has an inevitably masculinist edge in this context). In mid-century Ireland this is
a further riskily unorthodox Ulysses, an image of the poet trans-
ported by the hunger of desire.

Fallon's revisions of classical mythology in poems such as this are
congruent with his declaration in 'Sunday Morning' – that
Stevensian title, with its post-Christian connotations – that 'God is
dead, / His shadow what I throw for / Beyond into hurt and metaphor'. The 'hurt' is the wound inevitably attendant on the loss of
traditional faith and certainties; but the metaphors discover,
alternatively, a rich hoard of analogy and implication. In 'Lakshmi',
in particular, the 'dangerous bronze figure' of a Hindu goddess is
scrutinized in a punctiliously exact and almost entranced manner
until it reveals an altogether more eroticized religion than Irish
Catholicism: 'buttocks in motion, / . . . there was / Dancing here that
folded into a lotus'. The poem is an act of sympathetic intelligence,
at once reverent and voluptuous, in respect of this compelling
example of an alien religious culture: its interest in Eastern religion
and mysticism, which is evinced in other poems of Fallon's too, is at
one with what he calls elsewhere 'the larger toleration of the poem'.
Written in a political state in which the forces of reactionary Roman
Catholic censorship held sway, 'Lakshmi' may be read as an implicit
act of defiance.

Other mythological poems, however, such as 'Totem' and 'Boyne
Valley', have not so much a corrective as a correlative motive and
impulse; they bring Irish agricultural and historical reality into con-
gruity with mythological system. Behind 'Totem', and demonstrably
within the poem's narrative, is a farmer's putting-down of a sick
cow; but the incident is made ramifyingly emblematic when it is

regarded as sacrilegious by the adherents of what seems a 'primitive' religion:

> They knew it, the Totem people, the world
> Inside the world where man
> Makes metaphors
> For the animal.

Crossed with the evocation of a human death too, this killing – which the Totem people regard as 'murder' – prompts several stanzas on the way a primitivist religious view of life might continue to offer challenge to a briskly sophisticated, commonsensical, clear-minded rationalism, to which the poet's persona owes allegiance:

> . . . this old shambling skeleton in rawhide
> Is totally translated and taken over:
> Here in a way lies
> Everybody's mother
>
> Confusing certain formal issues, an
> Ambiguous body at best, straddling
> Source and origin like
> The first dolmen,
>
> Requiring the old almost religious
> Liaison, from whose
> Mysterious totem bones I must ask pardon
> For a pact broken . . .

This poem might well be read in tandem with some of Paul Muldoon's in which Native American experience and history are read into, or across, Irish Catholic experience and history; but whereas Muldoon's anthropology is turned and tuned prominently – although not exclusively – towards a politics rather than a theology, Fallon's here is an effort to hold in the balance with modern sophistication a genuine, unimpugnable and quite uncondescending sense of the emotional and spiritual validities of the ancient pieties. 'Here in a way lies / Everybody's mother' is the rueful acknowledgement that, psychologically, this is territory we all inhabit in relation to our sharpest experiences of familial piety and grief: so that, the poem implies without quite stating, similar communal experience is to be mourned when it vanishes; hence the sophisticated poet's asking pardon for the broken tribal pact. Many of Fallon's mythological poems, some of which seem very deeply meditated indeed, imply a similar wavering between a sense of the profit and a sense of the loss involved when the grand narratives of a still partly pagan Irish rural Catholicism are on the wane. If the world to the literary sophisticate no longer conforms to 'the world / Inside the world' known by the metaphors of these Totem people, Fallon's own new-minted mythological metaphor expresses the moment of self-doubt with consummately unpresuming tact. Constituting both appreciation and scepticism, 'Totem' rides the current of a transitional moment of Irish modernity in a way that makes the Stevensian title of 'Sunday Morning' the proposal of an alignment which is neither self-important nor disproportionate.

III

Discussing 'Stop on the Road to Ballylee' above, I hope I indicated how significant a poem I take it to be. Nevertheless nobody, I think, would want to cite its last three lines in defence of any claims made for Fallon before a disinterested but unpersuaded reader: there is little to be done with the lines other than to wish them away (just as the phrase about 'formal issues' in the lines above seems to have strayed into that poem, discordantly, from the language of scholastic theology). His uncertain judgement about bringing some of his poems to successful conclusion or resolution may be consistent with deconstructive or postmodern suspicions of closure – in which, I suppose, they might be read as a challenge to what has frequently been criticized as the brassily resolved clamour and clang of Yeats's endings, their too eager and, to some, suspect grasping after order and completion – but they are also one instance of a more general stylistic instability. Donald Davie is aware of, but also generous to, this defect, when he reads Fallon as 'a brilliant opportunist, and content to be so'.[12] At the end of 'Johnstown Castle', a further contribution to the extensive sub-genre of Irish 'Big House' poems, Fallon has a self-reflexive and engagingly poignant section in which he defines the effort and motivating power of self-revelation behind what he calls the poet's 'makeshift monologue'. The phrase does touchingly but justly characterize the provisional nature of some of the forms Fallon finds or stitches together from what happens to be to hand: poems can run through long stretches of *echt* Fallon only to dilapidate suddenly and unpredictably, although usually for no more than a few lines, into pastiche Eliot, Rilke, Muir, Dylan Thomas, Yeats himself (even after the argumentative challenge has been made), and Pound. Even in the last ten years of his life, he produced in 'Trevaylor' – his ear suddenly richly seduced, no doubt – a brilliant but altogether disconcerting pastiche of Sylvia Plath, which may also be read as a prayer to his many poetic mentors ('brilliant', because its inheritance of the Plath rhythm and imagery turns them to such profit; in these lines, when 'mirror', inherited from its many uses in Plath, is played against 'countenance', and when 'water' is 'fathomed' in a trope from Plath now turned entirely to Fallon's own original purpose):

> First, this
> Prayer, that you the people
> Gone over, ghosts, bright
> Narcissi, lean into my pool now
> And be this poem.
>
> Empty are
> All mirrors you do not countenance;
> The fabulous water is
> Fathomed by no horizons
> Till you come, till you appear.

For all the brilliance of their reflections, however, such mirrors may well end up by discountenancing the poet himself.

However, if makeshift is the price Fallon has to pay for following so closely on the feathered Yeatsian heels with his own large ambition, it is a makeshift in which he sometimes, nevertheless, shifts extraordinarily well for himself, and in which an aesthetic of patience, which is also an exemplary self-reliance, is very deeply inscribed. In a handful of poems written late in his life, makeshift in fact gives way to something more vibrantly self-assured. In such poems as the ninth part of the sequence 'The Small Town of John Coan (2)', 'A Bit of Brass', 'Body', 'Dardanelles 1916' and 'A Hedge Schoolmaster', Fallon manages a sudden, absolute final reckoning in which the old mythological interests and the Yeatsian dialogue cede to a newly summarizing strength. 'Dardanelles 1916', for instance, opens with the vivid memory of a local Connaught Ranger, Private Patrick Carty, 'stomping' into the family home on his way to the Front during the First World War. The poem takes the memory and transforms it into this:

> Filling the back kitchen, squinting
> Down from the roofbeams, shyly
> Shaking hands all round the family, smiling;
> Me he picks up and by God kisses me.
>
> Up there under
> The brown-white plaster an unknown soldier's face
> Is weeping.
>
> Do I remember more? The urchin daughters
> Bold for once and peeping
> Washed and ribboned through the door to wave
> Him off on the Mail, the 4.15, and away
> Where muted now in a long sand he lies, if not
> Entirely melted into
> The steadfast bony glare of Asia Minor.

There is a Poundian imagistic swiftness and fleeting impressionism in this, rendered more definite or concrete by the formal, almost classical inversion of the fourth line and its inclusion of the informal Irishism of that 'by God', which makes the child's astonishment immediate once again so much later now, in the time of the poem. The contrast between the concrete and the indefinite is vibrant in the poem's subject as well as its form, since its particularities – the naming of the Irish regiment, of Private Patrick Carty, and of the time of his train; the characterization of the shy young soldier; the sudden embarrassment felt by the child at his kiss – resolve or dissolve poignantly into 'an unknown soldier's face' and into his muteness and melting in the final lines. '*An* unknown soldier' is more anonymous even than '*the* unknown soldier', since, less particularized, it dramatizes the fact that his fate is shared with numerous others; and the poem visibly performs the transformation from named identity to anonymity when the three lines following the memory of the kiss appear to stamp his ghostly, disembodied, unnamed face into the roofbeams he stood under in the large-bodied spontaneity of his actual presence and name. Carty's namelessness in death is intensified by the fact that the poem implies a history of political and cultural amnesia too. This anonymity is clinched, terribly, in the alliterative sequence of 'muted' and 'melted'. 'Muted', particularly when it is contained in the exhaled sigh of the inverted phrase 'Where muted now in a long sand he lies', takes its edge from an etymology: it means 'terminally silenced', of course, but it also means 'excreted' (hawks 'mute' their faeces, in a usage probably near-archaic now, but not given as such in *OED*, whose last example is, nevertheless, from 1820). This sense is congruent with the peculiarity of the phrase 'a long sand', which appears to identify one such sand from the indistinguishable sands of the desert in which Carty is buried, and therefore suggests an individual, if invisible, grave or plot; and it is congruent too with the word 'melted' which carries the excretory dissolution even further. In the poem's final superb line, a long perspective is taken in a way that summons not only a tradition of English elegy, and elegy of the First World War, but, more particularly, I think, the poetry of Isaac Rosenberg, with its hauntingly reiterated imagery of moonlight and strange shadows, and such lines as those that open 'The One Lost', an address by an anonymous dead soldier to the mud in which he too is melted:

> I mingle with your bones.
> You steal in subtle noose
> This lighted dust Jehovah loans
> And now I loose.
>
> What will the Lender say
> When I shall not be found,
> Safe sheltered at the Judgment Day,
> Being in you bound?

This collocation may not prove an influence, exactly, but it does propose a communality of spirit; and, if this is accepted, then 'Dardanelles 1916' effects, as far as I am aware, a unique juncture between Southern Irish poetry and the English poetry of the First World War. In bringing Private Patrick Carty into an Irish poem then, Fallon is both organizing at least one appropriate memorial for the Irish dead of that war and asserting a communality of experience which subtly sabotages the aims of an over-insistent nationalist cultural aesthetic. 'Dardanelles 1916' also demonstrates how, on occasion, what I have called oxymoronically the gentle clash of registers in Fallon is not a stylistic liability but a formal resource: the variation in register here makes for an acutely alert and intelligent encounter with a difficult, manifestly long-withheld subject. Which all makes it richly appropriate that the penultimate poem in Fallon's *Collected* is 'A Hedge Schoolmaster'. A monologue by the classically-trained eponymous master in one of those Irish schools in which Catholic rural children were educated during Penal times, the poem is, throughout, a lament, a repining and a rebuke; but it becomes at last an index of defiance and a form of celebration, in which the poet Padraic Fallon clearly implicates himself, and with a characteristically learned metrical wit:

> No profit in it, or credit. Boors thrive
> But I eat afield with the crows;
> No goose gravy for Tom Euclid;
> The master feasts on the hedgerows;
>
> Yet, Pallas Athene, your true legionary
> In the last earthworks, the lone garrison, still
> Arrays himself in the delicate dactyls to
> Decline you to the barbarian.

IV Coda: 'A Flask of Brandy'

I would not want to end this essay on Fallon by too strongly giving the impression that only in the end does he win through to a definite style of his own, since this is, despite his stylistic uncertainties and hesitations, by no means the case. There are poems throughout his career which are perfectly achieved and resolved. One such, 'A Flask of Brandy', is written in a style entirely at the service of, and congruent with, its subject; it is a style, therefore, which, unrepeated in Fallon's *oeuvre*, exhausts itself in one swift act of intimate appropriateness. I first encountered the poem in the Dolmen *Poems* in 1974 and it has stayed powerfully with me ever since:

> You, said the Lionwoman,
> Pliz, this errand, a snipe of brandy
> From the first shop. Here's money;
> And for you this penny.

And on my way I saw:
Item, a clown who waltzed on stilts;
A bear saluting with a paw;
Two pairs of dancing dogs in kilts;
Eight midget ponies in a single file,
A very piccolo of ponies;
Then the princess far off in her smile;
And the seven beautiful distant ladies:
And then –

Facing after the big bandwaggon, he
The boy in spangles, lonely and profound:
Behind him the Ringmaster, a redfaced man,
Followed by silence heavy as a wound,
And empty.

Quickly as two feet can did I come back
To the Lionwoman with her cognac.

You, said the Lionwoman;
Pliz to the window, said foreign gutterals in
The cave of the caravan.
I waited, errand done.

And waiting on one foot saw:
Item: a twitching coloured chintz
Moved by a lemontaloned claw:
And after a woman with her face in paints,
A throat thickened in its round of tan
On shoulders sick and white with nature;
Behind was a pair of bloomers on a line,
Blue; a table with a tin platter:
More else:

A black electric cat, a stove, a pot
Purring, and a wild red Indian blanket
Crouching sidewise on a bunk;
And some exciting smell that stunk
Till the lionwoman rising blotted out
All but a breast as heavy as a sigh
That stared at me from one bruised eye.

This is no doubt alert to previous novelistic, pictorial and cinematic circuses and symbolist pierrots, and may seem also curiously proleptic of such subsequent circus inventory poems as Paul Muldoon's 'Duffy's Circus' in *Mules*; but its circus is uniquely realized too in its grandly exuberant and exhilarating catalogue, which includes the dandyish Stevensian flourish of that 'very piccolo of ponies'. The exuberance is propelled by the buoyant playfulness of the poem's rhyme and off-rhyme (brandy / money / penny/ chintz / paints; and the witty internal rhyme in which the poetic line separates those 'bloomers on a line' from their colour, and first-syllable rhyme, 'blue'). This propulsion is itself initiated by the startling confidence of the *in medias res* opening, with its ungainsayably adult, and foreign-sounding, imperative instruction to the child-persona. The humorous foreignness of the four-letter monosyllable 'Pliz' is then itself matched or even trumped by its being 'rhymed', as it were, with the archaic four-letter dissyllable of the word 'Item', that initiation of catalogue in old ledger and computation, which seems both decorously appropriate to, but also exaggeratedly discrepant with, a recounting of childhood memories; and the comedy resides in the discrepancy. This may also be thought true of the contrast between the poem's title, which names a 'flask' of brandy, and its opening stanza, where this is, alternatively, a 'snipe' of brandy; so that the phrase of the title never actually appears in the poem. 'Snipe' in this sense has no dictionary sanction; and perhaps attention is actually called to this fact by the more correct usage of the title. *OED*, however, in defining the word as of doubtful origin, offers the German 'schneppe' as a possible obscure or dialect cognate; and this, presumably, is itself cognate with 'schnapps', the Dutch gin, which is possibly why the foreign Lionwoman would use it. The point, as far as the poem is concerned, is that the phrase 'snipe of brandy' has, like the repeated peculiar pronunciation of the word 'Please' as 'Pliz', an aura of otherness about it: the child is responding to the strange and fearful attractiveness of what the poem goes on to call 'foreign gutterals', in a usage which is itself either a misspelling or a knowledgeably obscure form of the word 'gutturals'.

This linguistic foreignness is then – and this is the poem's subject – rhymed with other things still foreign to, but in the offing of, this poet-child's experience: the narratives of anxiety, death and sexuality. The first of these is carried by the implications of the relationship between the boy in spangles, that isolated follower on the joyous bandwaggon, and the Ringmaster, redfaced and in a wounded, empty silence. What this might portend is not made at all explicit; but it is certainly feasible to read out of it some narrative of violent imposition and repression, a scene of sadism, a very minatory aporia at the heart of what otherwise appears a zestfully ludic poem. Death is on the scene too, since the woman's painted face and tan-thickened throat fail to conceal from this perceptive – indeed, all-seeing – child those 'shoulders sick and white with nature'; this is indeed a Hamlet-child whose poem also says, 'Now get you to my lady's chamber and tell her, let her paint an inch thick, to this favour she must come. Make her laugh at that.' But anxiety and death are themselves occluded in the end – literally occluded, 'blotted out' – by sexuality, by the child's sensing of what might reside in the atavistic, pre-rational 'cave of the caravan'.

The perturbations of female sexuality for this male child turn on the question of what a 'Lionwoman' – that definition prominent in the opening line – might be. Is it a woman in charge of lions, a woman dressed up as a lion, or a metamorphic, Ovidian woman who is also a lion (there is that disconcerting reference to her 'lemontaloned claw')? It could be, of course, that the child, in the way of young children, gets the naming word wrong: that when the circus performer is called, by others, 'The Lionwoman', he imagines a woman-lion, and then invents the reality out of his terrified imagination; and this would harmonize with the linguistically alert, creative and ingenious consciousness witnessed by the poem. If she is a woman-lion to him, however, she is feline in a way that concentrates the same kinds of sexual unease or dread from which T. S. Eliot recoils in his misogynistic quatrain poems, where, for instance, 'The sleek Brazilian jaguar / Does not in its arboreal gloom / Distil so rank a feline smell / As Grishkin in a drawing room', and where 'Rachel *née* Rabinovitch / Tears at the grapes with murderous paws';[13] and, reinforcing the feline association, the Lionwoman is of course accompanied by a black electric cat. She is, that is to say, a woman whose sexuality is strongly sensed, smelt indeed ('some exciting smell that stunk') by the boy; and the sudden eye-to-eye contact between boy and Lionwoman in the last lines – a contact in which the woman's eye, at the same height as the child's, is actually the 'eye' of her nipple – occludes everything in an overwhelming excitement of electric erotic consciousness, 'as heavy as a sigh'.

This is a brilliantly effective conclusion to a poem which might induce, from the moment the catalogue begins, a certain anxiety about its successful closure or resolution, particularly in a reader who knows the difficulty Fallon sometimes has in bringing his poems to effective conclusion: a catalogue-poem is surely among the most difficult to resolve satisfactorily, since the disparate energy of its detail needs to be drawn into an integrity which will not seem merely willed, specious or factitious (even if in some instances of the kind the resolution might, as it were, precede the catalogue: Michael Longley's 'The Ice-Cream Man', for example). By rendering familar figures of misogyny not as adult sexual terror and disgust, but as first childish response to an eroticism sensed as both fearful and overwhelmingly attractive, 'A Flask of Brandy' richly and correctively implies that this child's errand is actually far from done, and that his waiting has only just begun. The first intrusion into the otherness of erotic confusion and unspecifiable desire is the beginning of the errand of a lifetime; the errand, you might say, of learning how to live.

4

Keeping the colours new: Louis MacNeice in the contemporary poetry of Northern Ireland

I

In W. H. Auden's 'In Memory of W. B. Yeats', written shortly after Yeats's death in January 1939, he discovers what has since become a famous trope for the way a poet might survive beyond the grave: at the moment of his death, he says, Yeats 'became his admirers'. It is clear that to the poet Auden this process is necessarily neither consoling nor desirable, since the imagery presenting it is one of Orphic dismemberment, self-estrangement, castigation and, ultimately, alimentary transformation:

> Now he is scattered among a hundred cities
> And wholly given over to unfamiliar affections;
> To find his happiness in another kind of wood
> And be punished under a foreign code of conscience.
> The words of a dead man
> Are modified in the guts of the living.

There is an almost surreal element in the final metaphor there, in which the somatic process is made to bear the burden of an alien, non-somatic substance – 'words'; and the metaphor, a peculiar one, may well be derived from Hamlet's revelation of 'how a king may go a progress through the guts of a beggar'. Neither for the king nor for the poet is the process likely to be an altogether aggrandizing one; and it is unsurprising to find Stan Smith, although not for this reason, persuasively discovering in this poem a virtually proto-deconstructive Auden.[1]

I shall return to Auden's view of Yeats later, since it is complexly involved in the issues I want to raise here; but clearly it is also a way of introducing my topic. The poet Louis MacNeice has 'become his admirers' in the recent history of poetry and criticism in Northern Ireland in a way quite unpredictable to anyone who grew up thinking of him as an English poet of the 1930s, in the shadow of Auden; and there may, indeed, be some irony in the way the loner and refuser of various affiliations in the 1930s is now so well plotted into the organizing graphs of others' solicitations. The reappropriation of MacNeice has, however, been virtually coterminous with the development of the poetry of Northern Ireland since the mid-1960s; and it represents a concerted and strategically successful form of accommodation and recuperation of a kind for which I can think of no contemporary parallel, making a strong case for what Edna Longley pleads as the 'special, living sense' of the term 'intertextuality' in relation to Northern Irish poetry: 'a creative dynamic working upon mechanisms of tradition and cultural definitions alike'.[2] It could also be claimed that the revision of MacNeice's standing and place is one of the clearest manifestations, a litmus test, of the present strength and authority of contemporary Northern Irish poetry and criticism.

In generously promenading MacNeice, contemporary Northern poets are – although not in the conventionally melodramatic, oedipal, masculinist and capitalist Bloomian modes of struggle and swerve – registering attachment to a chosen precursor. The choice is individually self-interested as well as culturally propelled, and it is unsurprising to find MacNeice taking on different colours as he appears in the work of different poets. Derek Mahon, in a piece of wittily oxymoronic critical table-turning, admires him as '*profoundly* superficial' and famously discovers matter for celebration rather than derogation in his role as 'a tourist in his own country': 'of what sensitive person is the same not true?' he asks, with a certain engagingly self-interested disingenuousness.[3] Mahon's own work as a deracinated cosmopolitan sophisticate is undoubtedly being signalled in that assumed solidarity of sensitivity, and a covert effort of self-definition is the subtext of this excellent essay, which he has characteristically subsequently derided in print.[4] This makes it strange to find him writing, in 'In Carrowdore Churchyard', his elegy for MacNeice, which pointedly opens his Viking/Gallery *Selected Poems* of 1991, a poem so apparently at variance with his customary zestfully ironic modes. Subtitled 'at the grave of Louis MacNeice', the poem has the gravity and good faith of the elegiac country churchyard tradition it inherits:

This, you implied, is how we ought to live –

The ironical, loving crush of roses against snow,
Each fragile, solving ambiguity. So
From the pneumonia of the ditch, from the ague
Of the blind poet and the bombed-out town you bring
The all-clear to the empty holes of spring,
Rinsing the choked mud, keeping the colours new.

These lines pay a lovingly recreative homage to several prominent circumstances of MacNeice's life and work: to the poem 'Snow'; to the pneumonia which caused MacNeice's death; to the figure of the 'blind poet' which appears in 'The Casualty', MacNeice's elegy for Graham Shepard, a figure Mahon ingeniously interprets in his essay; to the poems of wartime London which MacNeice wrote from the perspective of a fire-watcher; and to the many significances of the word and concept of 'colour' in MacNeice's poetry and criticism. Themselves taking on the colour MacNeice has left in the poetic landscape, these almost palimpsestic lines bring the poem's opening trope of *paysage moralisé* – 'Your ashes will not stir, even on this high ground' – to appropriate resolution; and they implicate Mahon himself, with a kind of intimacy and warmth not characteristic of his work, in the essential effort of dedication which the moralized and written-over graveyard is punned into carrying: 'This plot is consecrated, for your sake, / To what lies in the future tense.' This 'high ground' is cousin, it may be, of that 'high star' shining at the end of MacNeice's 'Thalassa': 'By a high star our course is set, / Our end is Life. Put out to sea.' What lies in the future tense of MacNeice's example and effort is, that is to say, this poem itself, and, since it is the opening poem of a large *Selected Poems*, to some degree the rest of Mahon's poetry too. Since the poem was written in 1964, one cannot very well make the point that the 'bombed-out town' was then the Belfast of the Troubles as well as London, but occurring in a contemporary Northern Irish poet's *Selected*, the collocation is surely irresistible, and deliberately so on the poet's part.[5] The generosity of recognition here is made particularly telling by Mahon's use of the potentially grandiose or portentous vocabulary of the Christian religion. The language of 'consecration' may seem not inappropriate to this Christian graveyard, or to this son of the episcopal palace, and it is, indeed, modified by the 'humane perspective' into which Mahon's poem eventually opens; but it nevertheless appears less guarded, more confirmed in its generous impulse, than we might expect from the usually tempered intelligence of Mahon's poems, of which watchful discrimination and the subtleties of self-mistrust are the very air and ambience.

Mahon's elegy does, nevertheless, preserve a tact in relation to its elegiac reverence, knowing that to put a foot one step further on this high ground would be to fall on to the much lower ground of the sententious. I am not sure that Tom Paulin's earnest in the critical pieces on MacNeice in his collection *Ireland and the English Crisis* (1984) and the essay 'Letters from Iceland: Going North' (1976) do not fall on to such ground. Nevertheless, they offer original readings of a Paulin-like, or at least early-Paulin-like MacNeice who brings an anti-pastoral instruction – rather dourly, it may seem – in the way poetry should be 'responsible, relevant and social'.[6] If the word 'relevant' – that clarion-cry of the 1960s and early 1970s – sounds out now with an almost charmingly dejected and anachronistic pathos, Paulin's perception that, when MacNeice describes the Icelandic landscape, he is implicitly writing about Irish politics and landscape too, is a striking one. It supplies the relevance of Iceland to Ireland in Paulin's own early poem 'Thinking of Iceland' in *A State of Justice* (1977), where the way 1970s Donegal is imaginatively mapped on to 1930s Iceland is the originary instance of that resourceful and increasingly complex trope in Paulin of geopolitical and historical allegorizing, analogizing, juxtaposition and parallel, that sardonically investigative tracing of symptom and causation which has been the constant impulse of so much in his otherwise extravagantly protean poetic.

Mahon and Paulin, then, confess and parade the MacNeiceian affiliation at initiatory moments in their careers, seeking and confirming, or creating a mentor or progenitor in the place of their earliest poems. Michael Longley identifies the necessity, and virtually proposes the initiation of the programme, in his essay 'The Neolithic night: a note on the Irishness of Louis MacNeice' (1975), where he writes that 'judgements would be more precise if the Northern Irish context were taken more into account';[7] and, when the programme has been long under way, he observes in his own finest contribution to it, the edited selection of MacNeice published in 1988, that 'a new generation of poets from Northern Ireland has helped to change perspectives. They have picked up frequencies in his work which were inaudible in Dublin or London.'[8] However, the picking-up of such frequencies was easier for some Northern poets at early stages of their careers than it was for others. Mahon, Paulin and Longley share not only MacNeice's Ulster background, but also, in varying degrees, his Protestant religious background and his English connections. Seamus Heaney, on the other hand, tells us in his second collection of critical essays, *The Government of the Tongue* (1988), that he bought MacNeice's *Collected Poems* when he graduated, but thought that they derived 'from a mind-stuff and . . . a cultural setting which were at one remove from me and what I came from'.[9] This is said, significantly, in a second essay on Patrick Kavanagh, to accompany the by then well-known and frequently cited first in *Preoccupations* (1980). What Heaney found exemplary in Kavanagh there, and what he manifestly himself wished to emulate, was the ability to raise 'the inherited energies of a sub-culture to the power of a cultural resource'.[10] This has its denominational inflection: the subculture in question is, of course, that of the Catholic minority of the North. In the shared aim, then, Kavanagh is for Heaney recognition, confirmation and encouragement; MacNeice's 'mind-stuff' is clearly alien to the conditionings and trajectories of that ambition, even if Heaney is arguably desophisticating his earlier self a little to make the point. Mac-Neice's poems are, however, the essay has the honesty to admit, the focus of a more vaguely apprehended ambition too: 'I envied them, of course,' Heaney says, 'their security in the big world of history and poetry which happened out there.'[11]

Some influence may in fact be veiled by these remarks, since it is hard to believe that *Letters from Iceland*, and in particular 'Postscript to Iceland', dedicated to Auden, did not play some part among the many intertexts of *North*, with MacNeice's psychologizing of the alien territory – 'the North begins inside' – and its culmination in the minatory moment 'before / The gun-butt raps upon the door'. Nevertheless, it is only when Heaney himself becomes secure in that big world of poetry and history, and secure too in a cosmopolitan existence well beyond the scope of the original parish, that he finds adequate space for MacNeice in his criticism. In his essay 'The Pre-Natal Mountain: Vision and Irony in Recent Irish Poetry', MacNeice becomes the exemplar of a potential new perspective: he 'positioned his lever in England,' Heaney says, 'and from that position moved his Irish subject-matter through a certain revealing distance'.[12] The fact that distance and its capacity for alternative revelation are much on Heaney's own creative mind at this later stage of his career is clear from the entire orientation of his books *The Haw Lantern* and *Seeing Things*, where the interest in parable, in visionary transcendence and in the revisiting of earlier phases of the career in order to read them differently are all elements of a newly individualistic self-assurance, a position from which authoritative judgement may be made, from which satisfaction may be expressed without complacency, desire without velleity. If there is MacNeicean sanction for these new distances and perspectives, there are also more specific traces in particular poems. The title 'Parable Island', for instance, of a poem first published in a Festschrift for William Golding, derives from a phrase MacNeice uses in his book *Varieties of Parable*, which concludes with a discussion of Golding.[13] The title 'A Postcard from Iceland' clearly alludes to *Letters from Iceland* but also, perhaps, makes a graceful little bow of obeisance, a postcard being an altogether less significant missive than a letter. And 'The Disappearing Island' secretes an episode from the narratives of the voyages of St Brendan or Brandan, with which MacNeice was fascinated, and from which he derived a great deal of imaginative stimulus.

When Heaney speaks of MacNeice 'positioning his lever', he is employing one of those classroom metaphors that figure in both his poetry and his critical prose: here the lever recalls Archimedes and the physics lesson. These metaphors are compelling in their childlike immediacy and aura of nostalgia, but they are also sly in their authoritative, tutorial panache, as they measure, weigh and balance. In his writing about MacNeice, Heaney has something of a field day – one might say – with such figures. In 'Carrick Revisited', he says, 'the whole parallelogram of cultural and ancestral forces operating in MacNeice's life is discovered and thereby to a certain extent redressed'.[14] The geometrical metaphor here, which offers the sense of unwieldy properties and relations mapped and plotted into manageability by the effort of MacNeice's own work, is elaborately extended in Heaney's final lecture as Professor of Poetry in Oxford.

He uses the authority of his platform here to offer his own new geometry of modern Irish writing, by developing a binarism between Joyce's Martello and Yeats's Thoor Ballylee which he has employed elsewhere in his criticism. In a figure of extremely self-aware remapping, he presents the idea of a 'quincunx' of literary architecture. The quincunx establishes in relationship a central 'round tower' of what Heaney calls 'prior Irelandness' located at MacNeice's 'pre-natal mountain'; Spenser's Kilcolman Castle; Yeats's Ballylee; Joyce's Martello; and, finally and for the first time, 'MacNeice's Keep' – which is, of course, at Carrickfergus Castle. 'By writing his castle into the poetic annals', Heaney says, '[MacNeice] has completed the figure.' But it is, of course, Heaney who has completed the figure, in a bravura act of new geometrical reappropriation, an attempt to 'sketch the shape of an integrated literary tradition', one which includes, in MacNeice, a literature of the Protestant North lacking any sectarian dimension.[15] The act of writing Carrickfergus Castle into the annals in this way, when Heaney began by excluding MacNeice in favour of Kavanagh, has involved painful reorientation and realignment on his part too. If the reorientation is in part a further exemplification of Heaney's self-image as a poet-chieftain 'still parleying, in earshot of his peers' in the poem 'Terminus' in *The Haw Lantern* – and his career may well be read as a kind of elegantly self-revising parley – my word 'painful' for these reorientations is no mere figure. This lecture, which terminates with the geometry of the quincunx, originates in a tellingly baffled account of Heaney's anxieties when he was housed in an Oxford college room normally tenanted by a British cabinet minister on the day of the death of one of the IRA hunger-strikers in the Maze Prison, a man from a family well known to Heaney. It is, of course, to the point – although it is not a point Heaney makes – that the accommodating quincunx is a figure constructed exclusively from military architecture: towers, castles and keeps.

II

I do not wish here to take up further these implications of Heaney's figure, apart from mildly wondering where other less military and possibly less imposing Irish literary architecture might appear in the surface area of this quincunx: Kavanagh's farm, for instance, or Clarke's villa in Rathfarnham, or, indeed, Heaney's own cottage in Glanmore or even his office in Harvard: that is to say, the figure, despite itself and its own generous instinct, inevitably also appears to act as an exclusionary zone.[16] I want, rather, to turn to MacNeice again by remarking how, in one way, Heaney's identification of his work with the castle's keep, while it has its manifest ideological point, is strangely inappropriate in its suggestions of solidity and permanence. For all the differences of discovery and self-discovery that these later Northern poets articulate in their treatment of MacNeice, they are agreed on the essential mobility of imagination and position in the work. Honourably a tourist in his own country, says Mahon; 'His imagination is essentially fluid, maritime and elusively free,' says Paulin;[17] Michael Longley, in 'The Neolithic night', celebrates his empirical anti-systematizing; Heaney himself, in *The Place of Writing*, reads him in terms of 'distance' and 'doubleness'. Heaney's geometry and architecture, then, have the effect of hardening flux into the permanence of manageable form and identity, of appearing to make the fluidity of the work cohere into a more readily identifiable construct. This is at odds with the actual architecture of MacNeice's own poems, whose paradigm is the house of 'Variation on Heraclitus', where 'Even the walls are flowing', and where the variation proposes the theme 'One cannot live in the same room twice.' I assume that it was this kind of architecture that prompted Hedli MacNeice's metaphor in her short but pregnant piece 'The Story of the House that Louis Built', where this house is imagined as 'a handsome house with thick walls. The windows on the west side looked towards Connemara, Mayo and the sea. Those to the south scanned Dorset, the Downs and Marlborough – the windows to the North overlooked Iceland and those to the east, India.'[18] This impossible house is everywhere and nowhere, then, less the inscription of a geometry than the topography of opportunity: a good home for the imagination, but also, it may be, a good place for a younger generation to inhabit, offering possibility without foreclosure, invitation without domination. It is also a not altogether desirable house, perhaps, with a few broken windows and one or two bad views, since the notorious 'middle stretch' of MacNeice's career provides so much less threatening a challenge than the self-confident *magisterium* that is Yeats's progress. To mention Yeats, of course, is to recognize that the recuperation of MacNeice in contemporary Northern Irish poetry is in part a strategy for coping with that authority and scope, as MacNeice himself had to cope with it. When Paul Muldoon brings Yeats, Auden and MacNeice into poetic focus, he situates them at the opposite end of the architectural scale from Carrickfergus Castle, in a poem entitled for what was in effect a home for transients, '7, Middagh Street', in his volume *Meeting the British* (1987). Placed in the poetic equivalent of 'no fixed abode', they become free to circulate and permutate in a self-conscious display of the way literary history actually produces its future; the texts are circulated and permutated by this reader, Paul Muldoon, who is also the writer 'making it new' in an act of critical reading which is hubristic and unjust but also, as an effect of pleasure, adroitly persuasive.

Before examining these issues further in '7, Middagh Street', I want to look briefly at the other major way in which Muldoon makes MacNeice, in the Poundian phrase, 'of present use', since this may supply a frame for what I say. This is the citation of his dialogue with F. R. Higgins that supplies the alternative to an introduction for his *Faber Book of Contemporary Irish Poetry* (1986). The fact that the anthology has no introduction had its moment of notoriety; but its audacity, even its impudence – the genie vanishing to leave a great swathe of smoke above the lamp – has implications for the critical essay that is actually supplied in '7, Middagh Street'. The dialogue itself is manifestly intended to set Higgins up as fall-guy to MacNeice, with his atavistic and potentially fascistic talk of poetry and the blood and so on, compared to MacNeice's urbane modernity, and Higgins does indeed, in the passages quoted by Muldoon, live up to the reputation devastatingly hung on him by Patrick Kavanagh when he said: 'Almost everything about Higgins needs to be put in inverted commas.'[19] However, as Muldoon must know, the evidence is that this was not MacNeice's view of Higgins: in *The Poetry of W. B. Yeats* some penetrating critical remarks by Higgins are cited, and this in a book which cites no other authority on Yeats; and Mac-Neice also writes approvingly, if mutedly, there of the subtle elegances and excellent craftsmanship of Higgins's own poetry.[20] Heaney is astute when he points out that MacNeice's poem 'Suite for Recorders' has a kinship with Higgins and when he goes on to observe that in fact Muldoon's own poetry, with its sustained recuperation of Irish legendary and mythological material, complicates the apparently simple dichotomies of the Higgins/ MacNeice debate. In Heaney's reading of Muldoon 'the final irony . . . is that it was the ironist himself who produced the goods capable of transfusing new life into that apparently doomed and simple vision'.[21]

None the less, the ironist editor of the anthology is deliberately tipping the scales when he makes Higgins the name for utterly uncomplicated 'simplicities', even crassnesses, knowing that Higgins's interlocutor in that dialogue had, himself, a more complicated view; which is presumably why he allowed himself to be a participant in the first place. However, if the unfairness of this supplies a frame for what I shall propose of unfairness in '7, Middagh Street' too, it clearly derives from Muldoon's primary allegiance. If there is, as Heaney says, work of MacNeice's which may be held in the same sentence with Higgins's, one element which makes him so exemplary for Muldoon is the *odi et amo* feeling for Ireland which informs many of his Irish poems. In 'Carrick Revisited' the triangulation of Ulster, the west of Ireland and England plots a graph of affiliation and detachment; but the poem 'Valediction', in particular, with its tropes of enmeshment and escape, submission and release, seems to set a kind of template for numerous Muldoon poems. In it MacNeice actually articulates the desire to be, precisely, a tourist in his own country, as a way of arriving at temporary accommodation with the disconsolate thought that 'the woven figure cannot undo its thread'. The poem's venomous repudiations are cut across by the poignancy of particular interests and affections; and it is an oddly oxymoronic valediction which actually promises to return. The 'woven figure' which 'cannot undo its thread' may be an apt way of defining all those figures in Muldoon who are enmeshed in circumstance, domicile and parish – the emblematically named 'Brownlee' and 'Joseph Mary Plunkett Ward', for instance. But a Brownlee who has left, undoing the weave of his name, like those other mysterious disappearers in Muldoon, is also potentially coded into 'Valediction' in a figure of startling vivacity and originality:

> If I were a dog of sunlight I would bound
> From Phoenix Park to Achill Sound,

> Picking up the scent of a hundred fugitives
> That have broken the mesh of ordinary lives.

In '7, Middagh Street' Muldoon turns MacNeice himself, along with the other inhabitants of Auden's Brooklyn house on Thanksgiving Day 1940, into such a fugitive figure. There is a biographical compulsion behind Muldoon's affiliation with MacNeice: at the time Muldoon was writing the poem he had taken up residence in the United States after quitting a job with the BBC in Belfast; MacNeice in the time of the poem is in America lecturing, but contemplating a return to wartime England to take up a propaganda post with the BBC in London. This reverse symmetry, and others in their respective careers, may be why MacNeice leaves 'by the back door of Muldoon's' at the end of the poem. '7, Middagh Street' has been much discussed, but too frequently as if Auden and MacNeice were its only personnel really to count. I shall myself return to them, but I want first to say something about the place of the other personnel of the poem. It is well known that the fiction of '7, Middagh Street' is developed in part from a few sentences of Humphrey Carpenter's biography of Auden, published in 1981. In 1940 the expatriate Auden was living in a house in Brooklyn which he described as a 'menagerie';[22] a human and bohemian one which included, for brief periods, six of the characters Muldoon includes in his poem: Auden, Chester Kallman, Louis MacNeice, Carson MacCullers, the striptease artist Gypsy Rose Lee, and Benjamin Britten. The character Muldoon includes who appears not to have spent time in the house, but who was actually in America later in 1940, is Salvador Dali. Each speaks a monologue; and the monologues are entitled according to the forenames of the speakers – 'Wystan', 'Louis', 'Carson', and so on. The monologues are constructed as a kind of postmodern *corona di sonnetti*, that Italian form of seven interlinked sonnets which Donne uses in 'La Corona'. In Muldoon there are not seven sonnets but seven sections, in variations based on the number 7 (apart from one section, which I shall come to), as befits the house-number of the poem's title; and each section is linked to the subsequent one by a line or phrase repeated, a quotation completed or travestied. The whole poem opens with Wystan's citation of the opening line of John Masefield's once well-known school anthology poem 'Cargoes' ('Quinquereme of

Nineveh from distant Ophir') and closes with Louis's picking-up of the reference. This device of echo may also owe something to the Renaissance 'echo poem' tradition, the kind George Herbert uses in 'Heaven', for instance, and also, significantly, the form Yeats echoes himself in 'The Man and the Echo', the poem Wystan cites in the sequence. The numerological precision and the playing with complicated traditional poetic structures and devices is very much a feature of Muldoon's finicky aesthetic. This would seem a Joycean element in him, except that in Joyce the structural complication is always an effort towards density; in Muldoon it seems, rather, an element of the poems' airy thinness, the guyropes emphasizing the way they are only just holding down the buoyantly wind-whipped canvas. In '7, Middagh Street' the implication of the corona is that the issues raised by the poem's seven characters are irresolvable. The corona form, its theme with variations, insists that they will maintain a constant circulation, from Auden and MacNeice in the 1930s and 1940s to Muldoon and his Northern Irish mentors and peers in the present moment.

Those critiques of '7, Middagh Street' that concentrate more or less exclusively on the 'Wystan' and 'Louis' sections focus, not surprisingly, on the issues of art and action that those sections raise in relation to Yeats, and this is, of course, a major element of the poem's interest. The poem is also, however, greatly pre-occupied with issues of sexuality, in a way which may be thought to move into another phase and a newer complication the trope of sexual–political linkage which figures variously in many Northern Irish poems, notably by Heaney, by Paulin and by Muldoon himself. The fugitives gathered in 7, Middagh Street are not political fugitives, but fugitives from stiflingly conventional sexuality, or from sexual or emotional misery. Wystan is in New York for the sake of his gay lover, Chester [Kallmann], striking out for the new sexual frontier and the 'ghostly axe / of a huge, blond-haired lumberjack'; Gypsy is in love with the intellectual George Davis, finding him a way of escaping the mercenary over-protectiveness and ambition of her mother; Ben is in love, and sharing his life for the first time, with Peter [Pears]; Chester is obsessively drawn to the sailors of Sands Street; Carson has left her husband and is in love with several women, including Erika Mann, daughter of Thomas; and Louis, after a failed marriage, is having a relationship with Eleanor Clarke. In '7, Middagh Street' America is the new-found land of greater sexual permission.

This is why the ship that transports Wystan and Christopher at the opening of the poem is the 'quinquereme of Nineveh'. Separate poems in Muldoon's individual collections sometimes conduct a dialogue among themselves, and in *Meeting the British* the poem 'Profumo' initiates the reference to Masefield's 'Cargoes'. A sort of companion piece in reverse gender to Muldoon's outstanding earlier poem 'Cuba' (in *Quoof*, 1983), in which the attempted domination of a daughter by father and priest is the issue, 'Profumo' has a Muldoon-narrator forbidden by his mother even to mention the name of the erring cabinet minister in the spying-and-sex scandal in Harold Macmillan's government in 1963, even though he knows that she is secreting all the salacious details in the *News of the World* beneath her 'snobbish' hams. In her snobbery and prurience she attempts to thwart his desired relationship with a girl called Frances Hagan:

> Haven't I told you, time and time again,
> that you and she are chalk
> and cheese? Away and read Masefield's *Cargoes*.

The instruction is presumably offered as a sort of preventive measure or prophylactic. We know that it has been carried out by one of the artful formal jokes of Muldoon's work. The syntax of 'Profumo', like the famously static syntax of 'Cargoes', contains three noun phrases, lacking their copulae. If this is a mocking gesture by the poet-narrator at the presumptuous interference of the mother, subverting her instructions by turning them into a vehicle of ironizing judgement, it is also a formally ironic insistence on the reduction of opportunity and the sexual and social repressions of this family. The noun phrases lack their copulae just as narrator and Frances Hagan are prevented from anything remotely resembling copulation, in this poem in which even the name of the arch-copulator Profumo is occluded, present only in the hidden newsprint beneath the snobbish hams, but of course also present now, and prominently, as the title of the poem which the poet-son has learned to write partly, we assume, by taking the mother's advice.

Consequently, 7, Middagh Street is the place where copulation thrives, with, it might be said, a vengeance; and the act of vengeance is performed by the occupation of the mother's safely prophylactic poem and the turning of its gorgeous first seacraft into the vehicle of alterity. Sexuality, as Ovid knew, is the most provocative agent of metamorphosis; and, as John Kerrigan has shown in his brilliantly synoptic essay 'Ulster Ovids', Muldoon is a deeply Ovidian poet.[23] Wystan with Kallmann becomes different from himself and says 'I will not go back as *Auden*', and Salvador Dali turns into 'O'Daly' in Louis's perception of him. These are the paradigms of the poem's fluidly mobile figures and effects, one of which is the adducing of Yeatsian poetic tags for sexual behaviour: 'There's more enterprise in walking not quite / naked', for instance, according to the teasing Gypsy Rose Lee, and Carson thinking of her new women lovers as 'two girls in silk kimonos'. In this intermingling of poetry and sexuality, art becomes manifestly the vehicle of one sort of action: even an old anthology chestnut like 'Cargoes' can take you to a new-found land. This celebration of the metamorphic and the indeterminate is, perhaps, the real reason why the surrealist Dali appears in the poem. Kerrigan has made this an element of his critique of '7, Middagh Street': 'Muldoon's work', he says, 'thins in those texts which summon other linguistic consciousnesses but which, honourably, cannot accommodate their difference. What is Dali doing in Middagh Street, and why does he sound like Muldoon?'[24] This is an uncharacteristically literal-minded question, despite the implied relative approbation of that 'honourably'. Dali is there because this is a poem much preoccupied with metamorphosis, and surrealism is the major artistic mode of metamorphosis in our time, one to which Muldoon himself gives a kind of allegiance in the disciplined surreal of mimetic hallucinogenic experience in such poems as 'Gathering Mushrooms'. He is also there because the sexual, the scatological and the political are merged in his major canvases of the 1930s, as at least two of those categories are in this poem. And he is there because his eventual 'trial' by André Breton provides a central instance of the problematic relationship between art and politics with which, particularly in the shape of Wystan and Louis, the poem is also deeply preoccupied.

But Kerrigan means the question literally. Dali was not literally a guest at 7, Middagh Street, as far as we know, although he could have been. But he can be a guest at the house supplied by the poem because the poem punctiliously goes out of its way to make room for him. When Gypsy, arbiter of the arts, establishes a correlation between striptease and literature, she sets a programme for Muldoon himself: 'it's knowing exactly when to stop / that matters, / what to hold back, some sweet disorder . . . / The same goes for the world of letters.' Gypsy is quoting Herrick here, his 'Delight in Disorder', a poem on the pleasures of *déshabille*:

> A sweet disorder in the dresse
> Kindles in clothes a wantonnesse:
> A Lawn about the shoulders thrown
> Into a fine distraction . . .
> Doe[s] more bewitch me, then when Art
> Is too precise in every part.[25]

Muldoon's numerologically punctilious poem structurally slips its sleeve from its shoulder too when the penultimate poem of the Wystan section has only twenty instead of the expected twenty-one lines, and it does so also by including a Dali who was not there precisely because he was not there. This poem, that is to say, is not in any sense a re-creation of the circumstances of 7, Middagh Street on Thanksgiving Day 1940, but a metamorphic reinvention of them, continuous with Muldoon's reinventions of Irish legendary and mythological material in such poems as 'Immram' and 'The More a Man Has the More a Man Wants'.

But why, being there, does Dali sound like Muldoon? Surely because everyone in the poem does, and because this is really not an attempt to 'summon other linguistic consciousnesses'. It is, rather, an attempt to write a *corona di sonnetti* to the recipe MacNeice gives for the lyric in his essay 'Experiences with Images' – 'your lyric in fact is a monodrama'[26] – and perhaps even more particularly to the specifications of his poetic self-analysis in *The Poetry of W. B. Yeats*: 'As far as I can make out, I not only have many different selves but I am often, as they say, not myself at all.'[27] If you combine that with a striking remark by Muldoon in an interview – 'One of the ways in which we are most ourselves is that we imagine ourselves to be going somewhere else'[28] – then you have clues to the provenance and preoccupations of '7, Middagh Street'. There are no 'other linguistic consciousnesses' in this poem; in '7, Middagh Street' Paul Muldoon is not himself at all, seven times. There may indeed, in this, be a sardonic subliminal recognition of the ways in which some lyric poems and sequences may too readily presume to a ventriloquial dramatic ability: 7, Middagh Street is a long way from that other notable contemporary Northern Irish poetic address, Station Island, but it too is a communing with ghosts, some of them literary. The poem also contains, in its Dali section's references to Antaeus and a welded foot, one of those parodistic or revisionist allusions to Heaney which you now wait for in every new Muldoon volume, as you wait for the cameo appearances of Hitchcock in his own movies: one of the stamps of authenticity, one of the signatures (Antaeus falls in from the Hercules and Antaeus poems of *North*, and the welded foot derives – Monty Python-like, it may be – from 'Leaving Malibu' in *Station Island*). If Heaney's posture in the sequence 'Station Island' is the apparently humble one of bowing before the advice of masters – with a view, of course, to himself inheriting their mantles – Muldoon's is that of the impudent, presumptuous, disconcertingly brilliant pupil, self-interestedly and unfairly reading the work and careers of others (not exactly masters, or mistresses) as facets of his own self-recognition and self-development.

It is in this light that we should read the debate between Wystan and Louis about Yeats which has been the focus of most critical commentary on the poem. Wystan, characterizing Yeats as 'part-Rapunzel' and 'partly Delphic oracle', remembers the question in one of his last poems, 'The Man and the Echo', about the potential political effect of his play *Cathleen ni Houlihan* and asks:

> As for his crass, rhetorical
>
> posturing, 'Did that play of mine
> send out certain men (*certain* men?)
>
> the English shot . . .?'
> the answer is 'Certainly not'.
>
> If Yeats had saved his pencil-lead
> would certain men have stayed in bed?

> For history's a twisted root
> with art its small, translucent fruit
>
> and never the other way round.

At the end of the poem Louis, thinking of the fate of Lorca, whom he has been reading in the Wystan section, and of Auden's new quietist 'intent only on painting an oyster', replies that

> poetry *can* make things happen –
> not only can, but *must* –
>
> and the very painting of that oyster
> is in itself a political gesture.

Edna Longley has observed that the Wystan lines are sometimes cited as Muldoon's last word, but that the Wystan and Louis sections are, of course, in dialogue.[29] This is quite true; but it is unsurprising that more emphasis has been placed on the Wystan lines, since, whereas the Louis lines are a reasonably accurate transcription/recreation of what he actually says, mild-manneredly, in his book on Yeats, the Wystan lines are much harsher to Yeats than even the voice of the prosecution in Auden's dialogue about Yeats, 'The Public v. William Butler Yeats', also published, like 'In Memory of W. B. Yeats', in 1939. The lines Muldoon gives Wystan have the panache of absolute memorability and the brazenness of unfair aggression. It is instructive and revealing that one of the readers who appears to take them at face value is one of Yeats's finest editors, Daniel Albright, who cites them without further comment in a footnote to 'The Man and the Echo'.[30]

But of course they are unfair. That Yeats is capable of posturing probably no one would dispute, and some even of his *Last Poems* may be thought to maintain certain kinds of arrogance and self-importance. 'The Man and the Echo', however, seems to me not one of these poems, and its self-questioning is neither crass nor rhetorical. It is provoked by the closeness of death, which is what the poem is partly about, and by the closeness, therefore, of whatever kind of judgement Yeats believed in; and, in the poem, he does appear to believe in judgement. The question 'Did that play of mine send out / Certain men the English shot?' is the anxious prediction of a possible posthumous opinion of his own behaviour and works. Such anxiety is emphasized by a marked poignancy in the form of the poem, in which the 'echo', with its death-inflected responses, may suggest that the Delphic voice is merely the projection of human will and desire, a kind of Forsterian 'ou-boum' of failed transcendence. And Yeats was not the only person to ask the question: Stephen Gwynn, in his *Irish Literature and Drama in the English Language: A Short History*, published in 1936, just a few years before 'The Man and the Echo', noted the effect on him of seeing *Cathleen ni Houlihan*, with, of course, Maud Gonne in the title role: 'I went home asking myself if such plays should be produced unless one was prepared for people to go out to shoot and be shot';[31] and MacNeice concludes the penultimate chapter of his book on Yeats with an exactly comparable judgement, the one Muldoon revises into his poem:

> Yeats did not write primarily in order to influence men's actions but he knew that art can alter a man's outlook and so indirectly affect his actions. He also recognized that art can, sometimes intentionally, more often perhaps unintentionally, precipitate violence. He was not sentimentalizing when he wrote . . .

the celebrated lines.[32] In a review of the *Last Poems*, MacNeice says of 'The Circus Animals' Desertion' what I would want to say of 'The Man and the Echo': 'In this excellent and moving poem a self-centred old man rises above his personality by pinning it down for what it is.'[33] One may, indeed, say of 'The Man and the Echo' what John Berryman said feelingly, self-interestedly and finely of the Shakespeare of the *Sonnets*: that 'when [he] wrote "Two loves I have", reader, he was *not kidding*'.[34]

If Muldoon allows Wystan an intemperateness that overshadows Louis's critical equilibrium, however, it is perhaps because '7, Middagh Street' is a poem so radically opposed to the kind of 'certainty' Wystan isolates and witheringly ironizes:

> Did that play of mine
> send out certain men (*certain* men?)
>
> the English shot . . .?
> the answer is 'Certainly not'.

Wystan's query '*certain* men?' here takes up the ambivalence of the word 'certain', one of those words, like 'quite', which Christopher Ricks, in his book *Beckett's Dying Words*, defines as 'words of antithetical sense', noticing that Beckett makes much use of them.[35] 'Certain', according to *OED*, can either mean 'determined, fixed, settled; not variable or fluctuating; unfailing' or be 'used to define things which the mind definitely individualizes or particularizes from the general mass, but which may be left without further identification in description; thus often used to indicate that the speaker does not choose further to identify or specify them'. Muldoon here uses the antitheses as the vehicle of an antithetical condemnation. His interrogative, parenthetical, italicized repetition of the word 'certain' draws attention either to Yeats's refusal to specify, which makes the phrase 'certain men' sound condescendingly patrician; or to Yeats's assumption of the men's assurance, which seems altogether too self-assured about the effect his play might have had in provoking such 'certainty', and is therefore justly rebuked by the definitive assurance of the negative riposte: 'Certainly not'. In '7, Middagh Street' the certainty of certain men is the certainty that concludes the poem in the sectarian exclusions of Louis's final sonnet, in which the gorgeous quinquereme of Nineveh is stationary in the shipyards of Harland and Wolff, and, given the Cyclopian foreman in the works, not about to admit the presence of a MacNeice. For this, of course, is the certainty that gets everything wrong:

'MacNeice? That's a Fenian name.'
As if to say, 'None of your sort, none of you

will as much as go for a rubber hammer
never mind chalk a rivet, never mind caulk a seam
on the quinquereme of Nineveh.'

The quinquereme ends, in short, where it began: not at the beginning of this corona-poem, as the gorgeous ship of self-transformation, but in 'Profumo', where it is the agent of prophylaxis and the emblem of exclusion: 'None of your sort . . . will . . . chalk a rivet'; 'Haven't I told you, time and time again, / that you and she are chalk/ and cheese?' Masefield in the mouth of the socially and sexually exclusivist mother, and Masefield in the mouth of the sectarianly exclusivist foreman, bookend this poem with insistences on those intransigent certainties which lie outside the utopian space of the poem, that space in which sexual, social and political categories circulate and slide.

III

In conclusion, I want to turn once more to John Kerrigan's critique. He discovers in the poem 'an elaborate bookish whimsy which promises a long way round to empty-handedness'. 'Everything', he says, 'turns into something else through the unrelenting lightness of fancy.'[36] As it happens, the specific lines he has in mind when he says this, those at the very beginning of the Louis section, do seem to me, more or less, to merit the criticism. And such bookish whimsy is a danger sometimes lying in wait for Muldoon's rarefied, light-footed and humoured writing. I am not at all sure myself that he does not succumb in *Madoc* (1990), where the whimsy seems related to a certain irritatingly exclusive knowingness, too ready an assumption of understanding from an insider readership. For all its length and scope, *Madoc* has come, as a result, to seem an almost disposable element of the Muldoon *oeuvre*, demanding far more from a reader than the minimal pleasures it is ever likely to return justify.

For '7, Middagh Street', however, the word one wants is not 'whimsical', but a neologism Muldoon once reached for, only to deny himself, in an interview: 'whimful'.[37] His capricious, fanciful play with his reading is earthed in a sense of how reading, the play of the intellect among the texts of a culture, is the agent of transformation. The reading one does with the encouragement of '7, Middagh Street' is ramifyingly suggestive and inclusive: for instance, the connections very lightly proposed between MacNeice, Whitman, Lorca and Dali – threads spun finely through the poem which I have not had the space to unravel here – are provocatively congruent with its central interests, not merely decoratively adjunctive to them. There is instruction as well as delight to be gained here, however lightly, and the nature of '7, Middagh Street' as a poetic critical essay traces a suddenly vibrant and knowledgeable line back through Byron to Pope. The poem's transformative ingenuity, which culminates with Louis clocking in at Harland and Wolff, offers MacNeice one of the most 'unfamiliar affections' even Auden could have predicted for him; but the affection, drawing on a respect for what MacNeice managed to hand on in the way of usable potential, is wholly unwhimsical, the product not of fancy, but of fully engaged sympathetic imagination.

~ 5 ~

Strange letters: reading and writing in contemporary Northern Irish poetry

Are we letting go of the pen?
Jacques Derrida, *Dissemination*

I

Whether as poets or as critics, we have been writing in very textual times: works by poets are now called 'texts' probably far more often than they are called 'poems'. 'Poem', from the Greek *poiema* (a thing made), tends to suggest the idea of a maker – the poet or author – whereas 'text', deriving from the Latin *textus* (a web or something woven), emphasizes the way the literary work is sewn into the fabric of its relations with language itself and with all those historical, political and cultural forces operating within language. 'Poem' summons an originating authority; 'text' proposes an infinite dispersal or dissemination. 'Poem' speaks presence; 'text' inscribes absence. 'Absence', therefore, the notification that a word is elegy to what it signifies, is one of the key words in post-structuralist critical discourse.

'Absence' is also a significant word in Seamus Heaney. 'Sunlight' in *North* (1975), that poem of a domestic love persisting through ordinary human diminishments and attritions, opens 'There was a sunlit absence'; and the word casts into tender relief the poem's evocation of the vibrantly particularized presence, in Heaney's memory, of his aunt, who 'sits, broad-lapped, / with whitened nails / and measling shins'. The seminal poem 'Gifts of Rain' in *Wintering Out* (1972) offers 'I cock my ear at an absence': the almost audible absence, that is, of the 'soft voices' of the guttural Irish language which is no longer spoken on the land celebrated by the poem, although its persistence in certain forms of the English language now in fact spoken on that land is thematic in some of the volume's most significant poems, notably the 'place-name' poems 'Broagh' and 'Anahorish'. In the third section of the

'Station Island' sequence (1984), a meditation on the death of a child provokes the sense of an empty space, 'like an absence stationed in the swamp-fed air': which is an almost present absence that assumes a precise physical location, a posture and, in effect, a personification; and that line lies behind the conception of death as various kinds of 'clearance' in the sonnet sequence 'Clearances', written in memory of the poet's mother, in *The Haw Lantern* (1987). The word also figures hauntingly in the poem 'Hailstones' in the same book, where the experience of being hit by hailstones in childhood is set in the context of the experiences of a later life:

> I made a small hard ball
> of burning water running from my hand
> just as I make this now
> out of the melt of the real thing
> smarting into its absence.

Here, the referent of 'its' is uncertainly ambivalent, allowing us to read what is painfully 'absent' as either the vanished original experience, 'the melt of the real thing', or 'this' – that is, the poem – in the process of its composition. 'Hailstones' is therefore both an elegy for the experience it commemorates and a glimpse of the poet registering, in the act of making a poem, a sense that this text inscribes his own absence. The poet smarts into the poem's absence because to write is to separate yourself from yourself, to inscribe your death in the elegy of signification. The poem is therefore, paradoxically, at its most self-reflexively alert when it registers the death of authorial subjectivity, which is the life of the text: 'this open book, my open coffin', wrote Robert Lowell.

The self-consciousness of Heaney's grammatical ambiguity here genuinely aligns 'Hailstones' with the discourse of modern literary theory, and *The Haw Lantern* is a volume in which a preoccupation with the act of writing comes very much to the fore, even in a poetic output which is, from the beginning, frequently self-referential in the characteristically post-symbolist manner. The word 'writing', or one of its cognates, figures ten times in the book's thirty-one poems, and it has a newly insistent materiality continuous with its use in the work of such theorists as Barthes and Derrida. This element of creative–theoretical *rapprochement* has, in Heaney's case, as the reiteration of the word 'absence' suggests, an emotional basis, reminding us that, for all the notable richness and immediacy of its evocation, his work is always haunted too by loss, diminishment, transience and loneliness; and it is, of course, to the point that, as it develops, elegy is one of his poetry's most predominant modes. Taking off from this perception of interrelationship, however, I want to suggest here that the self-conscious or foregrounded interest in the reading and writing of texts is a significant element in some of the most interesting contemporary poetry of Northern Ireland. My chosen texts are poems by Heaney, Paul Muldoon, Tom Paulin and Ciaran Carson, all published during the 1980s; and, in tracing a relationship between Northern Irish poetry and literary theory, I want to suggest that it focuses an attention which may properly be called political.

II

'Alphabets', which opens *The Haw Lantern*, was written as the Phi Beta Kappa poem at Harvard University in 1984, and it is, appropriately, a poem about educational achievement. It opens with the young schoolchild learning to read and write in various classrooms, and it closes when the pupil has become the teacher (or celebrated international poet-lecturer) standing in the Shakespearian 'wooden O' of a lecture theatre. Heaney's own name does not appear directly – I shall discuss the way it does appear in a moment – but autobiography is implicitly coded into such details as the school 'Named for the patron saint of the oak wood'. This is St Columb, the patron saint of Derry, which derives from the Irish *doire*, meaning an oak wood: Heaney's secondary education was at St Columb's College, Derry. The emphatic and unexpected plural of the poem's title 'Alphabets' arises from the fact that this is, therefore, a Northern Irish Catholic education in which the growing child assimilates, or is assimilated into, the different scripts of not only the Latin (and English) but also the Irish alphabetical system. This divided heritage is proleptically announced when the child's earliest attempts at writing imitate the agricultural and natural forms of his first experience: he 'draws the forked stick that they call a Y', and 'A swan's neck and a swan's back / Make the 2 he can see now as well as say'. Such images, and one or two others in the poem, may share a manner with the 'Martianisms' of the English poetry of, notably, Craig Raine and Christopher Reid in the late 1970s and early 1980s, in which the world is also frequently read as a text, and as if by a child; but they also have a specific political dimension, deriving from the fact that the Irish alphabet is usually acquired only by a Catholic child in Northern Ireland, and in a context of nationalist affiliation, sentiment and, probably, disaffection with the existing political *status quo*. This poet's first writing, therefore, already – 'always already', in the Derridean phrase – inscribes what Tom Paulin, in another context, and using another Derridean word, calls a 'spiky *différance*'. It is redolent not of straightness, but of forking or bifurcation; not of unity, but of division; not of singularity, but of the binary fission which inscribes, and is prelude to, the maturing knowledge of those other binarisms of the culture in which this child learns to write.

The poem is, for Heaney, unusually elaborate in its orchestration, moving through the stages of its alphabets with a confidently formal but also intimate address. This oxymoronic tone, the tone of formal intimacy, at once private and podial, is exactly appropriate to the poem's commentary on 'writing'. Writing makes you 'other' or strange to yourself; it places, and publicizes, your intimacies in the formality and form of the work; its 'letter' draws you up the 'ladder' of academic and critical esteem; it reshapes pupil into teacher, child into poet. 'Alphabets', in drawing the two together, neither sentimentalizes the child nor fails to confess the satisfaction of the poet's success. It does, nevertheless, elegize the absent: the disappeared child; the bulldozed school and the school window where the globe stood; the earlier agricultural existence, whose appurtenances are now as dead as the dead letters of the Greek alphabet; and, above all, the absence, within the alphabet now being used in this poem, of that 'other writing' of Irish script, the writing in which 'the poet's dream' was first manifested. 'All gone', says the poem plangently towards its close; but 'Alphabets' rejects this consolatory dolefulness as its rhythm gulps and recovers in the concluding stanzas: 'All gone . . . Yet', in which a dying fall is turned into a rising, even levitating, final cadence and cadenza in which the tightness of the poem's organization is slowly released into an almost ecstatic celebration of the way the strangeness of writing supplies, or supplements, these specifically realized absences.

This difference made by writing is articulated in two striking tropes: the 'shape-note language' as 'absolute' as the miraculous writing in the sky seen by the Emperor Constantine (*In hoc signo vinceretur*, 'Under this sign you will conquer'), and the necromancer's 'figure of the universe'.

'Shape-note language' appears to be Heaney's private metamorphosis of the 'shape-note music' of North Carolina, which is a kind of wordless singing: the concept acts, therefore, as a metaphor for the almost Platonic form of the perfect poem, that alphabet which is permanently sought, but never finally achieved, which will offer a proper, adequate and earned consolation for the depredations of time. Its 'absoluteness' is its power of command and its promise: the miraculous sky-writing prophesied that Constantine would conquer under the sign of the Cross, thereby effecting a link between conversion to Christianity and imperial expansion. The trope as it features in 'Alphabets', therefore, makes the act of writing the always desirable, the always to-be-attained, the promise of dominion – even if this is an imperial idea translated out of the realm of political conquest into that of creative or imaginative endeavour, as it is also earlier in Heaney's work when, in his elegy for Robert Lowell in *Field Work* (1979), he asks the American poet, 'What was not within your empery?' Despite the liberalizing or idealizing tendency of this 'translation', however, Heaney is manifestly, in these figures, drawn to conceptions of writing as itself a striving for dominion, whether he is commemorating his own origins or lamenting the relatively early death of an elder poet. If this has its masculinist impulse and implication and also its *hauteur*, it is nevertheless psychologically accurate and convincing in a way that strongly argues the clear-eyed honesty of the feelings being expressed.

The idea of dominion is in fact given a greater intensification in the subsequent trope of the necromancer's figure. Heaney is alluding here to the Renaissance Neoplatonist Marsilio Ficino as he is described in Frances Yates's *Giordano Bruno and the Hermetic Tradition*. Ficino's 'figure of the world' is a magical talisman designed to gain benefit from the universe. Heaney's lines virtually quote Ficino himself in his treatise *Libri de vita* as Yates gives it. Ficino observes how someone will construct on the domed ceiling of the innermost cubicle of his house, where he mostly lives and sleeps, such a figure with the colours in it. And when he comes out of his house he will perceive, not so much the spectacle of individual things, but the figure of the universe and its colours.[1]

Yates remarks that:

these . . . works of art are functional; they are made for a purpose, for magical use. By arranging the figure of the world with knowledge and skill, the Magus controls the influences of the stars . . . The man who stares at the figure of the world on his bedroom ceiling, imprinting it and its dominating colours of the planets on memory, when he comes out of his house and sees innumerable individual things is able to unify these through the images of a higher reality which he has within.[2]

This kind of allusion is not characteristic of Heaney; his learning is usually less immediately visible, his circus animals less obviously on show. As my own spontaneous allusion to 'The Circus Animals' Desertion' here suggests, this procedure has its Yeatsian resonances (particularly since Yeats's own references are frequently, of course, to the Neoplatonist tradition), and there is, as in the earlier 'Triptych' in *Field Work*, a sense of the poem rising rhetorically to its occasion, with perhaps deliberate exceptionality; even, it may be, in this scene of writing-as-dominion, a sense that Heaney is showing his readers how he can do the Yeatsian thing too, when he wants to. Ficino's Neoplatonic, magical conception, therefore, powerfully reinforces the poem's sense of the dominion represented by writing: this 'figure of the world' – like the work of art, like the poem – enables the magus, or the poet, to control the universe by representing it, signifying it under some other shape or form. In addition, its magical-representational function, which is one of unification, may be joined in 'Alphabets' to a political one: it may be thought to act as the symbolic salve for the wound of cultural division (the forked stick and binary number) of the poem's opening section.

The rapturous intensity and the release of the end of 'Alphabets' also derive, however, from the way the Ficino-figure carefully elaborates the poem's previous imagery of the globe, which itself has strong traditional sanction as one of the standard tropes of seventeenth-century 'Metaphysical' poetry. It is a magical transformation of the child's 'globe in the window' by way of the theatrical Shakespearian globe (or Globe Theatre) in its second part. This image undergoes a further transformation as 'Alphabets' reaches conclusion, when the globe in the window becomes the globe of the Earth seen by the astronaut, and when the Shakespearian 'wooden O' of the prologue to *Henry V* becomes 'The risen, aqueous, singular, lucent O' in a soaring adjectival and rhythmic progression. 'Alphabets' is a poem alert to typographical emphasis, to the materiality of altered typeface, which may serve to beat louder what Derrida has wittily called the 'graphic percussion'. These upper-case Os – 'coloured', 'wooden', 'lucent' – are joined by others: 'Book One of *Elementa Latina*' and 'IN HOC SIGNO'. In the poem's opening section the young child is learning to make 'the letter some call *ah*, some call *ay*', and these upper cases may be thought to unite O and A, omega and alpha, final and first world, poet and child, when the great globe itself is compared to the ovum and to this poet's 'own wide pre-reflective stare' as he stands 'agog' at the plasterer's 'strange letters'. Being 'agog' is to make the sign of an omega with your face, to be open-mouthed in fascinated astonishment: so that the shape of the world is, so to say, present, in one of the shapes of writing, in the pre-reflective child. Similarly, the astronaut watches 'all he has sprung from' when he watches the Earth from his space capsule in a pun on the phrase 'sprung from' which has him both exceptionally raised from the world by the genius of technology and, like everybody, derived from the ovum, since the form or shape of our protean selves is present in the womb's primary shapelessness.

Such origins, however, are made strange in writing – in what might be read as Heaney's version of the Russian formalists' *ostranenie* ('making strange', which is actually the title of a poem in *Station Island*) – since what produces the child's astonishment is the plasterer 'writing our name there' with his trowel in the wet plaster on the gable end of the family home.[3] These 'strange letters' spell the proper name 'Heaney', we must suppose, but the poem does not include the actual name; rather, it effaces it in the child's incomprehension, since, 'pre-reflective', he cannot yet read. In doing so, it also effaces the poet's name at exactly the point at which we might expect it to figure, holding autobiography, and personal memory, at the arm's length of the third person. Spelling out so many other large proper names ('Christ', 'Shakespeare', 'Graves', 'Constantine'), 'Alphabets' withholds the name of the author and, therefore, the name of the father: that father who nevertheless casts his shadow over the poem in its opening line, or at its (and the child's) origin, and whose shadow looms so large in many other places in this poet's work too: 'A shadow his father makes . . .'. This asks to be read in the light of Derrida's much-discussed problematization of the 'proper', particularly the 'proper name'; and an elegiacally analytical remark of his apropos of Joyce seems entirely apposite here: 'this madness of writing', Derrida writes, 'by which whoever writes effaces himself, leaving, only to abandon it, the archive of his own effacement'.[4] That archive of self-effacement may leave its clearest trace in the upper-case O itself, which is persistent throughout 'Alphabets': its circular fullness suggests Platonic coherence and repletion, an ideally formal and unfracturable harmony, but it circumscribes itself around absence and emptiness. Defamiliarizingly 'strange', it also summons back that aisling ghost of the 'tenebrous thickets' in the poem's second section, the 'poet's dream' of Irish, this 'new calligraphy that felt like home', since for this Irish poet to know 'all he has sprung from' is for him to know, too, that the strange letters of the English alphabet will never make you fully at home to yourself.

III

Paul Muldoon's 'Paul Klee: *They're Biting*', from *Meeting the British* (1987), is a poem about reading and writing under the guise of being a poem about a painting. The painting hangs in the Tate Gallery, and the poem was originally published in *With a Poet's Eye*, an anthology (with reproductions) of specially commissioned poems about paintings – sometimes called 'ekphrastic' poems – in the gallery.[5] Many of the contributions to the anthology are what might be expected: dutiful, descriptive, moralistic, running on a fairly low voltage. Muldoon's poem is not like that. Although it begins by appearing to describe the painting quite punctiliously, it soon goes astray into a characteristically wayward rejection of the obvious. The intimate formality of address, the concentrated and single-minded seriousness of purpose of Heaney's 'Alphabets' could hardly be more different from the Muldoonian tone. The essential difference between the poets may be expressed by noting that, when writing appears in the sky in Heaney, the Emperor Constantine is being converted to Christianity; in Muldoon a plane is spelling 'I LOVE YOU' over Hyde Park. Light-hearted, playful, almost whimsical, Muldoon's poem seems the sauntering whistle of a disengaged *flâneur*, moving among the objects of his idle metropolitan gaze (which include the Klee painting, a post-card, a sky-writing plane and a fishmonger's window) with a democratically cavalier lack of discrimination or will-to-coherence.

Muldoon's playfulness is apparent first of all in his rhyming, an exuberant but also thin-lipped performance of the wried and the askew. The poem is written in rhyming couplets, although the opening and closing ones do not rhyme internally but, as it were, with one another: the opening lines read 'The lake supports some kind of bathysphere, / an Arab dhow', and the closing lines read 'otherwise-drab window / into which I might glance to check my hair'; so that 'bathysphere' in the opening line rhymes with 'hair' in the closing one, and 'dhow' in the second line with 'window' in the penultimate one. The poem is thereby, you might say, enclosed in rhyme: in imitation, presumably, of the frame that surrounds the Klee painting. This witty formal ingenuity, a kind of ludic Joycean cunning, goes so far as to construct the 'frame' not only from this over-arching rhyming, but also from alphabetical repetition, since the poem's second line, 'an Arab dhow', is anagram-atically contained within its penultimate one, 'otherwise-drab window'. You have to look hard, or read hard, to notice this; and the responsibility of careful scrutiny places you, as reader, in the same relation to the poem as the poet places himself in relation to the painting, trying to coax its indefinite figures into an appre-hensible narrative. 'At any moment all this should connect,' the poem says of the painting, articulating what the reader feels about the poem too, and articulating it, furthermore, at the very centre of the poem, where the issue is most pressing. In this perspectival reflexivity, as in other things, Klee and Muldoon are well consorted, and part of the pleasure of the original anthology is, of course, the discovery of which paintings its poets choose to write about: Muldoon's choice is, perhaps, the only almost predictable thing about his poem. Some of the painter's aphoristic writings have, as it chances, clear relevance to the poet: 'Painting, dreaming, and at the same time, as a third element, myself caught up in both'; 'Genius is the error in the system'; and, particularly, his insistence on 'the essential character of the accidental'.[6] The accidents of Klee's witty, teasing painting *They're Biting* in fact converge on what is not painterly image, but writerly or graphic punctuation-mark; not painting, that is, but writing. There is a large exclamation-mark down among the fish who are 'biting' on the anglers' rods; and this is, we may assume, the minatory pronouncement, from a world beyond them, of their impending death-sentences. Death is figured as the eruption into their submerged, aquatic, peaceful painterly world of the discontinuity and 'absence' of this other world of writing. Muldoon himself makes such an assumption when he concludes the poem by bringing the exclamation-mark into relation with the capitalized word 'NO', which he imagines a 'waist-thick conger' to be mouthing from the fishmonger's window of the penultimate line: the exclamation-mark, the poem says, appears 'as if I'd already been given the word'.

Muldoon also suggests the essential character of the accidental by writing, uniquely in *With a Poet's Eye*, and as the poem gradually makes plain, not about the Klee painting hanging in the Tate, but about a reproduction of it. The painting as it figures on a postcard, sent by an unnamed 'you', is already part of another narrative altogether: 'When you sent me a postcard of *They're Biting* / there was a plane sky-writing // I LOVE YOU over Hyde Park'. This is a narrative which has nothing to do with original paintings in galleries, but one made possible by the forms taken by the production and consumption of the image obtaining in what Walter Benjamin, making it the signal feature of modernity, famously calls 'the age of mechanical reproduction'.[7] This narrative, then, in some sense subverts the partly publicist purpose of the anthology in which it appears, since it makes it plain how we can all view *They're Biting* without actually visiting the Tate Gallery. It is also a narrative initiated only to be tantalizingly withheld by the poet. The circumstantial accidents of his reception of the postcard mean that, reading its narrative, he is also reading two upper-case writings, a graphic percussion sounded as resoundingly as Heaney's in 'Alphabets': the plane's 'I LOVE YOU', and the 'NO' imagined in the dead conger's mouth. There is a kind of

undecidable 'accident' about the grammar of the poem's concluding five couplets too, which makes it impossible to assert
anything about these circumstances. Does 'When you sent me' the
postcard mean when 'you' posted the card or when he received it?
Is the fishmonger's window actual or imagined? These upper-cases
of affirmation and negation are left to collide accidentally, without commentary, so that the reader wonders whether this is a story
of unrequited love, in which the plane's affirmation is answered by
the conger's negative, or whether it is a story about the way the
fearful consciousness of death, against which the conger com-
plains in terror, must always undermine the amatory and sexual
pleasures of life; or even whether it is a story about the dark
pathology of Northern Irish political circumstance, that 'NO'
rhyming with the resounding upper-case negatives of the province's gable-ends, 'NO SURRENDER' and 'ULSTER SAYS NO',
negatives beaten out with a more than merely graphic percussion
in the streets of Ulster on the twelfth of July; or whether, indeed, it
is a story that draws some of these elements together and
becomes, therefore, a story about how the fragile affirmatives of
personal love happen or survive in a context of huge metaphysical
and political negatives.[8]

Muldoon's vibrantly implicative reading of Klee's pictorial
writing has one further twist. The conger's complaint at his death
is the only thing that saves the fishmonger's window from
drabness: the dark negative of unjust, untimely and unpredictable
death itself transforms its immediate environment. The poles of
negation and affirmation cross here, positing – like the Klee
painting – an intimate relationship between death and art. The
poem implies that the painting implies that art may be voyeuristic
on death, or on the suffering of others; which is, of course, the
implication that many poems of contemporary Northern Ireland
articulate or address. In 'Paul Klee: *They're Biting*' the issue is
raised only, as it were, to be deflected by that gesture in which the
window containing the dead conger is said to have been glanced
into merely for the purpose of checking the narrator's hair. This is
a harmless but still narcissistic vanity that may, nevertheless, be the
first impulse to the making or 'reading' of a work of art, as
Heaney, for instance, makes himself the 'big-eyed Narcissus'
staring into the dark pool of himself in the poem 'Personal
Helicon' in *Door into the Dark*. The art of a Klee or a Muldoon,

however, for all its wit and play, will always do more than offer us back our own reflections. The window, whether framed as painting or as poem, may be a mirror first, but it is also a transparency onto pain.

IV

Where the terminology of post-structuralism seems within earshot of Heaney's 'Alphabets', it is foregrounded in Tom Paulin's volume *Fivemiletown* (1987). This absorption into the fabric of his poems of a technical critical vocabulary is striking, since Paulin was initially publicly hostile, as a literary critic, to such vocabularies and the methodologies they signal. I want to consider his use of such a vocabulary, and whether any irony attaches to it, in the poem 'Mount Stewart'. The volume *Fivemiletown* contains this poem and another actually called 'Fivemiletown'. Both titles refer to the same village in Co. London/Derry, their twinning emphasizing what Paulin calls the 'floating letters' of this place-name: it has floated out of the planter's original self-aggrandizement into the people's 'demotic', replacing the aggressive colonizing act with a topographical anonymity. The poem 'Mount Stewart' depends on the fact that, previously named Mount Stewart, Fivemiletown was founded by Sir William Stewart, the Jacobean planter; the place takes its demotic name, however, from the fact that it is five Irish miles from the nearest villages. 'Mount Stewart' is typical of Paulin's later poetic manner, with its curt, phrasally emphatic lines, the line-breaks almost always following syntax and therefore tending to the abrupt, the abrasive and the staccato; with the equally blunt, take-it-or-leave-it mixing of dictions which are usually, outside the poem, hermetically sealed off from one another (Northern Irish dialect, Derridean terminology, racy vernacular, the self-consciously oracular, the quotation of scholarly or journalistic documentary material); and with the impression of a drifting free association and a hinted, intermittent narrative which give whole poems the agitatedly analogizing quality of modern or post-modern *bricolage*. It is a risky, unique mode, whose effectiveness is almost entirely dependent on the creation of a trustworthy rhythmic progression, in which the reader is compelled by the textual voice in a way that makes for tolerance of the apparently incidental and digressive in the security that such impressions and details will eventually amount to more than the sum of their parts. At their best, the poems become a kind of semantic space or field of significant implication in which the juxtapositions and associations issue in the genuinely, even startlingly, unpredictable and insightful.

The poem 'Fivemiletown' appears earlier in the volume than 'Mount Stewart' and is more obviously an oblique narrative of sexual liaison – or at least of the desire for, and lack of it – although the poem also has political implications and resonances: the hero-narrator of the fragmentary episode notices 'an olive armoured car' and says of it that 'no more than I could, it'd never fit / the manor house's *porte cochère* / and white oriel'. This is a lack of 'fit' which places different political Irelands in mutually exclusive juxtaposition by employing a punning version of the architectural tropes frequent in Paulin: here, the failure to 'fit' is a literal spatial fact, but it is also an aesthetic, and presumably a social, lack of appropriateness. In 'Mount Stewart', the interpenetration of the sexual and the political is at once more intimate and more problematic, even though the sexual relationship itself figures as a more mutually satisfactory one. The poem's political meditation on the 'letters' of the name 'Mount Stewart' is elided into its sexual reminiscence by the flimsiest grammatical connection: the former is said to be 'like' the latter ('it's like I touched both your breasts / that time we were lying low / in the grassy mouth of the plantation'), but the terms of the similitude are never explained; and, indeed, this usage of 'like' almost hovers into the contemporary demotic of slang or hip patois. The poem then proceeds by repeating, even intensifying, that initial act of elision in a sequence of others not readily open to secure interpretation. They include a direct citation of what is probably Derrida's most famous observation, that *n'y a pas de hors-texte* ('there is nothing outside the text', as it is customarily translated); but this occurs in a parenthesis sealed off from the main text, so that its relevance is, challengingly, the reader's to interpret. They also include an italicized sentence from an architectural guide by Alistair Rowan on how the house Blessingbourne's 'finials' erupt *'into Elizabethan / of a whimsical / yet scholarly kind'*;[9] and finally they include a simile which makes the lovers' speech 'a bit like reading / an anonymous love-letter / before it gets written', which appears wilfully even more baffling than the poem's first similitude. The shorthand fluidity of these grammatical gestures means that the poem's narratives seem to float, like the letters of its place-name; they slip and slide around one another in an apparently random or aleatory play which has some rhythmic and accentual charm: it is, indeed, 'whimsical yet scholarly', in the poem's own borrowed terms. The parenthetical Derridean dictum casts its shadow, however, over both the political and the sexual narrative. Their interweaving feeds off the ambivalence in Derrida: if there is nothing outside the text, then we are all dominated and controlled by it, written into it; but if we understand that everything is text, then we are perhaps given the capacity (however practically limited) to deconstruct it, or to inscribe ourselves differently within it. Both the poem's sexual and its political narrative are, in fact, about the writing of texts. Sir William Stewart's seventeenth-century imposition of his name and power on the land is figured as an abrupt translation of agriculture into culture: he 'planted his own surname / on a few sloping fields', where the imposition is made to seem a usurpation. The Plantation of Ulster is subsequently and stealthily undermined by the local renaming and virtual anonymizing of it. For the poem's narrator, however, this place is memorable for an entirely private erotic delight: to him, it is actually neither 'Fivemiletown' nor 'Mount Stewart', but the 'imaginary . . . Mount of Venus', a sexualized landscape which may accord with the speculative and anonymous love-letter of the future also named in the poem, and which has, it may be, partly ironic correspondences with Seamus Heaney's politico-sexual tropes in *North*, notably in the poem 'Act of Union'. Licensed only by the mind's and the poem's imaginings, this third name for the place, which reads the desired woman into the landscape as a *mons veneris*, would represent a conversion of the topographical text from one of colonial power to one of venereal pleasure, from political authority to bodily *jouissance*. The poem becomes the scene of an erotically metamorphic onomastics.

Yet the text of this poem places no assured faith in the possibility of such a rewriting, because the text written on Ulster by the Plantation is not to be circumvented merely by attempting a personal translation of it into sexual reverie or imaginative poem.

Indeed, the interweaving of the two narratives is most visibly signalled by their having a common motif, which is, minatorily, that of surveillance. The planter's house sits on the land 'like a transmitter', and it may be that the lovers, who apparently come from different 'tribes' – that is, it is to be assumed, the Catholic and Protestant ones – are being observed by someone, or some agency, inimical to them. The implication is that the Elizabethan Plantation, which has produced notable architecture in this landscape, has also provoked 'tribal' mentality and the consequent atmosphere of suspicion and espionage. There is no privacy to be had from that 'text', no outside whatever to it, in this place. The erotic narrative and its dream of release are therefore locked into the political narrative, dominated and potentially manipulated by it. But this text that is the poem called 'Mount Stewart' does contain, in its one strikingly oracular line, the 'dream' of a 'plenitude' alternative to both these texts. This is prefigured by the lovers' bliss, in which they have managed to 'disappear from [them]selves', to transcend the appurtenances of tribe and community in, presumably, the self-forgetfulness of orgasm; and the poem concludes by registering the desire to inscribe this variant text – the carnal or amatory, imaginatively constructed or invented text – on the politically given text of the place-name:

> Now, in the dream of our own plenitude
> I want to go back
> and rap it as milk, jism, cinnamon,
> when it might be a quick blow-job
> in a 6-motel,
> or a small fear just
> in a small town
> in Ireland or someplace.

These lines define that desire in an off-the-cuff, muted, even (paradoxically) dejected kind of utopianism, in which the register of aspiration – 'want' – exposes itself to a more urgent or even potentially violent commandeering: the Ulster dialect verb 'rap' means 'seize by violence' or 'get by any means, scrape together'.[10] Nevertheless, this is also an act of liquefaction or dissolution, in which the crusted categories of political surveillance which make Mount Stewart or Fivemiletown the representative place of hostile watchfulness and suspicion, of profoundly alienated human con-sciousness, may be doused in the renovating fluids of, as it were, sexual and culinary art, the fluids of an oneiric alternative to set against, or dislocate, the depredations of unsatisfactory sex ('a quick blow-job') and utterly unsatisfactory politics ('a small fear', which is, it might be said, a kind of stoic oxymoron). This desired 'plenitude', furthermore, will be one in which the ultimate anon-ymity or disappearance may occur: the place will become nameable not as 'Mount Stewart' or 'Fivemiletown', and not even as the sexually mythologized 'Mount of Venus', but as just 'a small town / in Ireland or someplace'. It will become, that is to say, the neutral, original place in which a new politics may grow, 'planted' there by human desire, not by the will of 'some military man'. If there is nothing outside the text, this poetic text can at least contain, as dream and desire, an alternative to everything that writes the textual place at present. In a poem much preoccupied by proper names, as (I noted above) Derrida is, it is an alternative coded in the blissful dream of anonymity, the placelessness of not having yet come into a 'proper' identity.

V

The ways in which these contemporary poems of Northern Ireland are studiously self-reflexive in their preoccupation with the acts of reading and writing is, of course, in tune with the intense focus on the materiality of the signifier in post-structuralist literary theory. The political implications of this self-reflexiveness, however, may ultimately derive from the marginality of Northern Ireland itself as a 'province' or 'statelet' within the United King-dom, or as a territory which has yet to find its definitive political configuration. In 'Alphabets', Seamus Heaney venerates lovingly, within his English writing, the 'other writing' which once 'felt like home', recording a self-division, therefore, in the very act of his own inscription: to write is to be not at home to yourself or, at least, as 'The Tollund Man' has it in a quite different context, to be 'lost, / Unhappy and at home'. In 'Paul Klee: *They're Biting*', Paul Muldoon guardedly and secretly, with what we might call a serious levity, reads a (possible) Ulster negative out of an apparently politically innocent painting: a negative we are the

more encouraged to identify by the poem's context in a book
frequently charged with an oblique politics elsewhere too, and
defining itself so by the insinuation of its title, *Meeting the
British*, which is not innocent. In 'Mount Stewart', Tom Paulin,
still obliquely but nevertheless with a more polemical edge, reads
his textual sources – the writing of Jaques Derrida, the writing of
Alistair Rowan, the reading of an anonymous love-letter, and the
reading of the floating letters of a place-name renamed – against
the grain of one another in a mordant piece of new textual
bricolage; reading, we might say, towards a future. All three texts
therefore, may be regarded as intruding on a dominant cultural
and political text with their glosses and revisions from a margin.

And these poets do indeed share such marginality with influential modern literary theorists. Roland Barthes's work takes an
edge from his outsider homosexuality in the Paris of the 1950s and
1960s, Derrida's from his being Algerian-Jewish, Heaney's and
Muldoon's from their being Northern Irish Catholics (and therefore coming to maturity as members of a varyingly oppressed
minority), and Paulin's from his being a renegade Northern
Unionist whose politics are fascinated by, even as they despise, the
rhetoric of an Ian Paisley,[11] and find their utopian image in the
eighteenth-century republicanism of the United Irishmen. In fact,
of course, the material acts of reading and writing have always
been very attentively regarded in Ireland, since the collusion
between print and violence, between text and power, is manifest to
everyone in a politically unstable culture. In conclusion, therefore,
I want to quote Ciaran Carson's 'Belfast Confetti' from *The Irish
for No* (1987). Here are strange letters too when, after an
explosion, the pieces of type rain their confetti on Irish streets
named after British imperial victories. The disintegrating city of
Belfast is a text here which violently writes itself across the lives of
those caught inescapably in its labyrinthine web:

Suddenly as the riot squad moved in, it was raining exclamation
    marks,
Nuts, bolts, nails, car-keys. A fount of broken type. And the explosion
Itself – an asterisk on the map. This hyphenated line, a burst of rapid
    fire. . .
I was trying to complete a sentence in my head, but it kept stuttering,
All the alleyways and side-streets blocked with stops and colons.

I know this labyrinth so well – Balaclava, Raglan, Inkerman, Odessa
   Street –
Why can't I escape? Every move is punctuated. Crimea Street. Dead
   end again.
A Saracen, Kremlin–2 mesh. Makrolon face-shields. Walkietalkies.
   What is
My name? Where am I coming from? Where am I going? A fusillade of
   question-marks.

~ 6 ~

Examples of Heaney

Seamus Heaney and the art of the exemplary

In his tender, witty, unillusioned poem 'An Afterwards', in *Field Work* (1979), Seamus Heaney imagines himself confined after death to the ninth circle of Dante's Inferno, part of a 'rabid, egotistical daisy-chain' of 'backbiting' poets. When his wife visits him there (accompanied by Virgil's wife), his instinctive, spontaneous question to her is a question about the state of the art: 'My sweet, who wears the bays / In our green land above, whose is the life / Most dedicated and exemplary?' The ambitious competitiveness of the enquiry, set against the poignant question she asks him – 'Why could you not have, oftener, in our years / Unclenched, and come down laughing from your room / And walked the twilight with me and your children?' – ironically undermines any simply exemplary quality in the words 'dedicated' and 'exemplary'. The poem, with its own 'Indifferent, faults-on-both-sides tact', exposes the hurt that any poetically exemplary life is likely to inflict on those domestically closest to the exemplar. Nevertheless, frequently in Heaney's earlier critical prose 'exemplary' is a significant term of approbation. In *Preoccupations* (1980), his title for an essay on Yeats, revising one of Auden's by adding a question-mark, is 'Yeats as an Example?'. During its course Heaney defines what he sees as Yeats's attempt to outface history with imagination and asks 'Is this then exemplary?'; after recounting an episode of Yeats's biography in which he believes Yeats to have acted with a sly political cunning, he finds Yeats 'exemplary in his bearing'; and, where he identifies it, he presumes that Yeats's 'peremptoriness, [his] apparent arrogance, is exemplary in an artist'. Yet he eventually decides that in Yeats 'the finally exemplary moments are those when this powerful artistic control is vulnerable to the pain or pathos of life itself', and he would make the *Collected Poems* 'more exemplary by putting a kinder poem last': 'Cuchulain Comforted' in place of 'Under Ben

Bulben'.[1] Elsewhere, when Heaney scrutinizes various literary readings of Ireland in an uncollected essay, 'A Tale of Two Islands', he offers a contrary and deconstructive reading of Yeats's myths of an indomitable Irishry, throwing up his hands in exasperated relief: 'And imagine if Yeats had got away with it. Imagine if we had to take these images as exemplary, in the way we were instructed to.'[2]

The word which carries such a burden of definition in relation to Yeats is also employed when Heaney discusses other writers. In a piece on Osip Mandelstam written in 1974, at the time Heaney was writing the poems collected in *North* (1975), the adjective is given a forceful contemporary edge: 'Mandelstam's life and work are salutary and exemplary: if a poet must turn his resistance into an offensive, he should go for a kill and be prepared, in his life and with his work, for the consequences.'[3] When he reviews Robert Lowell's posthumous volume *Day by Day* (1977), he describes Lowell as 'exemplary in his dedication and achievement'.[4] In the partly autobiographical talk *Among Schoolchildren* (1983), he identifies a reading of Joyce as a crucial moment in his own development: 'if Joyce is exemplary in revealing that the conceptions, loyalties and ideals of cross-channel culture are not necessarily to be shared by our insular imagination, he is also exemplary in refusing to replace that myth of alien superiority by the myth of native superiority'.[5] And when Dante – who, since *Field Work*, has figured in various significant structural and thematic ways in Heaney's *oeuvre* – is discussed in 'Envies and Identifications: Dante and the Modern Poet', an essay which may be regarded as Heaney's 'What Dante Means to Me', that vivifyingly immediate essay of T. S. Eliot's, the adjective is made to signal an Eliotic continuity of classical, or classicizing, tradition: 'As the great poet of the Latin language, Virgil can walk naturally out of the roots of this Tuscan speech, a figure of completely exemplary force. Virgil comes to Dante, in fact, as Dante comes to Eliot, a master, a guide and authority';[6] and as, surely, Dante comes to Heaney in *Field Work*, *Station Island* (1984) and *Seeing Things* (1991).

In its elaboration of what 'a figure of completely exemplary force' might be to a poet – master, guide, authority – that sentence intimates how the effect of the word 'exemplary' in Heaney's prose is persuasively reinforced by an associated vocabulary of recognition, or rhetoric of tribute. The words which carry a virtually patented signature are: 'dedicated', 'responsible', 'enabling', 'confirming', 'authoritative', 'proper'. It is a rhetoric which deliberately compounds an ethical and an aesthetic judgement: it implies that the poet's life as well as his work (or the quality of the life, with its gestures and alignments, as it can be read out of the work) is in some sense accountable, available to scrutiny, proposed as pattern and imitation. Indeed, as the foreword to *Preoccupations* tells us, when Heaney decided to 'put the practice of poetry more deliberately at the centre' of his life (by resigning an academic post), this was in part a response to 'a half-clarified desire to come to poetic terms with myself by considering the example of others' in relation to some 'central preoccupying questions: how should a poet properly live and write? What is his relationship to be to his own voice, his literary heritage and his contemporary world?'[7] No doubt all true poets are consoled, encouraged or goaded by similarly exemplary instances, but it is very rare for the process to become as self-conscious, as articulate, or as rigorous as it does in Heaney. The word 'exemplary' functions in his criticism as a primary signifier of one of its essential qualities: its self-referential intimacy. In coming to poetic terms with himself by considering the example of others, in reading his authors as 'confidants and mentors' (as the *Preoccupations* foreword has it), Heaney is constructing a bolstering imaginative system of self-instruction, self-declaration, self-evaluation and self-rebuke. The anxious scruple of this inherits, perhaps, something of the hagiology of Heaney's native Catholicism, with the exemplary writer as secular poetic saint: a pattern for imitation, a measurement of progress, a recognition of approval. Certainly, Heaney's critical and poetic language has its obvious theological or sacerdotal overtones, and the posture of humility explicitly longed for at the end of the third section of 'Triptych' in *Field Work* is a posture frequently implicit in the work:

> Everything in me
> Wanted to bow down, to offer up,
> To go barefoot, foetal and penitential,
> And pray at the water's edge.

However, if the exemplary has its self-abasement, it also, as the elegy for Robert Lowell in *Field Work* makes plain, has its pride and even, perhaps, its vanity or self-regard. Lowell is admired in that poem for a commanding self-assertion, a wilful, imposed mastery and authority, one of whose metaphors is a 'night ferry / thudding in a big sea'; and the late Lowellian blank-verse sonnets of such volumes as *History* and *The Dolphin* are described admiringly as 'bullied out'. The poem's respectful admiration is extended, indeed, to a Lowell 'promulgating art's / deliberate, peremptory / love and arrogance'; and these are terms of approbation which echo the qualities only partially assented to in the Yeats essay ('this peremptoriness, this apparent arrogance'). Towards the end of the poem, which is entitled simply 'Elegy', Heaney remembers Lowell taking his final farewell from him 'under the full bay tree / by the gate in Glanmore', the cottage in Co. Wicklow that Heaney lived in during the period in which he knew Lowell. In the *Poetry Book Society Bulletin* piece that Heaney wrote when *Field Work* was nominated its 'Choice', he refers to 'the bay tree that grows half-symbolically in a couple of poems' in the volume.[8] That 'half-' prefixing an adjective or an adverb is a not uncommon Heaney usage (see 'half-clarified' above, for instance) and sometimes seems to signal an almost embarrassed tentativeness, in which the impulse to proffer is virtually equalled by the desire to withhold; but the bay tree in 'Elegy', even if only half-symbolic, is a register of Heaney's own ambition at least as much as it is an affectionate recollection of Lowell. Heaney's sharing the bay tree's shade with the recently dead acknowledged master poet inevitably suggests a kind of poetic inheritance, since the bay, of course, supplies the leaves that bind the poet's coronale of esteem ('My sweet, who wears the bays . . .?'). The knowing self-recognition of this may be thought to disrupt any proper elegiac tone in this 'Elegy', even if elegy is always self-preoccupied to some degree; and it is consonant with a rather fulsome passage in Heaney's memorial address for Lowell: 'When a person whom we cherished dies, all that he stood for goes a-begging, asking us somehow to occupy the space he filled, to assume into our own life values which we admired in his, and thereby to conserve his unique energy.'[9] This Lowellian recognition may be regarded as the clearest instance of the obverse side of Heaney's sense of the exemplary: not foetal or penitential now, but organizing his place in the firmament, the strong poet assuming his position among his peers.

This art of the exemplary, with its dual note of obeisance and 'apparent arrogance', of rebuke and vaunt, has its cultural and political sources and significations. Heaney's painstakingly articulate self-consciousness about his 'confidants and mentors' is impelled at least in part by the fact that, as a Northern Irish Catholic, he lies at an oblique angle to the English poetic tradition, as he makes plain in a number of poems; and he must consequently labour to create in his criticism his own personally sustaining 'tradition' of sought-out exemplars. If there is an element of the factitious in this, it is, so to speak, a necessary factitiousness, given Heaney's divided cultural origins; and he is more or less explicit on the point in 'Unhappy and at Home', an interview in 1977 with his close friend Seamus Deane, published in the defunct but influential Irish journal, *The Crane Bag*. Implicitly referring to that journal's own work of literary and cultural analysis – which turned out to be the breeding-ground of the much better-known enterprise of the Field Day Company – Heaney says there:

> I think we can now speak of an Irish tradition because there is a mounting confidence in the validity and importance of our own ground. If only because people are killing one another. There is a strong sense in a number of poets that the cross-channel tradition cannot deal any longer with our particular history. Discussion of what tradition means has moved from a sort of linguistic nostalgia, a puerile discourse about assonance, metres and so on, to a consideration of the politics and anthropology of our condition. I think that every poet in earnest in this country is scanning for an exemplar, Irish or otherwise.[10]

This is a remarkable passage, in some respects both disarmed and disarming. The sense that the Northern Irish violence itself provokes the 'importance' of the local Irish literary ground is nowhere so openly admitted elsewhere in Heaney: partly, perhaps, because the assumption has been so frequently the vulgar or glamorizing platitude of journalism and literary journalism, which any self-respecting indigenous writer would therefore wish to disclaim; but also because a wariness and scepticism about making any such identification informs some of his most significant poetic and critical work. There is also a straight-forwardly stirred excitement about the possibility of defining an Irish tradition in relation to a newly sophisticated 'politics and anthropology', and an utterly unguarded admission that this may well involve a self-conscious seeking-out of exemplary – that is, usable in a new context – case and instance. 'Scanning' revealingly combines the senses of 'being on the lookout for' and 'analysing a passage of verse': it is, that is to say, a word already instinct with the achievement, in poetic composition or writing, of the desire that it announces. This 'scanning' demands, in Heaney, humility and submissiveness to the exemplar, when one is recognized, but it also rewards itself with moments of approving self-assertion: the service to a community – which is, in Heaney's reading of it here, virtually the creation of a community – is also the fulfilling discovery of one's own latent resources.

That the effort is, indeed, being engaged communally and not only individually is apparent, to some degree, from the way Seamus Deane's own critical discourse employs the 'exemplary' adjective. In his essays Yeats and Pearse are 'these demanding exemplars'; Yeats's dramatic career is 'the most exemplary of all' ('no drama so clearly offers itself as exemplary of the kind of consciousness which it would like to promote and see prevail'); Derek Mahon's poems are 'exemplary sites wherein . . . opposed forces are locked together in a mutually sustaining embrace'.[11] Heaney acknowledges Deane as a critical mentor in the dedication of, and foreword to, *Preoccupations* and in the first footnote to 'A Tale of Two Islands'; and in the shared elements of their critical discourse it is possible to sense a community of critical, poetic, and cultural enterprise, inspired and prosecuted by these two Northern Catholics who assumed influential positions in the Republic and subsequently in the United States. The creative and critical effort is a process involving the rediscovery and recuperation of some Irish writers (William Carleton, Patrick Kavanagh) and a suspicious or revisionary reading of others (Synge, Yeats, Joyce) in the interests of creating a sophisticated reading of Irish literary and cultural history, a reading shadowed by the relevant international presences (notably Mandelstam, Lowell, Dante and the poets of post-war, Soviet-controlled Eastern Europe in Heaney's case). The effort eventually produced the Field Day theatrical and publishing enterprise, of which both Heaney and

Deane are directors; and its controversial history since 1980 has been the subject of a great deal of critical discussion.[12] My point here is simply to note the way it had at least part of its origin in the scanning for exemplars by this poet and this critic, and in the sense of new exemplary effort required in the Ireland of the 1980s which presses in their respective poetic and critical work; and also to point up the way the cultural movement took its edge of engagement from the situation in the North: the political violence there insisted on the necessity for the cultural reappraisal ('if only because people are killing one another'). In the remainder of this chapter, I want to consider some of the ways in which such scanning is decipherable as an informing presence in Heaney's own earlier poetry. Scrupulously self-critical, it constantly makes enquiry into its own resources and potential, its affiliations and responsibilities; into, in the end, its own exemplary status.

In the earliest poems, Heaney's self-instruction takes the form of a drawing of analogies between poetry and agricultural labour: he wants his pen to become a spade; his mother sets up 'rhythms' when she churns butter; a water-diviner acts as an emblem for poetic technique; a blacksmith is a relatively unlikely priest of the imagination when his anvil is 'an altar / Where he expends himself in shape and music'; a thatcher, with his 'Midas touch', is an implicit recommendation of poetic economy. Such exemplary instances of dedicated labour are also instances of service to a community, and the way in which the analogies allow Heaney to consider the activity of poetry as continuous with the community's work takes the edge of guilt and anxiety off the inevitable divorce from that community which education, and writing, in fact represent. When, in *Wintering Out* (1972), under the pressure of circumstances in the North, Heaney's work becomes, however obliquely, more politicized, its exemplary figures are drawn not from the immediate local community, but from that community's history. The poems keep company with 'the moustached / dead' and the 'geniuses who creep / "out of every corner / of the woodes and glennes"' in Spenser's *View of the Present State of Ireland*, and with the eponymous 'servant boy' and 'last mummer' who offer their poet-memorializer examples in behaviour: the servant boy with his 'patience' and his stubborn ability to remain 'resentful and impenitent'; the mummer's 'picking a nice way through / the long toils of blood // and feuding'. If, as critics have sometimes said, Heaney is giving a voice in these poems to those who have not previously had one in poetry – the mute inglorious *colonisés* of Irish history now sadly rebuking, or finally rebelling against, their colonizers (that representative 'Edmund Spenser / dreaming sunlight' on his Kilcolman estate in Co. Cork) – he also takes instruction from them in what is for him, too, a necessary dissimulation and obliquity, a sly, watchful wariness, a suspicion, cunning and courage. The servant boy, indeed, is 'wintering out / the back-end of a bad year' just as this poet's own *Wintering Out* is an attempt to weather the crisis of Northern Ireland after 1969.

In the richly complicated 'Gifts of Rain' in that book, these exemplary imaginative presences are figured for the first time as 'voices' heard, or overheard, by the poet, in a version of the classical trope of prosopopoeia which becomes a characteristic resource in Heaney:

> Soft voices of the dead
> are whispering by the shore
>
> that I would question
> (and for my children's sake)
> about crops rotted, river mud
> glazing the baked clay floor.

These voices from the Irish past are 'soft' because they are ghosts, but also because they are speaking what Heaney thinks of as 'guttural' Irish ('soft-mouthed' is the adjective attached to Irish speech in the poem 'The Guttural Muse' in *Field Work*). What 'Gifts of Rain' calls the 'antediluvian lore' of the old Gaelic culture and community can be picked up by the properly educated and alerted ear in this metaphorical flood, and it is necessarily exemplary. Questioned 'for my children's sake', these voices from a colonial and agricultural desolation must be attended to in the search for a more satisfactory future, particularly since the oblique shorthand of the phrase 'crops rotted' may, of course, point back to the failure of the potato crop which resulted in the Famine of the mid-nineteenth century, about which Heaney has whole poems in the two collections, *Death of a Naturalist* and *Door into the Dark*, that preceded *Wintering Out*. This is the crucial point, in this volume, at which the poetic and the political are collapsed together: the poet listening in, intimate with and responsively alert to the voices of his own community's ancestors, performs the function of handing on what has been temporarily consigned to silence ('I cock my ear / at an absence') but remains obdurate, resistant and rebuking. In articulating such communal strains, as they are intimately known by the individual self, the poem's 'I' becomes an exemplary figure. And *North*, which is controversially fierce and unrelenting, if also self-divided, may be read as a full assumption of the responsibilities implied by this self-conferred status.

It is not surprising, then, that the counselling voices of that volume have become considerably harder and harsher than those of *Wintering Out*. In its title poem, the violent Viking dead are 'ocean-deafened voices / warning me, lifted again / in violence and epiphany', where the voice is 'lifted' as a weapon would be; and instruction is offered, extraordinarily, by a 'longship's swimming tongue', which counsels the poet in what seems a withdrawn, self-entranced, patient art of brooding watchfulness, wakefulness and possible disappointment which will always, nevertheless, be also an art of trustfully assured clarity and illumination: 'Keep your eye clear / as the bleb of the icicle'. The longship's tongue in this poem advises in a way that appears to propose that the Vikings' warship, the prime instrument of their expansive aggression, can counsel this modern poet in the truest impulses and modes of his own poetic; which is, inevitably, for the poem to insist on this poet's own primal, visceral knowledge of the 'darkness' of Nordic barbarity and atrocity. The Vikings of the poem 'North' do, indeed, in a way that has attracted strongly negative criticism,[13] have an atavistic allure that skirts the scandalous; but skirting the scandalous, coming dangerously close to stumbling on kinds of recognition not normally made in civilized literary discourse, is very much part of this volume's purpose and point. It does this, I would argue, both under the extreme pressure of its historical moment, and in a form self-dividedly alert to its own potential to give offence; acts of offence, and the recrimination, or indeed revenge, consequent on the giving of offence, being the subject-matter of the volume.

In the second, more 'declarative' part of *North*, the exemplary counsellors are more sociable, and their voices speak not from history but from the ordinary human world; but they are still persistent.[14] The 'Singing School' sequence, indeed, makes the idea of the exemplary explicit as its poet takes counsel in how to behave properly as a poet caught up in a moment of extreme political turmoil. In 'Summer 1969', Heaney, who is in Madrid while Belfast burns, listens to anonymous advice: ' "Go back", one said, "try to touch the people". / Another conjured Lorca from his hill', offering as model the poet murdered during the Spanish Civil War; and in 'Fosterage' he takes tiro instruction in the 'lineaments of patience' from Michael McLaverty, the Belfast short-story writer. The whole sequence, with its epigraphs from Wordsworth and Yeats on their childhoods, is an enquiry, under the aegis of salutary mentors, into the sources and responsibilities of Heaney's own art. 'Exposure', the culminating poem of the sequence (and of *North* itself), may be regarded as the tentative, muted rejection of the kinds of exemplary status offered by his own community and culture, and the assertion of a new kind of exemplariness: more elusive and uncertain, still conscious of political obligation, but aware too that the self, if it is to be adequately realized in art, must be more than merely a socially exemplary self. The moment of recognition, in which the claims of imaginative freedom assert their pressures against the claims of the world which is the poet's *donnée*, is a moment also dependent on the acknowledgement of prosopopoeic voices of instruction; but in the well-known crucial lines of the poem the voices of human persuasion dissolve into the more symbolically resonant voices of an objectively correlative Nature: the 'friends' / Beautiful prismatic counselling' competes with the 'low conducive voices' of the rain which 'Mutter about let-downs and erosions' while still recalling the 'diamond absolutes' to a poet weighing what, after Mandelstam and Ovid, he calls his 'responsible *tristia*'. The rain here is the final counsellor in *North*: its quiet voices may 'mutter', but they too clearly employ a rhetoric of persuasion. They are 'conducive'; that is, they work towards an end: towards, indeed, an 'absolute'. The rain is therefore a counsellor who feelingly persuades the Heaney of 'Exposure' what he is: not committed to the solidarity of an original community, but anxiously, even guiltily, pledged to the complicated freedoms and responsibilities of the poem itself.

In *Field Work*, consequently, the exemplary presences are other artists (Lowell, Dante, Sean O'Riada, Francis Ledwidge) or renegade representatives of the community, such as the fisherman of 'Casualty', who complicate any simple, unitary sense of loyalty. Harmonizing with the voices of the rain in 'Exposure', these are all instructors in the ways not of communal responsibility, but of personal and artistic self-reliance. The predetermined contours of the culturally conditioned self are challenged now by the arrogance and autocracy of existential decision. In the book's opening poem, 'Oysters', the contingencies of history are commanded away in a gesture of impatient self-reliance: 'I ate the day / Deliberately, that its tang / Might quicken me all into verb, pure verb'. 'Deliberately' there, positioned at the head of a line after an emphatic enjambment, is relished: it is abrupt, decisive, severe. Yet it too has its pre-existent textual exemplar when the word figures in its adjectival form in the 'deliberate, peremptory / love and arrogance' of the elegy for Lowell. The 'freedom / Leaning in from sea' longed for in 'Oysters' also has its exemplar in the 'Casualty' fisherman, out on the sea beyond tribal complicities: 'I tasted freedom with him.' In *Field Work*, then, the solitude of artistic self-reliance is shadowed – consolingly, comfortingly, it may be – by a community of exemplars. The book has its anguished self-questioning ('How perilous is it to choose / not to love the life we're shown?'; 'What is my apology for poetry?'), but it has, too, an exceptionally high sense of the rewards of artistic mastery: the metaphors are imperial and regal when Heaney asks admiringly of Lowell, 'what was not within your empery?', and when O'Riada is 'our jacobite, / . . . our young pretender'. Indeed, just as the Lowell elegy has its 'arrogant' moment under the Glanmore bay tree, 'In Memoriam Sean O'Riada' has Heaney sharing O'Riada's royalty when, fishing together from a boat, 'mackerel shoaled from under / like a conjured retinue / fawning upon our lures'. As an implied metaphor for the material of an art (music, language) submitting to the artist, or (unflatteringly) for an audience's adulatory response to an artist, this has its imperial sway, and Heaney clearly finds the boldness, authority and presumption of such gestures deeply compelling and attractive. His being, as it were, partnered in this way when he makes them himself, however, suggests that he actually lacks the single-minded arrogance he finds exemplary in a Yeats or a Lowell. The kindness he locates in 'Cuchulain Comforted' everywhere tempers his own sensibility in *Field Work*, which is a generous, accommodating, and warm-hearted book that discovers its central figures and tropes not in arrogant isolation or disdain, but in the mutuality of marriage and of a reciprocal relationship with Nature.

Station Island (1987), however, undoubtedly does move towards a purer form of emotional and poetic isolation. It may be considered, indeed, a bringing to fulfilment of Heaney's art of the exemplary and a farewell to it as, in the volume's first two parts, the poet makes himself penitentially available to instruction and then, in its final section ('Sweeney Redivivus'), discovers a way of finally flying free of all exemplars and instructors, becoming suddenly, fiercely and exhilaratedly his own master, authority and guide. In the poems of Part I, Heaney's customary sensuousness of evocation and realization is chastened and distilled by the tendency of virtually all the objects of his scrutiny to scrutinize him in turn. In these self-reflexive cross-examinations, the inanimate world asserts a caustic, disciplinary presence: now it is things that become examples. Sloe gin, with its 'cutting edge', is 'bitter and dependable'; a lobster out of water is 'fortified and bewildered'; a piece of granite is 'punitive / . . . and exacting'; a kite is 'the strumming, rooted, long-tailed pull of grief'; a clatter of stones in the Burren is 'a sermon / on conscience and healing'. The character shared by these poems is an unappeasable restlessness and suspicion, an unease which is the opposite of self-approbation, and a manifest refusal to stay contentedly in any fixed position. Placing himself under the voluntary duress of the scrutiny of objects, this poet is resisting the involuntary duress of too recognizably fitting his own image. The stony sermon of these poems is preached by the poet against himself, anxiously resistant to both stasis and hubris.

In this, they share the penitential quality of the central 'Station Island' title-sequence itself, in which, inspired by the Dantean analogy, the poet on pilgrimage is visited by exemplary, punitive, instructive shades from his own past. Although the sequence is not, to my mind, by any means the best of Heaney, lacking narrative and dramatic momentum, it seems altogether a necessary poem for him to have written. Necessary, because it may be thought a paradigm of his exemplary art in the way it creates a large-scale form deliberately to challenge and rebuke its poet into confessional self-revelation. A pilgrimage through moments and phases of his past which exact present self-definition, 'Station Island' is a thoroughgoing and rigorous enquiry into its author's former certainties and presumptions, an enquiry which the presence of the exemplary ghosts renders with some poignancy and pathos. The claims they represent – familial, political, religious – are opposed by the poem's artistic exemplars: the nineteenth-century apostate or 'turncoat' William Carleton, and the twentieth-century apostate and voluntary exile James Joyce. At the end of the sequence, the recommendation articulated by the Joycean ghost would seem to suggest that this will be the final exemplary presence in Heaney's poetry:

> You lose more of yourself than you redeem
> doing the decent thing. Keep at a tangent.
> When they make the circle wide, it's time to swim
>
> out on your own and fill the element
> with signatures on your own frequency,
> echo soundings, searches, probes, allurements,
>
> elver-gleams in the dark of the whole sea.

It could be argued that these lines sentimentalize Joyce by making him seem less egotistically self-preoccupied than he was, more selflessly concerned with another's career, not sufficiently, in fact, disdainful or 'arrogant', and that Heaney's failure is registered in the way he gives Joyce here a marine imagery which is actually all his own, deriving from the same nexus as 'A Lough Neagh Sequence', 'Oysters' and 'Casualty'. Yet this may also be considered peculiarly appropriate, since the Joycean advice is, as it were, actually being taken in the lines in which it is offered, as Heaney swims out on his own by making 'James Joyce' a facet of his own poetic personality, a tone of his own voice. This would accord with Joyce's fleeting appearance in one of the lyrics of Part I, 'Granite Chip', part of the 'Shelf Life' sequence, in which the eponymous piece of granite is hammered off Joyce's Martello Tower and hurts the poet's hand, being 'jaggy, salty, punitive // and exacting'. When its prosopopoeic statement is the brusque '*You can take me or leave me*', this Joycean emblem seems much closer to the Joycean actuality than the advisory voice of 'Station Island'.

The latter reading, in which Heaney autocratically command-
eers the Joycean voice, would certainly be in keeping with the final
section of *Station Island*, 'Sweeney Redivivus', where he does
manage a truly Joycean arrogance by, paradoxically (it may be),
employing the Yeatsian device of ventriloquizing through the
mask or anti-self of 'Sweeney', which is inherited from *Sweeney
Astray*, his translation of the medieval Irish poem *Buile Suibhne*,
whose eponymous hero is a ruined, outcast, maddened king transformed into a bird. The fact that Sweeney in the Irish poem is a
king may put us in mind once more of the regal and imperial
metaphors of *Field Work*; but he is also a lyric poet who laments
his fate and celebrates aspects of the Irish landscape that he flies
over when he is ostracized by his tribe. Sweeney in the poem, then,
is a figure of hostility, suspicion and alertness: contrary, apostate,
and divorced from the accepted *mores* of his people. In 'Sweeney
Redivivus', consequently, he becomes the opportunity for Heaney
to voice contrary and hostile emotions of his own, emotions exhilaratedly free from what he appeared to value in much of his earlier
work as his deepest attachments, obligations and responsibilities.
These include, notably, a scathing rebuke to his own people ('And
seed, breed and generation still / they are holding on, every bit / as
pious and exacting and demeaned'), an 'arrogant' justification of
his own behaviour and celebration of his own capacity ('so I
mastered new rungs of the air . . . / to fend off the onslaught of
winds / I would welcome and climb / at the top of my bent'), and a
flyting of his critics which is also a disdainful and triumphant self-
affirmation ('Let them remember this not inconsiderable / contribution to their jealous art', with its almost quivering
enjambment). These are all instances in which Heaney becomes,
most unpredictably, what Yeats in 'Vacillation' calls 'the finished
man among his enemies'.

'Sweeney Redivivus' has not been universally admired, some
critics finding a discontinuity in the relationship between Heaney
and 'Sweeney' in the sequence, between 'self' and 'mask', and
remarking that several of its poems depend hardly at all on the
Sweeney figure or context and that they are, therefore, interchangeable with the poems in Part I. The criticism seems nugatory
to me, since, in a book whose three parts clearly call across to one
another in their different but congruent ways of defining a self
and a self-development, this may well be regarded even as a

strength. The point is that in 'Sweeney Redivivus' the mask of Sweeney acts as a means for Heaney to interiorize the exemplar to the point where the voices of poet and exemplar are inextricably one. They are twinned, indeed, or 'twined', since one of the earliest poems in the sequence imagines the head 'like a ball of wet twine / dense with soakage, but beginning / to unwind'. This figure may be read as combining a comically self-deprecating representation of Heaney's distinctive and much-photographed facial and capillary appearance with the notification that in this sequence a density of cultural conditioning is beginning to be scrutinized newly and, possibly, undermined: 'unwind' would then carry, in addition to its sense of the unravelling of a ball of string, the more colloquial sense of 'relax'. It could therefore be thought part of the development of the sequence that some poems should seem almost to cast themselves free of the Sweeney figure: 'Holly', for instance, 'The Old Icons' and 'In Illo Tempore' seem to derive only from Heaney's 'own' voice and experience and yet to be in debt to what we might call the 'discipline' of Sweeney for their sharp, strict, unembarrassed self-declaration. In this respect, these poems mark a new kind of self-reliance in Heaney's work. The foreword to *Preoccupations* insists that 'the self is interesting only as an example', and the sense of self in Heaney, from *Death of a Naturalist* to 'Sweeney Redivivus', would seem to bear this out: the self is an 'example' of divided loyalties, of cultural conditioning, of artistic endeavour, of filiality, paternity, relationship in marriage. 'Sweeney Redivivus', however, begins the recognition, which fuels much of Heaney's subsequent work, that the self is interesting no longer as an example, but as an exception, and that it can issue, as well as receive, instruction.

'The Spoonbait', in *The Haw Lantern* (1987), contains a figure for what Keats calls 'soul-making' which returns, as 'Alphabets' does, to the primary scene of instruction or example, the classroom of early childhood, for its significantly variant emblem of liberation: a spoonbait once contained in the child's pencil case which is now 'Risen and free and spooling out of nowhere'. In doing so, the poem defines a moment of major transition in Heaney's *oeuvre*, emblematizing a disburdening which is the prelude to what *Seeing Things* (1991) will define, in a sequence of poems, as 'lightening'. 'Then exit', says the poem, 'the polished helmet of a hero'; which is, we may take it, the figure of the exemplar leaving under the poet's instruction, but also with a final flourish of admiring gratitude from him.

Heaney's Joyce, Eliot's Yeats

No ambitious Irish writer after Joyce – whether poet or prose writer – can avoid him, even if some contemporaries have advertised their attempts to do so;[15] and Seamus Heaney has made a virtue of the necessity, foregrounding the relationship in both his poetry and his critical prose. The twelfth, concluding section of the long poem 'Station Island' (1984) offers, as I noted above, what is undoubtedly Heaney's most significant engagement with the figure, personality and reputation of Joyce. In its dreamlike or visionary pilgrimage, 'Station Island' stages a series of Dantean recognitions on Station Island, or St Patrick's Purgatory, the traditional Irish place of pilgrimage on Lough Derg in Co. Donegal. They culminate, back on the mainland, in an encounter between its subjective poet and the shade of Joyce, in which this Joycean revenant counsels the poet – who is presented throughout as more pliable than the 'straight' Joyce – in the virtues of a separation from the *mores* of family, place and religion, and offers the promise or reward of what appears a more satisfactory artistic fulfilment. This is figured in sexual terms which combine, it may be, a Joycean licence with a more Barthesian textual erotics or *jouissance*: 'Cultivate a work-lust / that imagines its haven like your hands at night // dreaming the sun in the sunspot of a breast'; where the erotic feeling is extraordinarily, but tellingly – in this portrait of the Catholic artist as a middle-aged man – displaced from the self and its agency onto the agency of a neologized object ('work-lust') and a personified bodily part ('hands . . . dreaming'), a metonymic figure which makes the self more passive than active in relation to the nevertheless deeply desired and richly imagined erotic fulfilment.

Heaney's large ambition in staging this encounter is emphasized by its poised allusiveness: Joyce is made to advise the poet returned from his penitential pilgrimage in something of the spirit in which the 'familiar compound ghost' advises T. S. Eliot in 'Little Gidding', the last of the *Four Quartets*, in a passage which manages a magnificent imitative approximation of Dantean *terza rima*, the form Heaney also adapts, although quite differently, in some sections of 'Station Island'. Behind 'Little Gidding', and therefore also behind 'Station Island', as context and allusion, is the fifteenth canto of the *Inferno*, in which Brunetto Latini predicts a future for Dante, offers him encouragement in the journey towards a salvation he has himself tragically lost, and poignantly draws the poet into a reminder of their earlier collaborations ('we were scholars in our time'). The context is adduced and illuminated in what is probably Heaney's most significant uncollected essay, 'Envies and Identifications: Dante and the Modern Poet';[16] and it is clearly not without relevance that the Brunetto Latini passage was translated – superbly, in my judgement – by one of Heaney's most notable early poetic exemplars, Robert Lowell, in his volume *Near the Ocean* (1967). Eliot's ghost is genuinely 'compound' – that is, developed from separate primary sources, and representative of various original poets – where Heaney's is entirely singular, if unnamed. Nevertheless, the drafts of *Four Quartets* published by Helen Gardner in *The Composition of 'Four Quartets'* clearly indicate that it was Yeats – the Irish poet Yeats – who was uppermost in Eliot's mind while he was writing the poem; and I am labouring the fact of Yeats's Irishness here since Eliot does so too, strikingly, in those drafts, and I shall return to them at the end of this chapter.

'Station Island' has met with a mixed critical reception, and, as I noted above, I have expressed reservations myself. Denis Donoghue has been particularly harsh to the ambitiousness of this Joycean section. He says that 'Eliot was wiser in making his master a compound figure rather than an individual. Heaney's invocation to Joyce can't escape being brash, as if vanity were inscribed in it from the start. In any case Joyce is supposed to urge Heaney to strike out on his own, write for the exhilaration of it, and let others wear the sackcloth and ashes. It is not clear what sacrifices Heaney has made for the sake of being an Irish poet.'[17] In the light of this acerbity, I want to think about the passage again, since it now seems to me more complex than I had originally thought, and since I believe that it inscribes something much more interesting than vanity, despite the deliberateness of the very august company it keeps.[18]

In offering the poet of 'Station Island' both goad and consolation, the figure of Joyce is making explicit what the whole poem has already obliquely implied: that on this pilgrimage to an ancient Irish Catholic site Seamus Heaney, well-known Irish Catholic poet, is taking what one of the shades in the poem calls his 'last look' at the repressions and restrictions of Irish Catholicism before freeing himself into a newly self-dependent artistic, and perhaps religio-political, freedom. Some of the shorter lyrics in the *Station Island* volume reinforce this sense of the Joycean example. In 'Granite Chip', in the 'Shelf Life' sequence, Heaney's meditation on a piece of stone taken from Joyce's Martello Tower in Sandycove implicitly associates the Joycean character or writing with the granite's emblematic significance as a 'houndstooth stone', a 'flecked insoluble brilliant': 'jaggy, salty, punitive // and exacting', it says *'Seize the day'* and *'You can take me or leave me'*. The Joycean arrogance and absolutism test and measure Heaney's own *complaisance*, hurting him into an awareness of its limitations: *'You can take me or leave me'* may be read as the convinced self-assurance which will always embarrass the solidarity of community. More delightedly, that voluptuous poem about the voluptuous, 'A Bat on the Road', proposes an erotic Joycean trope for the *jouissance* which such an increase in isolation might bring the poet, taking the story of Davin's bewildered encounter with the pregnant peasant woman in the Ballyhoura hills in *A Portrait of the Artist as a Young Man* as an emblem for the seductive invitations, the 'rustles and glimpses', of the poem's own promise to its creator.

The final section of 'Station Island' also centrally alludes to the *Portrait*. Addressing Joyce (as Stephen addresses Dedalus) as 'old father', Heaney refers to Stephen's well-known diary entry for 13 April:

> That tundish has been on my mind for a long time. I looked it up and find it English and good old blunt English too. Damn the dean of studies and his funnel! What did he come here for to teach us his own language or to learn it from us. Damn him one way or the other![19]

Heaney's describing this as 'a revelation // set among my stars' is a perhaps 'jocoserious' – Joyce's portmanteau word in *Finnegans Wake* – indication of a superstition akin to Joyce's own: the poet shares the astrological sign of the diary entry, since his birthday is also 13 April; and one can imagine the young Heaney responding with glee to this on his first reading of the *Portrait*, a book in which most Catholic adolescents, of both sexes, have characteristically had little trouble in recognizing themselves. But the religious implication of the word 'revelation' is made explicit when Heaney identifies the diary entry's 'password' as 'the collect of a new epiphany // the Feast of the Holy Tundish'. Where Joyce adapted liturgical terminology towards aesthetics, with the result that the word 'epiphany' became a central term in literary Modernism, Heaney adopts a crucial word in the *Portrait*, 'tundish', as the day of commemorative celebration in his newly heterodox liturgy. At the end of this poem entitled for an Irish Catholic pilgrimage, the Joycean feast – we might say – erases the orthodox feast-days of Catholicism, substituting for them the liberating permission of the Joycean linguistic and cultural-political triumph. The diary entry in the *Portrait* is an erasure and a substitution too. Remembering Stephen's earlier civil but bruising encounter with the English Jesuit dean of studies in an episode of the novel that has become a central text in modern Irish literary criticism, it makes the Irishman's English, the ability to say 'tundish' instead of 'funnel', a matter for steadying resolve where formerly, smarting after his encounter with the Dean, Stephen had made it a matter of anxiety and humiliation:

> He thought:
> —The language in which we are speaking is his before it is mine . . .
> His language, so familiar and so foreign, will always be for me an acquired speech. I have not made or accepted its words. My voice holds them at bay. My soul frets in the shadow of his language.[20]

The 13 April entry, then, turns this corrosive envy and resentment into a lacerating pride; the inferiority of a 'subject people' becomes the superiority of the writer who bends a familiar foreign language (that culturally and politically charged oxymoron) to his own native, but novel, purposes. The Joycean triumph over linguistic servility relocates English as an instrument of rebellion, a language in which the Irishman can damn the Englishman ('Damn the dean of studies and his funnel!'), relishing the Calibanic 'profit' of a 'curse' in the act of celebrating a newly linguistically assured, even authoritative, self. Which is why Heaney, at the end of 'Station Island', inflates the little local difference between 'funnel' and 'tundish' into the self-mockingly pompous 'Feast of the Holy Tundish'. At the end of his poem of Catholic pilgrimage, this poet's allegiance is transferred from the feast-days of Catholicism, those signs of the solid community – 'braced and bound / Like brothers in a ring', as the ambiguous simile of 'Casualty' in *Field Work* (1979) puts it – to this new secular linguistic feast which celebrates the continued momentum given to succeeding Irish writers by the Joycean example. The exemplary quality Heaney locates in Joyce is dutifully and, it seems, humbly recognized by the filial submissiveness ('old father'); but the lines of the passage in which Heaney gives a voice to Joyce, with their recommendation to 'fill the element / with signatures on your own frequency, / echo soundings, searches, probes, allurements // elver-gleams in the dark of the whole sea', may assert a more (Harold) Bloomian kind of recuperation: the strong poet decisively swerving from the admired but inhibiting precursor. For, as I have observed above, these are some of Heaney's own most character-istic signatures: the nouns of the passage have a distinctively Heaney-like, rather than Joycean, quality. Even though Joyce is addressed as 'old father' in 'Station Island', then, this poetic son ventriloquizes for the father in his own most familiar figures and tropes; and this may well be read as an almost parricidal act, denying paternity even in the act of asserting it, making 'James Joyce' a function of the work of Seamus Heaney.

However, as I have also argued above, Heaney's figuring of exemplary instances for himself in his own work frequently does combine vaunt and self-abasement, and elsewhere he readily bends his knee to Joyce. The extreme linguistic self-consciousness of the volumes *Wintering Out* (1972) and *North* (1975) has, as it were, the Joycean permission or *imprimatur*, and Joyce is cited or quoted a number of times in both books. There is, notably, the citation of another sentence from the passage on the encounter with the dean of studies ('How different are the words *home*, *Christ*, *ale*, *master* on his lips and on mine') as the epigraph to the usually under-regarded poem 'The Wool Trade', which offers an instance of the English language, in the form in which it is spoken in Northern Ireland, as also the continuing testimony to a repressive political and industrial culture, in which tweed is a cloth inevitably 'flecked with blood'. There is too the reverberant use of Leopold Bloom at the end of 'Traditions'. That poem is explicit on the matter which implicitly informs most of the poems in these books, the divided heritage of any Irish person, whether Northern or Southern, Catholic or Protestant; and at its close Bloom represents, as he does during the 'Cyclops' episode of *Ulysses*, a 'sensible' (the poem's word) view of Irish nationality. It is a matter of simply being born in the country, even if you are born there, like Bloom, as a second-generation Hungarian Jew. 'What is your nation, if I may ask?' demands the rabid nationalist and anti-Semite in 'Cyclops': ' "Ireland", says Bloom, "I was born here. Ireland" ';[21] which is the line with which Heaney brings the plurally entitled poem 'Traditions' to its conclusion. Bloom's pacific and reconciliatory example is pursued in those poems in *Wintering Out* that develop a politicized linguistics, attempting to find a utopian space within a shared dialect where Northern Catholic and Protestant may be reconciled. The place-name poem 'Broagh', for instance, celebrates the mutual ability of Northern Catholic and Northern Protestant to pronounce this name, 'Broagh', which the strangers find 'difficult to manage'; and that tiny instance of solidarity is offered as an emblem for an alternative future. *Wintering Out* may derive from Joyce not the apparently heroic aim of Stephen at the end of the *Portrait* – to forge in the smithy of his soul the uncreated conscience of his race – but the more muted and ironically self-deprecating aim of envisaging linguistically a hitherto uncreated political and cultural consciousness; that is an aim which may also be read in the linguistic inventiveness and experimentalism of both *Ulysses* and *Finnegans Wake*.

It is also manifestly to the point, in thinking about Heaney and Joyce, that, in 'Summer 1969', in the sequence 'Singing School' in *North*, Heaney pictures himself in Madrid at the time of the first riots in Belfast guiltily 'suffering / Only the bullying sun' and 'sweat[ing his] way through / The life of Joyce'. Here, the reading of what is presumably Richard Ellmann's biography of Joyce will have supplied one example of an Irish writer who did not suffer feelings of guilt during his self-enforced exile from an Ireland which he nevertheless continued to write out of himself as long as he lived. Yet it is also clear in *Wintering Out* as a whole, and then more intensely and problematically in *North*, which side of the cultural and political divide the poet Seamus Heaney is on. However deeply some form of reconciliation is desired by these

poems, the actual politics of Northern Ireland in the late 1960s
and the 1970s meant that, if you were a Catholic, the divisions of
your fractured tradition were characterized by fear, resentment,
anger and the first stirring of confident witness and rebellion; and
these things demanded articulation too. The violence of the
Unionist opposition, as it made itself visible after the Civil Rights
protest marches of the late 1960s, seemed to insist that the Irish
Catholic poet speak for his 'side', and both *North* and, to some
extent, *Field Work*, the volume that followed it, in such poems
as 'Triptych' and 'The Toome Road', take on this burden, and take
it on as burden – oppressively, self-laceratingly, constrictedly.
These are, to my mind, necessary poems which articulate those
elements of resentment and hostility at the bottom of the
republican-nationalist psyche at the level at which they have genuinely operated: that is, at a level beyond the access of conventional
political arrangements and, of course, now also well beyond the
access of a utopian literature or meliorist cultural politics, whatever optimisms are possible in the wake of the 1998 referenda. Yet
the potential embarrassment of this deliberate shouldering of the
burden is, I think, the subtext to be glimpsed beneath the dreamer-
poet's encounter with the figure of Joyce in 'Station Island'. In
order to speak with authority, honourably, from the Catholic
position in the earlier poems, Seamus Heaney assumed it after
1972 with some easily readable public gestures, immersing himself
in some of its social forms and structures of feeling. The biography is well enough known: he moved from the North to the
South, from Belfast to Dublin; he left a teaching position in
Queen's University, Belfast and eventually took one up in a
Catholic teacher's training college in Dublin (once run exclusively
by nuns); he contributed to an Irish Catholic theological journal
an article called 'The Poet as a Christian' in 1978.[22] He was, that is
to say, visibly and publicly assuming, in a time of crisis, positions
against which Joyce had uttered, through his autobiographical
self-representation Stephen Dedalus, his *non serviam* sixty years
earlier. For Joyce, the great act of rebellion had been the rejection
of Catholic Ireland; Heaney's reaction to the British State in
the North of Ireland involved, on the contrary, his articulate
allegiance to a Catholic Ireland which, if very different from
the one Joyce had left, nevertheless maintained clear continuities
with it.

The final section of 'Station Island' therefore recognizes and confesses, faced with the Joycean alternative, that the price of solidarity is too high, that community can demand collusion, that to be co-opted is to be artistically constricted. It also recognizes that it is very late in time, and in his own life, for such a realization to be made. The reference to the poet's birthday in the 'Holy Tundish' passage is picked up devastatingly by the Joycean shade when he offers his opinion of the cultural anxieties it manifests. They are, he says:

> a waste of time for somebody your age.
> That subject people stuff is a cod's game,
> infantile, like your peasant pilgrimage.

In 1984, when the poem was published, Heaney was forty-five; whereas the Stephen Dedalus who writes the diary entry about the tundish has just left university. The Joyce depicted in the opening lines of the 'Station Island' passage is, of course, a much older Joyce, speaking posthumously, in a version of the way he appeared in his final years, as the blind, bony-handed author of the 'Anna Livia Plurabelle' section of *Finnegans Wake*; and he speaks with the authority reserved for age. Yet the potential embarrassment remains that the essential counsel Joyce gives is given by a man who himself put that counsel into practice when he was much younger; and in so far as 'Station Island' is a poem about the loss of faith, forty-five is an unusually late age for such a crisis to occur. The sometimes overwhelming sense of constriction during the poem derives from Heaney's painful attempt to extricate himself from religious and social forms which are deeply imprinted on his psyche but which he has intellectually outgrown; the poem derives its moments of greatest tension from the dramatization of both an anxiety about its own instinctive pieties and a guilt about what it might mean to abandon them. In this sense, its Dantean form might well be regarded as the opportunity for obliquity, since the psychological and emotional crises dramatized at different 'stations' of the pilgrimage are rendered with a figurative and symbolic intensity which never requires their explicit discursive articulation. The preoccupation with the poet's own age suggests, however, that, having learned the Joycean linguistic lesson early in his creative life, he has had to wait until middle age to presume for himself that divorce from first allegiance and affiliation which is the other and, it may be, even the consequent Joycean example.

The earlier decision to speak out of, and on behalf of, the community may be read, therefore, as the very real 'sacrifice' that Heaney has made for the sake of being his kind of Irish poet, even if the melodrama of that word is precisely what the poetry does not invite; and it is certainly congruent with the structures of feeling inherent in Northern, rather than Southern, Irish Catholicism. That is to say, it contains a strong element of anti-State subversiveness, quite the opposite of the traditional association of Catholicism with repressive State control in the Republic. However, the 'sacrifice' has undoubtedly had its rewards too: the obedience of the poet has earned new permissions of the language. In Heaney's earlier work – which is resolved into completion and almost ceremonially waved farewell to in the *Station Island* volume – the major political perturbation in contemporary Britain and Ireland has been brought to one of its most clarifying literary articulations, and the attempt to render a uniquely Northern Irish experience in a uniquely Northern Irish tongue has been central to that process of deconstructing the concepts of centre and periphery which may be one of the most lasting efforts of contemporary poetry in English. If James Joyce is made the patron saint of that effort in the poem 'Traditions', he is also the exemplar of a further solitude, a deeper isolation, at the end of 'Station Island'. The father may indeed be rejected there; but he is rejected precisely in the act of expressing the necessity for such rejection. Unlike the exemplary saints of Irish Catholicism – the St Patrick, for instance, in whose name the pilgrimage to Station Island is made – the exemplary witness of James Joyce is that examples are to be rejected: go, says Heaney's Joyce (jeering where the earlier Heaney would honour), and do thou otherwise.

The poetry Seamus Heaney has published since *Station Island* may well be read under this initiatory rubric. *The Haw Lantern* (1987) and *Seeing Things* (1991) in particular represent a decisive break not only with the emotional structures of his own earlier work, but also with the most seductive shackles of all, those of that 'Joycean complex' whose origins Seamus Deane locates in the work of William Carleton, the Catholic apostate who figures in the second section of 'Station Island': 'the renegade from his people who nevertheless is their true interpreter, the writer sick of the politics he cannot escape, the genius made miserable by Ireland'.[23] It may well be that Heaney's long schooling in the ways and dialect of the tribe, and his rejections in maturity, not in adolescence, have genuinely opened his path to a more 'neuter' possibility, as the word is used in the phrase 'neuter original loneliness' in 'Triptych'.

The poem 'Fosterling', in *Seeing Things*, may intimate as much in its now amazed pleasure, rather than guilty embarrassment, about the length of time such recognitions have taken him: 'Me waiting until I was nearly fifty / To credit marvels'. It is also the case, however, that in a modern Ireland in a state of what seems permanently metamorphic self-reassessment, it is possible to be analytically judgemental or even satirically rebuking while still maintaining loyalties and attachments. The 'Joycean complex', that is to say, may well long since have frozen into convention and caricature; it may have become the almost sentimental or melodramatic reflex of the disaffected. Heaney's ability to locate the complex as it is incarnate, and where it was a vital necessity, in its major representatives – Carleton and Kavanagh, as well as Joyce himself – and to make poetry of its suasions and invitations in 'Station Island', suggests both the strength of his desire to overcome it and his ability to do so. In this sense, ironically and paradoxically, it may well be that the ultimate example of Joyce in the work of Heaney is not merely the example of how to go and do otherwise but, specifically, the example of how not to be or become James Joyce.

Before concluding, I want to return to one of Eliot's drafts for 'Little Gidding'. In the published version of this passage in *Four Quartets*, the compound ghost's words about the responsibilities of poetic language are made to focus on one of Yeats's major late preoccupations, old age itself, and some of Eliot's lines in the section specifically play a variation on Yeats's sequence 'Vacillation', in *The Winding Stair and Other Poems*, with its remorse for 'Things said or done long years ago, / Or things I did not do or say'; but the Irish poet's nationality forms no part of the representation. The draft version is very different. Helen Gardner's transcript is a palimpsest of alternatives, but what follows is one way of reconstructing it. The familiar compound ghost speaks:

> I also was engaged as you should know
> In fighting for language: here, where I was tutored

> In the strength and weakness of the English tongue
> And elsewhere; when the political flame had dampened
> Another people with an archaic tongue
> Claimed me. I, and another, saved them.
> I spent my life in that unending fight
> To give a people speech:
> From which, by my example, you may learn.[24]

Eliot knows here that Yeats's own intolerable wrestle with words and meanings is an intensely political matter, an 'unending fight', as it had to be for a poet who inherited, even if very differently from Heaney, the fractured traditions of Irish speech and writing and the complex fate of being an Irish poet. The lines may be interpreted as meaning that the Irish needed to be saved from their 'archaic tongue' (their 'first' language) by finding themselves properly expressed in Yeatsian English, an English which attempted to draw on the resources of Irish as they were made available to Yeats by the translations of his friends at the time of the Irish Literary Revival; in which case, this would be a more cogent treatment of the issue than Eliot's bland and even neutralizing observation in a lecture on Yeats delivered in Dublin in 1940, a year after that poet's death: 'The point is, that in becoming more Irish, not in subject-matter but in expression, he became at the same time universal.'[25] It is impossible to imagine the passage from the draft fitting decorously into the published version of 'Little Gidding'. There, what is unending is not fight but reconciliation, and specifically not the fight of an Irish poet with the English language, but a reconciliation between the warring parties of the English Civil War: now, in 'Little Gidding', 'united in the strife which divided them', and revealing to T. S. Eliot (expatriate American and naturalized British subject) that 'History is now and England'. To that resounding peroration the Irish question raised by Eliot's Yeats would have been, as the Irish question has sometimes been in English history, a tedious distraction.

But what Eliot has repressed in 'Little Gidding' returns even more obviously than this in 'Station Island'. 'I, and another, saved them', Eliot has his Yeatsian figure say. Who is this 'other', unnamed here and entirely invisible in the poem's published version? It is, we may presume, the just perceptible shade of James Joyce.

~ 7 ~

A languorous cutting edge:
Muldoon versus Heaney?

Since what follows is an account of the behaviour of two Irish
male poets, I want to begin with a kind of counter-epigraph from
a dialogue by two Irish women poets, Medbh McGuckian and
Nuala Ní Dhomnaill. McGuckian remembers how she first
encountered Seamus Heaney when she was a student at Queen's
University, Belfast, in the late 1960s and early 1970s. 'In my final
year,' she says, ' '72, I had him in a seminar, and he was just a
wonderful mediatrix.' 'Yes,' agrees Ní Dhomnaill, 'sometimes I
think about Seamus that his great strength is that he is actually a
woman – a great big benevolent mountain, standing protectively
behind you, like your mother should do.'[1] The tongue-in-cheek
generosity of the notion, which, accepting Heaney into the
sorority, may be intended to administer a reproof to some of the
feminist criticism he has received, is perhaps vitiated a little by the
information, conveyed at length in the subsequent conversation,
that the two writers had quite spectacularly difficult relationships
with their mothers and identify these as the source of their
creativity.

I

Several years ago Paul Muldoon published a poem in the *Times
Literary Supplement* which, for some reason, he has never collected. A characteristic piece of cheeky Muldoonian whimsy,
'Caprice des Dieux' imagines the contemporary poets of Northern Ireland as a rather extravagant cheeseboard. The sophistication and expensiveness of some of its cheeses may be a little dig at
those socially upwardly mobile meals eaten in several contemporary Ulster poems in which, as it were, Maxim's puts soda
farls on the menu, in which the expensive restaurant becomes the
scene of primal guilts. This is a sub-genre probably initiated by
Muldoon's own 'Paris', in *Mules* (1977), with its disingenuously

astonished exclamation 'Chicken Marengo! It's a far cry from the Moy'; part of the joke being that, conceivably, it is not, since the Moy, Muldoon's home town in Co. Armagh, was designed by its eighteenth-century founder, James Caulfield, Earl of Charlemont, on the plan of the Lombard town of Marengo. The genre might also include Heaney's 'Oysters', with its anguished and anguishing 'bivalves' in *Field Work* (1979) which disturb social and aesthetic serenity, and 'Away from it All' in *Station Island* (1984), which contains a hyper-articulate lobster shared with Czeslaw Milosz, who is subsequently christened 'Coleslaw Milosz' by Muldoon in his short volume *The Prince of the Quotidian* (1994). In any case, in the poem's limpidly witty combination of flyting and celebration, the poet John Montague is a *Port Salut*, Derek Mahon is 'wrapped in vine-leaves / or *au poivre*', Michael Longley is a '*Brie / of Betty Smith L.P.'s*'; and so on, until Muldoon himself is the goat's cheese, 'Caprice des Dieux', of the poem's title. Heaney, along the way, is a 'monumental / *Emmenthal*'.[2]

Muldoon as the fickle French cheese 'Caprice des Dieux', then, dances his goat-like capers around the sturdily resistant Dutch monument of Heaney's Emmenthal. For years now, Muldoon's caprice has included coded references in his own poems to the various inscriptions on the Heaney monument. I want to examine one or two of them. First, that stanza in 'The More a Man Has the More a Man Wants' in the volume *Quoof* (1983), where Muldoon's shape-changing hero Gallogly stops for a moment to take sustenance:

> Gallogly lies down in the sheugh
> to munch
> through a Beauty of
> Bath. He repeats himself, *Bath*,
> under his garlic-breath.
> *Sheugh*, he says. *Sheugh*.
> He is finding that first 'sh'
> increasingly difficult to manage.
> *Sh*-leeps. A milkmaid sinks
> her bare foot
> to the ankle
> in a simmering dung hill
> and fills the slot
> with beastlings for him to drink.

This is doubly allusive to, and doubly parodistic of, Heaney. As Gallogly pronounces the Ulster dialect word for 'ditch', *sheugh*, he remembers Heaney's place-name poem 'Broagh' in *Wintering Out*. Written during the meliorist, Civil Rights phase of Northern Irish history, that poem makes of the shared ability of Catholics and Protestants to pronounce the local place-name 'Broagh' – which 'the strangers found / difficult to manage' – an implicit emblem for the possibility of reconciliation. Muldoon's parody, written many years later, out of a more exhausted and despairing historical moment, is presumably an indictment of such naivety. This is phrased as another kind of Irish pronunciation, which is no longer a shared ability but, rather, a disability: the rural gaucheness (or stage-Irish drunkenness) which cannot get Standard English pronunciation right. That this rephrasing, as it were, is combined in 'The More a Man Has the More a Man Wants' with an allusion to a pathos-filled moment at the conclusion of Heaney's *Sweeney Astray*, his translation of the medieval Irish *Buile Suibhne*, might appear a swipe at the various ways in which Heaney's status as an 'Irish' poet makes itself too readily available to, or accommodable by, English and American critical expectations, or audiences. Muldoon, this kind of parody might imply, instinctively withdraws from such alignments and associations, even though he is himself formed by a cultural complex almost identical to Heaney's – Northern, Catholic, rural, Queen's University-educated, latterly American academic emigrant (to Princeton, whereas Heaney has been at Harvard). The stanza offers us a Paul Muldoon who, once tutored by Seamus Heaney in the School of English at Queen's, goes and does quite otherwise. He is the impudent, presumptuous, disconcertingly brilliant pupil wilfully running rings around his earliest mentor; the ludic postmodern in caper around the stern and strict Romantic/Modernist; the witness to subjectivity as a play of signifiers deconstructing the claims of the authoritative, integral self.

Secondly, this brief squib from *The Prince of the Quotidian* (1994), which seems less than grateful for a Christmas card:

> The mail brings 'literature' from Louisiana
> on various plantation tours
> and a Christmas poem from Doctor Heaney:

the great physician of the earth
is waxing metaphysical, has taken to 'walking on air';
as Goethe termed it, *Surf und Turf.*

This would be, I assume, a reference to the moment when Heaney exchanges the bog and mud of his earlier work for the visionary water, light and air of *Seeing Things* (1991). Any such vision is dragged bathetically back to earth by Muldoon when he figures it in terms, now, of a rather downwardly mobile meal in an American diner: surf and turf, seafood and steak; with Goethe appearing here, presumably, as the great Romantic exemplar become the unwitting harbinger of this much depleted kind of Romanticism, in which *surf und turf* substitutes for *Sturm und Drang.* In a similarly bathetic act of subversion, Muldoon's 'literature' (or advertising material) about plantation tours in the American South arrives with fortuitous appropriateness along with the 'literature' (or high art) of Heaney's Christmas poem; which might imply that those earlier poems of Heaney's, in the volume *North* (1975), for instance, were also a 'plantation tour', a tourist's trip to the Elizabethan Plantation of Ulster and its historical consequences being undertaken by someone who no longer lived there. This tiny poem – almost a paradigm of the Muldoonian allusive method, loading every rift with ore – also remembers both Edna Longley's polarizing of Heaney and Muldoon in one of her numerous critical references to them – 'What is physical in Heaney', she says, 'becomes metaphysically problematic in Muldoon'[3] – and Heaney himself in his essay 'The Pre-Natal Mountain: Vision and Irony in Recent Irish Poetry', where he says that Muldoon's 'swerves away from any form of poker-faced solidarity with the political programmes of the Northern Catholic minority . . . have kept him so much on his poetic toes that he has practically achieved the poetic equivalent of walking on air'.[4] Muldoon's poem, therefore, impudently implies that it has taken Heaney a little while to catch up with him. And Heaney does, indeed, seem to be alluding to some of his own earlier poetic procedures, notably in *North*, when he uses that word 'solidarity'. Muldoon notoriously prints nothing from *North* but its dedicatory poem in his *Faber Book of Contemporary Irish Poetry* (1986); and this implied view of the book and its collusiveness with political programme is, of course, continuous with Edna Longley's egregious criticism of it.

Which is to say, it is impossible to consider the relationship or antagonism between Muldoon and Heaney without taking stock of what Edna Longley – a Northern Irish insider if ever there was one – has already made of it. She turns it into a paradigm of Irish historical and literary-historical revisionism, in which not only Heaney, but also the Field Day enterprise of which he is part, is undermined. In this scenario – and it is extensively presented in Longley's densely referential essays – Muldoon's awareness of Heaney runs a long way past his official citations and parodies. It includes, *inter alia*: 'The Right Arm', in *Quoof* (1983) – Muldoon's poem about the place-name Eglish – as a counter to Heaney's 'place-name' poems in *Wintering Out* (1972); 'Come into My Parlour', in *Why Brownlee Left* (1980), as a subversion of 'Digging' in Heaney's first book, *Death of a Naturalist* (1966); 'The Boundary Commission', also in *Why Brownlee Left*, as a challenge to the terms of 'The Other Side', also in *Wintering Out*; 'The Frog', in *Quoof*, as a savage critique of 'Act of Union', in *North* (1975); 'The More a Man Has the More a Man Wants', the long poem that concludes *Quoof*, as a text in which Muldoon plays a sophisticated internationalist Joyce to Heaney's nationalist Corkery; and the Southey and Coleridge of 'Madoc', the long poem in the eponymous volume published in 1990 – that cruel fantasy of Romantic pantisocracy in action – as an allegory of Heaney and Muldoon in America.[5] Similarly, again and again in Muldoon's work Edna Longley finds evidence of parodistic or travestied versions of the staple figure of the father in Heaney's, and she describes this as Muldoon's 'running demurral with Heaney'.[6] One of the lessons of all this may be that if Muldoon had not existed, Edna Longley would have had to invent him; and, indeed, to some extent – to the extent that she, like Heaney, was one of Muldoon's teachers at Queen's, and to the extent that the citation of the two has become a characteristic and sometimes, it seems, ingenious or even far-fetched binarism in her work – she has. In doing so, she has conceivably underestimated the degree to which doing the opposite is also a form of imitation. The real subversion would surely be the self-assurance of disregard.

II

Given the apparent needle and niggle of all this, how has Heaney behaved and responded? Pretty well, it would have to be said. He has consistently championed Muldoon's work. His radio review of Muldoon's second book, *Mules*, was published in *Preoccupations* (1980), Heaney's first critical book, and therefore gave this poet, still in his early twenties, status along with such other contemporaries in the original Heaney canon as John Hewitt, Brian Friel and Robert Lowell. He has written appreciatively of him in the essay I have already cited, 'The Pre-Natal Mountain', which was originally delivered as one of the inaugural Richard Ellmann Lectures at Emory University, and also in his pamphlet *Place and Displacement* (1985), both of which for a while, in the way of Heaney's vividly eloquent critical writing, supplied the critical terms by which Muldoon was appreciated and judged.[7] The latter is particularly notable for Heaney's apparently deferential and graceful acknowledgement that he is himself the butt of the Muldoonian joke in 'The More a Man Has the More a Man Wants', when he says that in it, the 'old alibis of heritage, tradition, folklore, Planter and Gael, and a whole literature and discourse posited on these distinctions (including poems by his contemporaries) are rifled for tropes and allusions until, within the fiction of the poem, they themselves are imputed with fictional status'.[8] This sounds astonishingly like Heaney willingly erasing a significant part of his *oeuvre* at his pupil's bidding; and he must, of course, have agreed to the very selective selection Muldoon published in his *Faber Book*. *North* itself, scrupulously self-inspecting as it sometimes is, notably in the poems 'Strange Fruit' and 'Whatever You Say, Say Nothing', nowhere gives the impression that it would agree to impute to its attachments and solidarities anything as potentially undermining as 'fictional status': in fact, quite the contrary.

Even more notably, Heaney made a point of adducing Muldoon when he was awarded a prize by the *Sunday Times* in 1988. The prize was presented to Heaney by the paper's reviewer, the Oxford don John Carey, who had not long before published a tandem review of Heaney's *The Haw Lantern* and Muldoon's *Meeting the British* which – gleefully, it seemed – seized the opportunity to turn a celebration of Heaney into the occasion of a swingeing disparagement of Muldoon.[9] Heaney's acceptance speech was subsequently published in the *London Review of Books*: which is to say, he ensured that it became a matter of public record. Accepting the prize, he bites the hand that feeds him (as, interestingly enough, he had his 'freedman' in the poem of that title in *North* prophesying for himself: 'Now they will say I bite the hand that fed me'). After very briefly thanking Carey, he rebukes him: 'It is not so long ago indeed that I experienced a sharp regret that John Carey's unstinted praise of work that I had done had also provided the occasion for his fierce underestimation of work by a friend and countryman of mine.'[10] This rebuke, which is itself 'fierce' to Carey's literary judgements, then becomes the opportunity for a more general attack on the reflex anti-Irishness of the British press in the wake of a recent, exceptionally frightful atrocity in Northern Ireland. The uncustomarily polemical mode of this is a sudden reversion by Heaney, under extreme pressure, to the manner of some pieces on the situation in the North which he had published in English journals in the 1960s and 1970s. To account for his behaviour, he cites Robert Lowell's observation 'on another occasion' that 'every serious artist knows that he cannot enjoy public celebration without making subtle public commitments'. What he does not say is that this 'other occasion' was Lowell's public letter to President Lyndon Johnson in June 1965 when, after initially accepting an invitation to read at the White House, he withdrew in protest against American foreign policy (it was, of course, the period of the Vietnam War).[11] It seems peculiarly characteristic of Heaney that he should register his protest while nevertheless attending the event itself: the gesture has decision, hesitation, courtesy and bravery in it all at once.

Heaney's phrase in the speech for Muldoon, 'friend and countryman', is an arresting one: its echo of Antony in *Julius Caesar* suggests that he has, despite his professed geniality, come to bury Carey, not to praise him. And the word 'countryman' registers a double solidarity: Muldoon is both a compatriot and from a very similar Ulster Catholic rural background. As poems by both make clear, this involves knowing, at certain stages of their lives, the perpetrators of other atrocities in Northern Ireland, or their families. In the speech, Heaney makes it plain that, in his view, the British State is the perpetrator of atrocities too, and that therefore the British press has no automatic right to the moral high ground, although it assumes it. In the act of rejecting the political opinions of the *Sunday Times* even while accepting a prize from the paper, Heaney is also rejecting any complicity that readers of Carey's review might assume him to have with the paper's literary judgements; and the rejection is made by emphasizing, even exaggerating, a chosen solidarity of identity and identification. By himself approving Muldoon (although he does not actually name him – but, then, this audience will know exactly who he means), whose less charming way of being 'Irish' is so different from his own, and so disconcertingly difficult for Carey to acknowledge, Heaney is self-justifyingly refusing to occupy what he calls 'the token role of the poetic Irishman'. Muldoon on this occasion is, you might say, Heaney's access to a way of being uncharacteristically uncharming and utterly uningratiating, even if the speech does conclude in a tone of almost equable aesthetic assuagement rather than in the forceful political challenge it articulates elsewhere. Carey consequently becomes, you might say, the 'stranger' who finds both Heaney and Muldoon 'difficult to manage', as he must have been in the disconcerting process of discovering, in front of an audience, during this speech.

Heaney's public recognition of Muldoon is reinforced by the poetic recognition he gives him in the brief and beautiful poem 'Widgeon' in *Station Island*. Dedicated to Muldoon, the poem's fiction reports an anecdote in which 'he' observes how, while plucking the little wild duck of the poem's title, he discovered 'the voice box', and 'blew upon it / unexpectedly / his own small widgeon cries'. The poem is a wonderfully dense and ramifying little lyric, its simplicity the flower of deep meditation; and I have written about it elsewhere in terms of its intimation of the relationship between poetry and suffering.[12] For my purposes here, however, it is its articulation of the idea of poetry as ventriloquism that interests me. The poem's anecdote is given to Heaney by its dedicatee, Muldoon; and the poem is therefore the generously reciprocal acknowledgement of the gift, the turning of anecdote into art. But – equally and oppositely – it is an appropriation of the anecdote, a seizing on it for its own opportunity, even a devouring of it: the widgeon is, after all, being prepared for the table. As such, the poem is, too, an allegory of itself. 'While he was plucking it / he found, he says, the voice box' remembers that hoariest of old critical clichés about the poet 'finding his (or her) own voice'. A reductive other anecdote or narrative therefore lies below the apparent generosity of the gesture here: the narrative of how a poet, Paul Muldoon, finds his voice, 'unexpectedly', by initially sounding out through – impersonating, indeed, in the etymology which derives the word from *impersonare*, which means 'to sound through' – Seamus Heaney. The generous recognition of influence is checked in flight, therefore, by a serene self-assurance; and the gift is returned to the giver.

As it chances, Muldoon reviewed *Station Island* in the *London Review of Books* in 1984 and – perhaps not entirely unexpectedly, although still brazenly – isolated 'Widgeon' for particular praise, even while registering a wariness about much of the rest of the volume. Muldoon is a true critic of poetry only in his poetry itself – in the brilliant literary essay that is '7, Middagh Street' in *Meeting the British* (1987), for instance – and this prose review is a relatively lacklustre affair. However, it rises to lustre of a kind when, at its climax, this pupil offers counsel to his former tutor:

> In the unlikely event of a truly uninvited shade being summoned up in some reworking of the 'Station Island' sequence, I suspect that its advice to Seamus Heaney would be along the following lines: 1. That he should, indeed, take the advice he gave himself as long ago as 1975 – 'Keep your eye clear as the bleb of an icicle' – but take it quietly rather than rehearse it again and again. 2. General Absolution is too much for even a Catholic confessional poet to hope for. 3. That he should resist more firmly the idea that he must be the best Irish poet since Yeats, which arose from rather casual remarks by the power-crazed Robert Lowell and the craze-powered Clive James, who seemed to have forgotten both MacNeice and Kavanagh.[13]

Muldoon's first publication was a pamphlet called *Knowing My Place*; this is putting Heaney firmly in his. This is not the place to enter into a discussion of whether Heaney has taken the anti-hubristic advice; but criticism of the poet must take stock of the issue and the charge.[14]

III

What one might regard as Muldoon's pointed reappropriation of 'Widgeon' in this review, however, suddenly – 'unexpectedly', indeed – reclaims the ground of contestation from political history, where Edna Longley too frequently locates it, for literary history – and literary history of, surely, the Bloomian kind. Longley, in discussing Muldoon and Heaney, nowhere refers to Harold Bloom; and elsewhere she objects to his theory as individualism and Romantic subjectivism 'run mad'.[15] I have myself referred to it as the 'Promotions Board' theory of poetry;[16] and certainly in Bloom Romantic subjectivism chimes all too harmoniously with American masculinism, even if these are, in particular cases, in fact modified by his own melancholy about the neo-Freudianism of his theory, with its distressing news that poetry is the sublimation of aggression. However, Seamus Heaney and Paul Muldoon are Irishmen – 'countrymen', indeed – who have made successful academic careers in the United States; and some of Bloom's categories of 'revisionary ratio' seem appropriate to their relationship. In Bloom's theory, it is, of course, essential that the precursor poet be dead; and in fact if you were wholeheartedly to relate Bloom to Heaney and Muldoon, you might discover the common precursor in Robert Frost. I can imagine a nice little essay that would offer Heaney's and Muldoon's antithetical readings of Frost within the framework of Muldoon's antithetical reading of Heaney; but it would itself be a 'nice' – that is to say, a complicatedly detailed – job, and it would be attended by the usual anxiety that Edna Longley has, to some extent, already got there before you. For my purposes here, however, I do think the Bloomian theory can be applied to this relationship of the living, and for two reasons. First, because both Heaney and Muldoon have known the theory for as long as it has been around, Heaney as a professor of literature deeply read in Romanticism, Muldoon as a voracious dabbler among the texts who has spoken in an interview of his assent to Bloom ('What Bloom said about the anxiety of influence makes sense').[17] Secondly, because a masculinist, neo-Freudian theory of poetic stress, which reads literary history as the Freudian 'family romance', may seem peculiary appropriate to a relationship between Irish 'friends and countrymen' who have been so closely kinned in various forms of precedence and subsequence too: as teacher and pupil, mentor and charge, both of which may be read as versions of what Bloom calls precursor and ephebe; as Irish poets published by the London firm of Faber & Faber (and I assume that Heaney was to some degree instrumental in organizing the publication of Muldoon); as Irish-American emigrant East Coast, Ivy League academics. The difference made by the fact that the relationship is between two living poets is, I propose, that in it a Bloomian species of melancholy and anxiety occasionally obtains, yes, but is sometimes transformed too into something at once poised, resistant and calm, the sharing of a difficult inevitability that restores to poetic interrelationship a benignity and mutuality effecting a return of the repressed generous impulse.

Be that as it may, when Heaney uses the word 'swerve' of Muldoon – 'his swerves away from any form of poker-faced solidarity' – he is using the major Bloomian word, the word that translates the first of his six 'revisionary ratios', the word *clinamen* (taken from Lucretius). And Muldoon's poem 'The Briefcase', which immediately precedes the title poem in the volume *Madoc*, may also make an explicit Bloomian reference. Its dedication mimics and reverses Heaney's to 'Widgeon':

The Briefcase
for Seamus Heaney

I held the briefcase at arm's length from me;
the oxblood or liver
eelskin with which it was covered
had suddenly grown supple.

I'd been waiting in line for the cross-town
bus when an almighty cloudburst
left the sidewalk a raging torrent.

And though it contained only the first
inkling of this poem, I knew I daren't
set the briefcase down
to slap my pockets for an obol –

for fear it might slink into a culvert
and strike out along the East River
for the sea. By which I mean the 'open' sea.

This briefcase is, you might say, another kind of widgeon; but instead of the little plucked wild duck about to be eaten, this is the skin of a once-live eel disconcertingly likely to revert to its first state. In this, 'The Briefcase' is very much the epigraph poem for 'Madoc', in which such forms of exploitative transformation are endemic: in 'Madoc', as it were, 'The woodchuck has had occasion / to turn into a moccasin' again and again. Eelskin, though, is Heaney's clothing, since his first long poem, 'A Lough Neagh Sequence', in *Door into the Dark* (1969), takes as its overt subject-matter the life-cycle of the eel; and, at the end of *Station Island* (1984), as we saw in the two preceding chapters, the arch-mentor, James Joyce, counsels Heaney to 'fill the element / with signatures on your own frequency, / echo soundings, searches, probes, allurements, // elver-gleams in the dark of the whole sea'. Muldoon's inability to produce an obol is, no doubt in similar vein, a reversal of Heaney's earlier mentor poem, 'Fosterage', from the 'Singing School' sequence in *North* (1975), where his acknowledgement of Michael McLaverty, the Belfast short-story writer, concludes in gratitude that he 'fostered me and sent me out, with words / Imposing on my tongue like obols'. Where Heaney's obol has mythic and sacramental connotations – the rite of passage as a laying-on of hands and a taking of Communion – Muldoon's is just the banal bus-fare coin that you cannot quite manage to reach, encumbered as you are with an unputdownable briefcase.

Heaney's price is, this must intend, too heavy for Muldoon to pay, even to the ferryman who will take him across the River of Posterity. Instead, the briefcase, made of its Heaneyish fabric, must be held at arm's length – suspiciously, anxiously – despite the fact that its owner knows that it contains that punning 'inkling' of his own poem. The 'fear' registered here is presumably the fear of belatedness and subsequence and, still, of competition: the poem's attitude is one of perpetual, self-protective vigilance. However, that anxiety may well be countered by its American setting and idiom ('waiting in line', not 'queuing up'; 'the sidewalk', not 'the pavement'), neither of which is at all common in Heaney, despite the length of his American residence. They insist that this eel has come a long way from Lough Neagh, even if it has, nevertheless, a yearning to return: as Tim Kendall points out, the East River would be the direction the briefcase would have to take if it were to head back to Ireland from New York.[18] In this respect, the poem is at one with a recent strain in critical writing about Heaney, exemplified notably by Michael Allen's article 'The Parish and the

Dream: Heaney and America, 1969–1987', with, in particular, its
contrary and revelatory reading of the seminal poem 'Bogland'.[19]
The conceit of Muldoon opening himself up to America, where
Heaney imports his Ireland there with him, may be one reason
why the word 'open' is so oddly foregrounded, rendered emphatic
inside inverted commas, at the end of this poem. But there may be
another reason too.

At the end of his introduction to *The Anxiety of Influence*,
Harold Bloom defines his sixth 'revisionary ratio', 'apophrades',
or the return of the dead:

> The later poet, in his own final phase, already burdened by an
> imaginative solitude that is almost a solipsism, holds his own poem so
> open again to the precursor's work that at first we might believe the
> wheel has come full circle, and that we are back in the later poet's
> flooded apprenticeship, before his strength began to assert itself in the
> revisionary ratios. But the poem is now *held* open to the precursor,
> where once it *was* open, and the uncanny effect is that the new poem's
> achievement makes it seem to us, not as though the precursor were
> writing it, but as though the later poet himself had written the
> precursor's characteristic work.[20]

I would not want to claim that, exactly, of Muldoon's latest work;
nor, of course, would I wish to locate him in anything like 'his own
final phase'. But I would claim that, in *The Annals of Chile* (1994),
the magnificent long poems 'Incantata' and 'Yarrow' come into
new possession of modes and tones that Heaney has long since
managed; and they are, significantly, elegiac modes and tones.
They are, that is, appropriate to grief, loss, and anxiety about one's
own mortality. Although such things have figured often enough in
Muldoon's previous work, they have not figured there with such
sustained application or, I suggest, with such intensity. When an
'apophrades', or a return of the dead, itself becomes subject-
matter – as an ex-lover, the painter Mary Farl Powers, is directly
addressed in 'Incantata', and as Muldoon's mother, Brigid Regan,
is alternately approached and withdrawn from, mourned and
judged, in the fluctuating forms of 'Yarrow' – then caprice may
indeed, if it is managed with cunning and care, remain an element
of the articulation, but it can hardly persist as a dominance in the
structure. Both poems, in their negotiations with personal pain
and private grief, appear to desire a space of uncontaminated

authenticity in which direct and memorable lyric utterance may be made. They desire this even, as the complicated, 'exploded-sestina' structure of 'Yarrow' in particular makes apparent, when they know the difficulty of discovering any such space in the complex entanglements, the endlessly ironizing and self-ironizing technologies of representation, that constitute the postmodern condition. The poem appears to ask, in effect, how your memory might find the proper frame to freeze when your finger is always, figuratively as well as literally, on the remote control of the video: when, that is, you have such free and ready access to so many self-modifying or even self-cancelling sources of mnemonic regret that to pause at any one is to be reminded more of your own powers of reconstruction than of any pure poignancy of original event.

For the Paul Muldoon of 'Yarrow', painful memory insists, nevertheless, on isolating frames, and one name for the space such frames create will always, I suspect, be for this poet 'Seamus Heaney'. This would be the Heaney who, in a 1988 interview, spoke with (even for him) quite extraordinary, and affecting, eloquence about what he looked for in poetry; and it is not without interest that he uses here, once again, the adverb of the poem 'Widgeon', in its adjectival form: 'the preciousness and foundedness of wise feeling become eternally posthumous in perfect cadence . . . something sweetening and at the same time something unexpected, something that has come through constraint into felicity'.[21] Something perhaps – unexpectedly – not unlike what Muldoon manages in 'Incantata', which, from its riot of reference and self-revelation, and from the constraint of the cruel necessity that it commemorate the death by cancer of a former lover, produces a final desire, or howl, that Mary Farl Powers, his addressee, might 'reach out, arrah, / and take in your ink-stained hands my own hands stained with ink'. Only in the eternally posthumous, ink-stained cadences of the poem can such posthumous meeting and reconciliation occur; but these are also the perfect, paradoxical cadences that register the abjection of the loss.

IV

In his essay 'The Makings of a Music' in *Preoccupations*, discussing Wordsworth's ambulatory compositional methods,

Seamus Heaney reminds us of the 'suggestive etymology' of the word 'verse'. It derives, he says, from the Latin *versus*, 'which could mean a line of poetry but could also mean the turn that a ploughman made at the head of the field as he finished one furrow and faced back into another'.[22] The poet whose first poem in his first book, 'Digging', famously rhymes the pen and the spade, culture and agriculture, would clearly be fascinated by the derivation. In concluding these remarks on the relationship between Muldoon and Heaney, I want to appropriate it to another end. Muldoon's and Heaney's verses take the antagonistic sting from the hostility of opposition, from the word *versus* ('against'), even while recognizing that argument, disputation and competitiveness have their legitimate, even necessary, place in poetry. Their oppositions are, rather, the turns made by friends and fellow-countrymen as, on occasion, they find themselves ploughing the same field; they are turns which recognize affinity and inter-relationship and perhaps understand also that only shared labour will get the richest harvest in. Where this is the field of Irish poetry itself, Heaney and Muldoon are two of the most significant workers in it, although there are others – such as Ciaran Carson, Tom Paulin and Medbh McGuckian – who could be comprehended by the same trope when Seamus Heaney figures in their poems too. As an interpretation of this behaviour, I want, in conclusion, to offer two propositions in note form, in the way Muldoon offers his advice to Heaney in his review of *Station Island*:

1. The relationship between Muldoon and Heaney, which is ultimately one element, the most significant one, in a tissue of interrelationships between contemporary poets of Northern Ireland, offers evidence of an exemplary poetic community, in which the option is taken for a set of liberating oxymorons: generous wariness; satirical approbation; deviating recognition – what Muldoon, writing about Byron, calls 'the languorous cutting edge'.[23] It is one in which the most painfully difficult matters of cultural authority – where the fear is that one's footfalls may be 'already pre-empted by their echoes', as Muldoon's prose-poem 'The Key', in *Madoc*, puts it – are negotiated at the level of brave articulation and explicitation, rather than suppression or sublimation; where potential damage and danger are faced, not flinched at; and where, as a result, they act as furtherance, not

hindrance. In so doing, they become luminous with future potential.

2. In the work of Heaney and Muldoon the matter of Northern Ireland continues to be articulated as a crucial element of the debate between two major Irish writers. Indeed, in the mid-1990s books of both – Heaney's *The Spirit Level* (1996) and Muldoon's *The Annals of Chile* (1994) – this 'matter' proves as indigestibly and indefatigably present as ever, the source of bile, pathos and grief. Their work therefore keeps these issues in circulation at a level of cultural authority, sophistication and subtlety which acts as challenge and affront to the expediency and opportunism of British and, to a large extent, Irish political consensus. If contemporary Irish poetry makes nothing much happen, in the classic Auden formulation that Muldoon chivvies at in '7, Middagh Street', it nevertheless persists, in an outstandingly refined form in the dialogue I have been delineating here, as 'a way of happening, a mouth'.

~ 8 ~

Resident alien: America in the poetry of Derek Mahon

The Ulster writer, says Hewitt, 'must be a *rooted* man. He must carry the native tang of his idiom like the native dust on his sleeve; otherwise he is an airy internationalist, thistledown, a twig in a stream . . . He must know where he comes from and where he is; otherwise how can he tell where he wishes to go?' This is a bit tough on thistledown; and, speaking as a twig in a stream, I feel there's a certain harshness, a dogmatism, at work there. What of the free-floating imagination, Keats's 'negative capability', Yeats's 'lonely impulse of delight'? Literature, surely, is more than a branch of ethics. What about humour, mischief, wickedness? 'Send war in our time, O Lord!'

Derek Mahon, *Journalism*

The passport picture is perhaps the most egregious little modernism.

Paul Fussell, *Abroad*

I

The most interesting and inward criticism of Derek Mahon has always made a point of the peculiar status of place in his work. Although numerous place-names figure in it, it always appears, nevertheless, profoundly unsettled or displaced. A contemporary poetry of departures, one of its characteristic locations is the seashore; and that, as John Kerrigan has persuasively shown, is a location haunted – at least at the back of this poetry's mind – by the exile's lament in Ovid's *Tristia*.[1] At the same time, however, the poetry has little truck with the tropes of exile familiar from a great deal of modern Irish literature. Because an effort of detachment seems the very spirit in which many of Mahon's poems are written, the nostalgia consequent on exilic attachments is, for an Irish poet, singularly lacking, and this despite the fact that some of the poems appear to make play, even in their titles, with exactly such tropes: witness 'Thinking of Inis Oírr in Cambridge, Mass.', for instance. If this poem is, on one level, a contemporary companion to the Romantic yearning of Yeats's 'The Lake Isle of Innisfree', it substitutes for that too a more convinced, and therefore modernist, sense of the fictionality of all the locations of such longing: the poem's 'dream of limestone in sea-light' may be a scale for the measurement of all subsequent experience but, admittedly oneiric, it makes Inis Oírr acknowledgedly an imaginative construction, rather than an actually existent place in an idealized Irish West. When Mahon remembers Inis Oírr in Cambridge, Mass., that is to say, it is with a Proustian kind of memory which understands how 'les vrais paradis sont les paradis qu'on a perdu'.

This nimble avoidance of rhetorical cliché no doubt has much to do with Mahon's origins as a Belfast Protestant, although to labour this point might well be to fall into other sorts of cliché, as Seamus Deane does when he observes that Mahon's urbanity 'helps him to fend off the forces of atavism, ignorance and oppression which are part of his Northern Protestant heritage'.[2] It may well be that it is precisely this kind of unsubtle and embattled version of a 'heritage', and the frozen discourses of identity which have surrounded much contemporary Irish cultural debate, that the displacement or strange placelessness of Mahon's work is designed to avoid or even, at an obliquely sophisticated level, to impugn. Remembering how Seamus Heaney works to establish place in poems like 'Anahorish' and 'Broagh', and how even Paul Muldoon establishes the Moy in place in his earlier poems, it is remarkable to be told by Peter Denman, in a lively and revealing study of Mahon's notorious revisions, that in successive versions of some poems, place-names get substituted, becoming, Denman memorably says, 'equivalents in the gazetteer of anywheres'.[3] Places in Mahon, Kerrigan observes in a nice paradox, 'are more important than where they are';[4] and in fact some poems can hardly bring themselves to admit that places are actually where they are. Of 'A Lighthouse in Maine', for instance, the poem says: 'It might be anywhere – / Hokkaido, Mayo, Maine; / But it is in Maine', where the rhythm teeters towards uncertainty even as it attempts to establish assurance, and where in any case the pass has been sold by the subjunctive, which suggests the irrelevance of the whole attempt at such topographical clarification. Very frequently in the poems, reinforcing such displacements, one place is viewed from another, often in a destabilizingly ironic topographical or historical perspective: Inis Oírr from Cambridge, as we have seen; Belfast from London in 'Afterlives'; Kinsale from Penshurst in 'Penshurst Place'; the relatively treeless North of Ireland from a pastoral English woodland in 'Going Home'; the Belfast of Mahon's childhood from seventeenth-century Holland in 'Courtyards in Delft'; Treblinka and Pompeii from 'A Disused Shed in Co. Wexford'.

Such displacements have their consonance with a set of personal and cultural assumptions in Mahon, in which he famously celebrates what others have derogated as Louis MacNeice's being a 'tourist in his own country'; and Hugh Haughton is surely right to read into this Mahon's self-identification with the condition of the modern *déraciné* intellectual, and against a common, predominantly nationalist, credo of Irish poetic stability or rootedness.[5] But these displacements in the poetry also appear to carry the burden of some less voluntary displacements in Irish historical experience. In 'A Garage in Co. Cork', contemplating the 'picturesque abandon' of the eponymous deserted garage, and making a poignantly belated little Ovidian myth out of it, the poet wonders of its inhabitants, 'Where did they go? South Boston? Cricklewood?'; and the almost unwilled purposelessness of their leaving for these interchangeable American and English locations, which nevertheless constitutes their fate, becomes another lesson in how 'We might be anywhere but are in one place only'; and this in turn is a Cavafy-like lesson, for those who are confined to such places, in the 'intrinsic nature' of any future likely to be available to them. In Mahon's best-known poem, 'A Disused Shed in Co. Wexford', which is indebted to J. G. Farrell's novel *Troubles* (1970), the pitiful, clamorous, supplicating mushrooms represent, in part, the class or caste of the Anglo-Irish that fell, or was finally pushed, out of power and history in the 1920s, even though they may also figure other types of endangered species too, such as the contemporary Protestants of Northern Ireland. It could also well be that such specifically social and cultural disappearances and terminations lie behind the finely tuned and frequently invoked apocalypticism of Mahon's work, in which displacements and unsettlings of this kind are caught up into the largest potential unsettling of all, that of nuclear catastrophe; but they also surely restore, by the back door – the back door of that disused shed, maybe, into which the poet-photographer intrudes his 'light meter' – and in an imaginatively renewed form, the familiar Irish trope of exile. These poems implicitly refuse what Mahon has called, again in relation to MacNeice, 'the histrionic and approximate sense in which the word is used in Ireland';[6] but their inwardness with *émigré* and *déraciné* Irish experience makes it not sentimental for Edna Longley to have said of Mahon that 'he receives a defenceless spirit into the protectorate of poetry',[7] even if one ought to modify this by observing that it is in fact to defenceless bodies, as well as a defenceless spirit, that his poems give sanctuary or succour.

II

These various kinds of displacement put their pressures on the ways in which America is perceived in his work, and perceived in relation to Ireland, as it frequently is, particularly latterly. In the introduction to the anthology he coedited with Peter Fallon, the *Penguin Book of Contemporary Irish Poetry* (1990), Mahon draws America into the radius of Irish poetry when he drily observes that the countries are 'determined . . . by transatlantic neighbourhood'.[8] This three-thousand-miles-apart 'determination' is, we must assume, in fact not so much geographical as historical: Mahon is presumably alluding here to the presence of Irish America as a determinant in modern and contemporary transatlantic aesthetic and cultural relations, and also to what his 'Joycentenary Ode' calls, in its pastiche Finneganese, 'the gineral californucation' which has 'revolationized / Ourland beyand raggednition'; but the anthologist's insistence on the wide narrowness of the Atlantic Ocean supplies a self-referential rationale for some of his own littoral locations, and it also offers what we might regard as an epigraph to one of his finest poems, 'The Globe in North Carolina', which closes *The Hunt by Night* (1982).

Hugh Haughton has described the way this poem inherits and transforms one of the stock tropes of seventeenth-century Metaphysical poetry, that of the globe, and how, further, it is formally indebted to Andrew Marvell.[9] Mahon's variant octosyllabics, which he employs in other poems, too, may well share in what T. S. Eliot famously characterized as a 'tough reasonableness beneath the slight lyric grace' of Marvell's poems:[10] they supply a nimble, alert, dexterous mode for meditation and self-reflection, for an apparently reasoned effort towards clarification. Yet, as Haughton also recognizes, these are Marvellian octosyllabics very much indebted to the use Robert Lowell makes of the form in *Near the Ocean* (1967), and crucially in 'Waking Early Sunday Morning' and 'Fourth of July in Maine', those tensely exacerbated combinations of private reflection and political speculation. Any consideration of Hiberno-American literary relations in the 1970s and 1980s must centrally involve Lowell, who also figures prominently in Seamus Heaney. Whereas, however, the Heaney of *Field Work* (1979), and perhaps to some extent of the earlier volume *North* (1975), is indebted primarily to the iconoclastically and conversationally free-verse Lowell of *Life Studies* and *For the Union Dead*, and to the aggressive lyric disruptions of his later blank-verse sonnets, Mahon's sophisticated urbanity is drawn to what we might regard as the effort towards an existentially negative sublime in the Lowell of *Near the Ocean* (whose very title, indeed, defines the locale of many of Mahon's poems). In Mahon, as in Lowell, that is to say, the tough reasonableness of Marvell's civilities – which was itself won out of a distressed imagination of civil war – is disturbed and distressed by things unamenable to reason; and in both, the octosyllabics are the formal representation of the only momentary resolution of almost ungovernable anxieties that the poem makes possible. In Lowell and then in Mahon, the ruffled poise of the octosyllabic couplet is a form bruised or even mauled by an apocalyptic sense of history which may well, in Mahon's case, take its initial inspiration or impulse from his own contemporary imagination of civil strife in Ireland. As elsewhere in both poets, therefore, irony becomes a principle of form, discrepancy a fundamental mode or principle of historical perception.

In Lowell's 'Waking Early Sunday Morning', mid-1960s America and the Vietnam War are the source of the ultimate anxiety, and the poem advances, in its final stanza, a negative sublime that is climactically and despairingly self-definitive:

> Pity the planet, all joy gone
> from this sweet volcanic cone;
> peace to our children when they fall
> in small war on the heels of small

> war – until the end of time
> to police the earth, a ghost
> orbiting forever lost
> in our monotonous sublime.

In Mahon's 'The Globe in North Carolina', as in many of his poems, the ultimate distress is ecological, the poet fearing that a characteristic 'scepticism / And irony' might 'be dumb'

> Before the new thing that must come
> Out of the scrunched Budweiser can
> To make us sadder, wiser men.

The Coleridgean allusion there makes this poem too a kind of survivor's tale; and, just as 'Waking Early Sunday Morning' moves in conclusion to a perspective beyond the great globe itself, Mahon's poem also takes what it calls, neologistically, the 'theoptic' view, as the globe which spins to the poet's finger-tips in the poem's opening lines – 'The earth spins to my finger-tips and / Pauses beneath my outstretched hand' – eventually metamorphoses into 'our peripheral / Night garden in the glory-hole / Of space, a home from home'. Heaney's 'Alphabets', in *The Haw Lantern*, plots a not dissimilar trajectory, and it is feasible that the long perspectives taken in a number of the contemporary poems of Northern Ireland may well have a cultural or political dimension. They register both the exacerbations and the desires of poets unwilling to bow to factional interest; indeed, when Mahon imagines himself returning to Ireland from America in Part xvii of 'The Hudson Letter', the theoptic becomes political too: 'I can see a united Ireland from the air.' In 'The Globe in North Carolina', however, the imperative is more manifestly metaphysical. The poet as astronomer at the beginning of the poem develops a 'theoptic' view until, in a self-reflexive image of the kind that Christopher Ricks has identified as characteristic of some Northern Irish poetry, and that it shares with English metaphysical verse, 'America is its own night-sky':[11]

> Its own celestial fruit, on which
> Sidereal forms appear, their rich
> Clusters and vague attenuations
> Miming galactic dispositions.

> Hesperus is a lighthouse, Mars
> An air-force base; molecular cars
> Arrowing the turnpikes become
> Lost meteorites in search of home.
>
> No doubt we could go on like this
> For decades yet; but nemesis
> Awaits our furious make-believe,
> Our harsh refusal to conceive
> A world so different from our own
> We wouldn't know it were we shown.
> Who, in its halcyon days, imagined
> Carthage a ballroom for the wind?

These remarkable lines have somewhere behind them, I think, the description in the 'Ithaca' episode of *Ulysses* – that other long perspective taken in modern Irish literature – of the Dublin night sky as a 'heaventree of stars hung with humid nightblue fruit'; but they require, too, the slight exoticism of their transatlantic location for the startlingly vertiginous play they make with their contemporary revision of medieval and Renaissance concepts of microcosm and macrocosm. It is, in part, as though Mahon's witty lexical refinement is searching for a form that will allow him to combine, without undue attention or stress, the almost self-parodying precisions or pedantries of the words 'sidereal', 'attenuations', 'nemesis' and 'halcyon' with the word 'turnpikes', that most routine vocabulary of American topography which nevertheless strikes the un-American ear with an open-road, empty-space, freewheeling attractiveness. Indeed, the word 'America' itself figures in the poem with an aura of the exotic or the glamorous about it too, as it does in the work of some other cisatlantic poets who grew up in places and periods of utter non-californucation: a notable example being the Ted Hughes of *Birthday Letters*.[12]

It may seem heavy-handed and contrary to the spirit of Mahon's poem, with its suave, if 'salt', astringency, to insist that its premonition of ecological catastrophe is neither narcissistic nor merely glamorously nihilistic, as his intimations of apocalypse have sometimes been accused of being, but that in fact it secretes an ethics or a politics: since to remind us that nemesis awaits the make-believe of self-interested ignorance, our 'era-provincial self-regard', has its corrective impulse. This is why the extraordinary conception of the Earth itself as only a 'home from home' is followed by the annotation of the 'Devotion we can bring to it', a devotion which may be – and this is the poem's own phrase – 'true / Salvation'. Yet, as if himself turning wilfully from the possible sententiousness of this underlying theme, Mahon ends 'The Globe in North Carolina' by veering away from a conclusion in some version of the anticipated sublime, the kind of emotionally and argumentatively appropriate conclusion to which Lowell comes in 'Waking Early Sunday Morning'. Instead, he bravely and surprisingly digresses by opening his final stanzas, and then closing them, with those marks of ellipsis characteristic of a later Lowellian manner:

> . . . You lie, an ocean to the east,
> Your limbs composed, your mind at rest,
> Asleep in a sunrise which will be
> Your mid-day when it reaches me;
> And what misgivings I might have
> About the true importance of
> The 'merely human' pales before
> The mere fact of your being there.
>
> Five miles away a south-bound freight
> Sings its euphoria to the state
> And passes on; unfinished work
> Awaits me in the scented dark.
> The halved globe, slowly turning, hugs
> Its silence, while the lightning bugs
> Are quiet beneath the open window,
> Listening to that lonesome whistle blow . . .

The drifting ellipses, which announce the sudden veering-away from a poem of social and cosmic meditation towards a love poem, here destabilize the Lowellian sublimity with what might appear an almost auto-deconstructive dissonance, one that diverts climactic closure into something more like irresolution or incompletion; and this is, we may take it, the ultimate importance of elsewhere in Mahon. 'America' may provide the exoticism of the theoptic view, and may establish the Earth itself as only a home from home – unnervingly, but also in a way that existentially adapts a Christian metaphysics – but there is an elsewhere, 'an ocean to the east', which is itself a closer home for the displaced poet. It is at this point, returning to the image of the globe on the desk with which the poem began, that Mahon most clearly inherits the timbre of the seventeenth-century metaphysical love-lyric. Indeed, the effectiveness of these stanzas is of a kind that opens a negotiation with the wistfulness of pastiche, which it nevertheless forecloses immediately by citing the alternative wistfulness of that staple 'lonesome whistle' of American country-and-western music, a kind entirely appropriate, of course, to this North Carolina location. That this poem finds its form by returning finally to an opening image, but returning there only in an unpredictable digression, may be regarded as one of the strongest instances in Mahon of that stylish combination of composure and discomposure, of finish and process, *brio* and melancholy, that holds so many of his poems in profitably unresolved tension. The combination may, indeed, be written in little into that elegant lexical move from the derogatorily quoted phrase 'the "merely human"' to the bravura assurance of the *in propria persona* phrase 'the mere fact of your being here', where the move, which is that made by the whole poem, is from misgiving dismay to a steadying resolve, and is enacted by the restoration of a vanished etymology to the word 'mere', so that its use in the second phrase is suddenly vibrantly and piquantly Shakespeare's: 'absolute, entire, sheer, perfect, downright', as *OED* tells us.

What the lines also do, however, is to introduce to the poem in a complex way the issue of gender which has already been raised by the epigraph from Voznesensky ('There are no religions, no revelations; there are women'). When 'The Globe in North Carolina' takes the theoptic view, it includes a theme familiar from many of Mahon's poems, the death but possible further life, or afterlife, of the gods, the quasi-Stevensian attempt to locate in consciousness some form of transcendence in a post-Christian period and in a post-religious sensibility. This leads to the poet's apostrophe to the moon mythologized as Selene:

> Great mother, now the gods have gone
> We place our faith in you alone,
> Inverting the procedures which
> Knelt us to things beyond our reach.

This continues in the vocative until immediately preceding the ellipsis before the final two stanzas, which I have already quoted; and that ellipsis, as we have seen, introduces the apostrophe 'You lie . . .'. There is a gnomic, riddling element in some of Mahon's work which has not, strangely, been much picked up on by his critics, but which may well be connected with his obsessive revisionism; here it consists, for the first-time reader of this poem, in an uncertainty about whether the 'You' being addressed here, after the ellipsis, is still the moon, the 'Great mother'. The effect, that is to say, is to have the prominently gendered moon goddess waver or warp across the dissolve of the ellipsis into the less prominently gendered but (we assume) also female lover of the poet as she lies composed in sleep. The poem shares an element of its imagery with 'Courtyards in Delft', which opens the volume, *The Hunt by Night*, that 'The Globe in North Carolina' closes. In the former poem, 'the pale light of that provincial town / Will spread itself, like ink or oil . . .'; in the latter, 'Night spreads like ink on the unhedged / Tobacco fields and clucking lakes'. The similes in both cases are, of course, self-reflexive in ways entirely appropriate to their preoccupations, foregrounding the activity of painter and poet in poems which are, in part, enquiries into the sources and value of artistic and poetic composition or representation: significantly, at the end of 'The Globe in North Carolina' the poet reminds himself, and us, that 'unfinished work / Awaits me in the scented dark'.

The sharing of that simile, however, may alert us to the fact that not only seventeenth-century poetry but seventeenth-century painting too is involved in 'The Globe in North Carolina', as it is in 'Courtyards in Delft', in a volume which makes other references to paintings and takes its title from a work by Uccello, to which 'The Globe in North Carolina' itself also makes reference. I am suggesting that it is conceivable that behind the image that opens the poem there may well lie Vermeer's painting in the Louvre known as *The Astronomer*, one of the very few Vermeers to represent only a male figure, in which the eponymous astronomer leans forward to touch his globe as light pours onto it from the window in front. But even if no such specific allusion is being made, I still think that we can interpret the poem's move from an apostrophe to the mother to one to the lover in something of the way Edward Snow, in his book on Vermeer, conceives of what he calls the 'intricate relation' between three Vermeer paintings, *The Astronomer*, the similarly male representation of *The Geographer*, and the much better-known female representation of *Woman Holding a Balance*:

> The male figures reach out through consciousness in an attempt to map, to encompass the limits of their world, to grasp the realm beyond as thought or image or microcosm; yet in doing so they instinctively tighten their grip on the material dimension that supports their speculations. The woman locates more intuitively (both in her measuring and by virtue of her presence) the center, the balance point, and, suspending it, gently touches down.[13]

Snow also reads that gentle touching-down as a benediction; and, in turn, reading that against the quoted painting of the Last Judgement before which the woman stands in the intricately allusive Vermeer, he says: 'There could scarcely be a greater contrast between this gesture and that of the Christ in the background of *Woman Holding a Balance*, whose upraised arms preside over the apocalyptic destruction of everything that is graced by, and abides in, Vermeer's art.'[14]

The image of the female lover composed, and in repose, at the end of 'The Globe in North Carolina' is similarly positioned against apocalyptic destruction, and, indeed, the poem's images of microcosmic America are prominently gendered as masculine: the 'hardware in the heavens'; the phallic lighthouse of Hesperus; the air-force base of Mars; and the equally phallic cars 'Arrowing the turnpikes'. I am not, of course, suggesting that Mahon's work is collusive with seventeenth-century stereotypes of masculine exploration and feminine intuitive balance. What I am suggesting is that 'The Globe in North Carolina' finds its ultimate elsewhere in the difference of gender, and that in the calm repose of that recognition, as it terminates a poem fraught with the deepest global anxieties, it offers its own constructive celebration of what might be opposed to the cosmic destructiveness whose possibility it also conjures. 'No doubt we could go on like this / For decades yet', the poem says, where 'go on' carries the colloquial sense 'talk to little purpose or effect' as well as the stronger sense of 'proceed'; but not, the implication must be, if 'The mere fact of your being there' convinces us of the devotion that should attend on the mere fact of being.

III

Among various others of Mahon's poems in octosyllabics are the verse letters 'Beyond Howth Head' and 'The Sea in Winter', written in the 1970s. Both have named addressees, like Auden's 'Letter to Lord Byron' and 'New Year Letter'. The form was, for Auden, 'light verse', but both of his letters have, nevertheless, serious concerns, even if these are managed with a certain levity of tone. In Mahon, as in Auden, 'light verse' is an effort to open solitude or even solipsism into sociability, since the letter assumes that it has at least one auditor or correspondent, just as it also assumes, although in a different way, what, as we have seen, many of Mahon's poems do: the coexistence of at least two places being brought into significant relation, the place written from and the place written to; verse letters, in this, following ordinary letters in what Charles Lamb in his essay 'Distant Correspondents' (which is itself in the form of a letter) calls 'this grand solecism of *two presents*' in which '*my Now*' encounters '*your Now*'. In 'Letter to Lord Byron', Auden, setting an ambition for himself, tells his addressee: 'You are the master of the airy manner.' Nothing in Mahon's octosyllabic letters is ever quite so airborne, however, that it does not aspire to a further negative sublime; and both of his verse letters climax in chilly declensions – 'I who know nothing go to teach / While a new day crawls up the beach' in 'The Sea in Winter', and 'I put out the light / on Mailer's *Armies of the Night*' in 'Beyond Howth Head'.[15] The poems are wry, disaffected, 'less deceived', with a kind of icy celebration of contingency and debris made in the face of an obvious melancholy, dejection or morose apocalypticism, and, in the case of 'The Sea in Winter', in the face of an anatomization of the political culture of the North of Ireland, to which Mahon has temporarily returned – 'Portstewart, Portrush, Portballintrae – / *Un beau pays mal habité*' – which perhaps matches Lowell's state-of-the-Union poems in *Near the Ocean* with its own state-of-the-Union address.

Despite these poems, and the fact that Mahon subsequently wrote a series of prose letters from New York for the *Irish Times*, it was quite unpredictable that his return to poetry after a ten-year gap between the interim collection *Antarctica* (1985) and *The Hudson Letter* (1995) would be prominently, in 'The Yaddo Letter' and the lengthy title sequence itself, via the verse letter, now newly constituted formally in irregularly rhyming loose pentameters, rather than octosyllabics, although the form does occasionally permit a short run of tetrameters; and part of the unpredictability of such a thing for Mahon is the fact that, unlike other prominent modern Irish poets, he had not previously employed anything resembling the long poem or sequence. In relation to the earlier work, Seamus Deane observes that the general mood of elegy is 'no more than an inflection away from satire',[16] and the forms adopted in 'The Hudson Letter', with their faint but distinct echoes of the eighteenth-century heroic couplet, inflect these poems further in that direction, although we should also note that satire is traditionally itself an element of elegy (as it is, for instance, in 'Lycidas'), and also that the Horatian verse epistle and the Juvenalian verse satire are audible classical precedents. At the same time, these are very capacious discursive forms in which the poet's self-presentation is more straightforwardly sociable and apparently autobiographical than anything previously in Mahon, and more open to the contingent and the provisional. In fact, the initiation of the form in 'The Yaddo Letter' serves as the vehicle for Mahon's address, from a writer's colony in upper New York State, to the children in England whom, as a divorced father, he rarely sees (Parts IX and XI of 'The Hudson Letter' are also addresses to his daughter and son). 'The Yaddo Letter', it may be, stays just on the right side of the maudlin and the sententious, if indeed it does, and in Part XI of 'The Hudson Letter' the poet satirizes himself as a 'Polonius of the twilight zone' and actually quotes that prolix and preposterous Shakespearean father at several points. If the maudlin and the sentenious are tones occasionally at least at the edge of earshot in the sequence, however, this kind of familial intimacy also serves to anchor it in the frayed anxieties, exacerbations, self-doubts and guilts of the quotidian in a way that wilfully distresses the poised, melancholy perfectionism of earlier Mahon which, however much one might admire it, could hardly be expected, itself alone, to maintain viability throughout an entire career, even if the volume's sometimes negative or indifferent reviewers have thought otherwise. The element of routine ongoingness in the sequence is also carried by its intermittent address to a 'you' who appears to be a lover offering a possible alternative to the more immediate personal distresses alluded to during it.

'The Hudson Letter' is a lengthy, eighteen-part verse letter sent from the banks of the Hudson River in New York City, where this poet now displaced into American exile establishes one further maritime location as his *mise-en-scène*: 'a rented "studio apartment" in New York / five blocks from the river', on the island of Manhattan. The poet who admires Louis MacNeice for being a tourist in his own country now becomes, as he says in Part VI, 'an undesirable "resident alien" on this shore', enjoying that official status in which one is not a citizen but has 'lawful permanent residency' in the United States. The sense of a temporarily anchored rootlessness which the official legal phrase conveys is, it could be said, the condition to which all Mahon's work aspires; and this passport identity provides the impulse for an unpredictable extension to, and variation of, the Mahon lyric, an ironically alert and adroit representation of the solitary poet among his predicaments. Indeed, 'The Hudson Letter' may be regarded as one in a long line of Mahon's poems about poets, some of them about *poètes maudits*, except that this is now a *self*-portrait as poet, and one taken, as it were, from the inside.

If tonal variety and the representation of a discursive subjectivity distinguish 'The Hudson Letter' from Mahon's earlier work, however, the sequence shares with it, and outdoes it in, an intense literary and cultural allusiveness. Its eighteen sections are prefaced with epigraphs from a wide range of sources, including Albert Camus, Louis MacNeice, Gerard de Nerval, Eugene O'Neill, Woody Allen, Scott Fitzgerald, Susan Sontag, J. M. Barrie and Oscar Wilde, and these convey the strong sense of a cultured writer riffling through his bookshelves, living among and in his texts. The poem contains all sorts of other quotations from, and allusions to, poems and poets, including other famous poet-visitors to, and residers in, New York, such as Lorca, Dylan Thomas, MacNeice, Auden and Hart Crane. It also refers extensively to novels, philosophical texts, movies, plays and music. It is interspersed with upper-case citations of the texts prominent on the streets of the New York which the poet walks as a latter-day *flâneur*: advertising hoardings, newspaper headlines, neon signs, graffiti. And it contains some less identifiable quotations from, I imagine, sources such as gazetteers, *National Geographic*-type journals and newspapers; embedded quotations from the titles of other texts (Paul Tillich's *The Courage to Be*, John MacCormack's 'I Hear You Calling Me', Saint-Exupéry's *Vol de Nuit* (*Night Flight*), and Alain-Fournier's *Le Grand Meaulnes* (*The Lost*

Domain), for instance); identified quotations which make sections of the poem read like wittily and engagingly raconteurial conversation – as when Part XIV, for instance, reports Noel Coward's opinion that King Kong clutches Fay Wray 'like a suppository'; and joke or phoney citations which send up the whole idea of citation, as when Part II offers a self-image of the poet–professor grading papers 'with the radio low / as Pascal said we should'. It includes too that more invisible kind of quotation which is translation, version and pastiche: Part II, 'Last Night', is a poem resembling Hitchcock's *Rear Window*, which is itself alluded to in Part XIV (a section on *King Kong*, watched on video, dedicated to Fay Wray); Part V, 'To Mrs Moore at Inishannon', is a pastiche letter from a late nineteenth-century emigrant from Cork to New York; Part VII, 'Sneaker's', is a kind of 'found poem' constructed exclusively from snippets of bar-room conversation and monologue; Part VIII is a version of the Tereus and Philomela story from Ovid, intercut with reflection and critical commentary, and including a draft cancellation; Part XIII, 'Sappho in "Judith's Room"', is a monologue by Sappho in contemporary New York which includes translations from her poems; and Part XIV, 'Beauty and the Beast', begins as an excellent pastiche of the camply insouciant pretend-aimlessness of the Frank O'Hara of such poems as 'The Day Lady Died':

> I go nightshopping like Frank O'Hara, I go bopping
> up Bleecker for juice, croissants, Perrier, ice-cream
> and Gitanes *filtre*, pick up the laundry, get back
> to five (5!) messages on the answering machine . . .

The element of the bravura in these performances, which makes the poem virtually a compendium of citation, produces a zest which is not now compounded with melancholy, as it is in the earlier Mahon; and the sense of the writer performing himself in a stable and viable solitude, of the contemporary intellectual constructing an existence from the cultural representations available to him, and available as sustenance and delight, is intense in the sequence. The proliferating referentiality is also, however, an insistence that, even though this letter has its dedicatees, it is, in the end and, indeed, even in its inception, primarily a letter from the self to the self: the poem is a compellingly inward demonstration of the contemporary ways in which solitude can be managed without self-pity. Its dense textuality is also testimony to the way a contemporary, postmodern consciousness is itself a textualized subjectivity, already written as well as writing. Indeed, in this regard, it is perhaps not too fanciful to see the sequence as secreting a series of references to that Ur-poem of modernist textuality, *The Waste Land*. It contains, as *The Waste Land* does, a pub scene; the mythical material of Tereus and Philomela; many drifting megalopolitan crowds; as we have seen, an immense amount of literary reference, quotation and pastiche; and, in the persona of the poet himself, a character, like some of those in Eliot, in a state of nervous extremity ('O show me how to recover my lost nerve!', he says in the opening section). The Derek Mahon who, in his earlier sequence 'A Kensington Notebook' – in a form which brilliantly pastiches the quatrains of 'Hugh Selwyn Mauberley' – offers a view and a critique of Ezra Pound at work in London before the First World War on the enterprise of international Modernism, here places himself as the knowledgeable inheritor of the already-writtenness of that literary Modernism, although one who has made the opposite transatlantic crossing. Citation in Eliot and Pound sometimes takes on the aspect of nightmare, however, where the fragments, for all that they might shore one against ruin, nevertheless emphasize the ruin too; whereas in Mahon it is more manifestly ballast, part of the effort of pleasurable self-recuperation, and entirely at ease with its own cultural pluralism and non-differentiation ('Thank God for the VCR').

In addition to the local epigraphs and references, the whole poem is itself prefaced by three further epigraphs, one of which is the stanza from Keats's 'Ode to a Nightingale' in which the nightingale's song is invoked as the great Romantic figure for a permanent imaginative solace: 'the self-same song that found a path / Through the sad heart of Ruth when, sick for home, / She stood in tears amid the alien corn'. Keats's poem is alluded to several times in the sequence itself, and its symbolic nightingale appears, along with a range of other birds, at various further points within it, acting as a little leitmotiv organizing principle in this otherwise apparently random poetic structure. The Keatsian epigraph is intended, presumably, to introduce the trope of exile, emigration, alienation, even as it deflects the 'histrionic and approximate' Irish sense with which the word has been used into a remembering of its provenance in Romantic and post-Romantic literature more generally. The point of the epigraph would tally with the sense of the Earth itself as a 'home from home' in 'The Globe in North Carolina': that is, it offers a conception of exile as a fundamental human pattern and predicament, rather than a too readily available national appropriation.

This does not prevent the poem, however, from presenting, in several of its sections, specific situatings of Irish emigrant experience: that of the late nineteenth-century Bridget Moore, in the pastiche letter to her mother which forms Part v; and, in Part xvii, that of Yeats's father, the painter John B. Yeats, who moved to New York late in life, never to return to Ireland. These specific Irish-American instances are complemented, however, with vivid considerations of the actual contemporary homeless and dispossessed, those who sleep in cardboard boxes in New York City, and who are given a section to themselves, Part xii, the punningly entitled 'Alien Nation'; and Mahon identifies with these in the radical sense that, as he says there, 'I too have been homeless and in detox.' This is, obviously, the personal experience which yawns as a chasm below the perilously achieved lucidity and stability of the steadying pentameters of 'The Hudson Letter' and which, presumably, accounts for the ten-year gap in Mahon's writing career. Just as Mahon as poetic self-portraitist in the sequence inherits the figure of the poet from previous poems of his own, so in this respect too he himself becomes one of those derelicts, down-and-outs, beggars and tramps, one of the outsiders and the alienated who figure frequently in his own earlier work. In this way, it might be said that 'The Hudson Letter' receives the defenceless spirit of its own poet into the protectorate of his poetry, to very poignant effect and without the self-exacerbating bravura which can sometimes accompany such kinds of revelation in more straightforwardly 'confessional' modes of modern writing. If the Keatsian nightingale supplies Mahon's poem with an epigraph which offers one of the most conventional of all Romantic analogies for the utterance of the poet, the poem itself, in its various representations of birds, transforms that inherited symbol into a trope which embraces this once apparently destitute poet and his companions in dereliction and abandonment too, when Part vi explores an image of exotic ornithological species which have escaped during a storm in New York and whose chances of survival 'are less than fair':

On ledge and rail they sit, Inca tern and Andean gull, who
fled their storm-wrecked cage in the Bronx Zoo
and now flap in exhilaration and growing fear
above Yonkers, New Rochelle, Bay Ridge, the whole 'tri-state area',
a transmigration of souls, crazy-eyed as they peer
through mutant cloud-cover and air thick with snow-dust,
toxic aerosol dazzle and invasive car-exhaust,
or perch forlorn on gargoyle and asbestos roof,
fine-featured, ruffled, attentive, almost too high to hear
the plaintive, desolate cab-horns on Madison and Fifth:
like Daisy's Cunard nightingale, they belong in another life.

As an image of displacement, and as an emblem for the almost
hopeless attempt to survive in a world choked by pollution, these
lines inherit a great deal from Mahon's earlier work, and the plangency of their long perspective forms a memorable addition to the
range of his 'theoptic' views. What is newly poignant in them,
however, is the implicit human relevance and empathy: this 'transmigration of souls' does duty for the numerous other human
transmigrations in the poem too.[17]

This unillusioned but resilient universalist's theoptic view ap-
preciates, in Part x, named 'Auden on St. Mark's Place', the resolve
of that other exile and poetic aerialist ('as the hawk sees it or the
helmeted airman'): 'in the darkest hours / of holocaust and
apocalypse, cheap music and singles bars, / you remind us of what
the examined life involves'. 'The Hudson Letter' too is testimony
to a well-examined life: confessional in acknowledging its poet's
own distresses, but seeking neither sympathy nor forgiveness.
There is no autocratic Yeatsian casting-out of remorse here: the
poem is instructive in its capacity to cope, to endure and to
empathize; and it is exemplary in the quality of its unsentimental
but deep affections. It is entirely appropriate, then, that the Yeats
to whom allegiance is given in the sequence is Yeats *père*, the
improvident man but affectionate father in his letters to his son,
and the bravely resilient recommender of the virtue of being, in his
own words quoted at the end of this section (Part xvii), 'an exile
and a stranger'. John B. Yeats is, elsewhere in that section, discovered making his own empathetic response to a young Irish
exile; and 'The Hudson Letter' concludes in Part xviii, 'The
Small Rain', with a universalization of affectionate sympathy and

involvement made while contemplating 'the moon's exilic glare', that ultimate elsewhere always visible from wherever one is. This is a climactic long and inclusive perspective, one further theoptic view, and, finally, a secular, humanist prayer. Coming at the end of this complex, many-layered and very powerful poem – a new kind of poem, indeed – in which this poet has found a mode of unsentimentally direct, if tempered, address, its cadence of sympathetic renewal has great resonance and authority, particularly when we remember that it inherits the cadence of the mushrooms' plea from 'A Disused Shed in Co. Wexford' (' "Save us, save us," they seem to say'):

> I think of the homeless, no rm. at the inn;
> far off, the gaseous planets where they spin,
> the star-lit towers of Nineveh and Babylon,
> the secret voice of nightingale and dolphin,
> fish crowding the Verrazano Bridge; and see,
> even in the icy heart of February,
> primrose and gentian. When does the thaw begin?
> We have been too long in the cold. – Take us in; take us in!

9

To stop the bleeding: the poetry of botany in Michael Longley

I

In *The Ghost Orchid* (1995), Michael Longley has a character-istically brief, indeed single-sentence, poem called 'Mr 10½ *after Robert Mapplethorpe*'. The poem is a meditation on a 1976 photograph of Mapplethorpe's entitled 'Mark Stevens (Mr 10½)'. It is one of the images sealed off by separating red pages in the standard Jonathan Cape edition of Mapplethorpe's work: one of those erotic or (as Mapplethorpe thought of some of them him-self) pornographic images, which 'plays with the edge', in the phrase which Arthur C. Danto, in the volume's accompanying essay, tells us Mapplethorpe used.[1] The image is that of a white male torso viewed from neck to upper thigh and bent to the right over some sort of table or box. Naked except for a pair of leather chaps, the torso displays on the table a circumcised penis whose astonishing flaccid size makes it quite clear how Mark Stevens came by his pseudonym. This is Longley's poem:

> When he lays out on a market stall or altar
> His penis and testicles in thanksgiving and for sale,
> I find myself considering his first months in the womb
> As a wee girl, and I substitute for his two plums
> Plum-blossom, for his cucumber a yellowy flower.

This poem swims buoyantly on what Hugo Williams has called, in a poem, 'the sea / of post-war British photograph poetry',[2] since it behaves so unexpectedly and unpredictably, reading its photo-graphic text with such wayward, oddly angled intelligence. The photograph might have prompted, after all, a number of responses. Longley might have responded with a meditation on the particular line or 'edge' which distinguishes the erotic from the pornographic in Mapplethorpe, the kind of meditation Roland Barthes offers in relation to another Mapplethorpe image in his book on photography, *Camera Lucida;*[3] or he might have noticed what Barthes would almost certainly have thought the *punctum* of the photograph, a tiny tattooed devil on the torso's upper arm, which – given the altar-like nature of the display – might have prompted a meditation on the strange persistence in parodied form of Mapplethorpe's native Catholicism. Alternatively, the photograph might have given rise, as it does in Danto's essay, to an account of the paradoxical combination in Mapplethorpe of erotic or pornographic content with a chaste classicism of form. These would all be interesting and informative, but in the end obvious, critical ways of representing or interpreting the photograph. Longley's way is not like these ways; and in its unlikeness it seems to me entirely characteristic. I want to try to say why.

The poem's sinuous single sentence inspects the image and finds it wanting: it reads the masculine display, this putting of the penis on a pedestal, as an arrogance requiring the correction of deflation. In reading arrogance into the image, Longley is, arguably, moralizing it in excess of the facts. There is nothing intrinsic to it to justify his remark that this penis is 'for sale', for instance, unless this implies not prostitution but simply the fact that Mapplethorpe paid his models: but then, what painter or photographer does not, when his, or her, models are studio models? Similarly, Longley's title makes Mark Stevens anonymous as 'Mr 10½', whereas Mapplethorpe's title prominently and punctiliously gives him his proper name. Danto has argued that this lack of anonymity evidences a trust between photographer and model of a kind which very precisely differentiates between pornography and eroticism. I would also say that such moralizing tends to miss something else about many of Mapplethorpe's images, including this one: the fact that, when the initial shock of, or erotic reaction to, the image has worn away, as it does quite quickly, the residue is often a kind of comedy, and often also, as in this photograph, a comedy of discrepancy. Mapplethorpe, that is to say, is serious enough, but not *that* serious; although, indeed, the casual, even whimsical humour of the Longley poem may itself include precisely such a recognition.

However, if Longley overinterprets, he does so in the interests of reducing male presumption and arrogance and of reminding us of the instabilities of gender differentiation. This huge displayed phallus is relocated at its point of origin in the womb where, prior to sexual differentiation, it was not yet phallus at all, but a non-specialized shape. It is probably worth saying that the poem is physiologically knowledgeable here in a way that people are, sometimes – surprisingly, it may be – not. The point has been made with brilliant wit and aplomb by the scientist and popular-science writer Stephen Jay Gould, in his essay 'Male nipples and clitoral ripples', where he says that if you ask the majority of people why men have nipples they can't tell you, being ignorant of what he calls 'the most elementary fact of sexual anatomy – the homology of penis and clitoris', an ignorance prompted by the pervasiveness of the functionalist model in evolutionary theory. Gould writes:

> The external differences between male and female develop gradually from an early embryo so generalized that its sex cannot be easily determined. The clitoris and the penis are one and the same organ, identical in early form, but later enlarged in male fetuses through the action of testosterone. Similarly, the labia majora of women and the scrotal sacs of men are the same structure, indistinguishable in young embryos, but later enlarged, folded over, and fused along the midline in male fetuses.[4]

Gould's insistence on the point is, of course, continuous with his sense that such physiological knowledge may have consequences in psychology and sociology. If the penis is a clitoris too, that is to say, its arrogant place on the pedestal may not be so securely held or, possibly, even desired: competition won't count. I think this is Longley's point too, and he is finely discriminating to have made it – given its complexity and its ramifications – in such an exquisitely brief and witty poem.

My theme is botany in Longley, however, not physiology, and this essay is probably taking an inordinately long time to broach it. But, on the other hand, perhaps it is not, since by broaching botany through physiology – human physiology – it is holding in the same thought things that are almost always held together in Longley's poems too. As they are, of course, in 'Mr 10½', where the unreconstructed penis and scrotum are two plums and a cucumber, the penis and scrotum reconstructed as clitoris and vagina are plum-blossom and a yellowy flower. In these figures Longley has appropriated the Mapplethorpe photographic image to the most consistent imagery of his own poetry, an imagery of botany – of plant, wildflower and herb – through which some of his most central preoccupations are insinuated; an appropriation emphasized by the languid revision of Mapplethorpe's New York chic into the Northern Irish demotic of that 'wee girl'. On the other hand, Longley's biomorphism here is continuous with Mapplethorpe's own, where his flower pictures – of calla lily, poppy, baby's breath, chrysanthemums and orchid – rhyme their flowers with the human genitalia. In Longley's poem 'Mr 10½' it is almost, therefore, as though the male floral rhyming of Mapplethorpe is being revised into the female biomorphism of a Georgia O'Keeffe, those flowers which enfold, invite and caress rather than assert, rise up and strut.

II

If physiology is read under the figure of botany in 'Mr 10½', then, it is an instruction in the way botany in Longley is instinct with human significance. It is a botany frequently eroticised, and in ways sometimes subversive of masculine norms; it offers a series of figures for the processes of psychological identity and differentiation; it attempts to act as palliation for the afflictions of history and mortality. Before all of these metaphorical and figurative functions, however, botany in Longley is what it is. As in the other botanical poets named in his work – John Clare and Edward Thomas, but also those momentary botanists of the battlefields, Isaac Rosenberg and Keith Douglas – the naming of species is itself a rich poetic resource. There is in Longley a sweet lyricism of the onomastic, ambivalently caught between spontaneous delight and something more melancholy and wounded.

Edward Thomas is, as Seamus Heaney has said, the 'sponsoring presence from the literary tradition' for this strain in Longley – 'a sponsorship with just as much political significance as we want to assign it'[5] – and certainly such poems as Thomas's 'Old Man', 'Lob' and 'Household Poems' seem generative of Longley's own most characteristic processes. At a very early stage in his writing career he clearly deeply internalized and newly synthesized the way such poems 'like the names', as 'Old Man' has it – 'And yet I like the names'. Longley's poetry likes the names too – nowhere more so than in 'The Ice-Cream Man', in *Gorse Fires*, where the liking of the names builds into a perfectly cadenced catalogue:

> Rum and raisin, vanilla, butter-scotch, walnut, peach:
> You would rhyme off the flavours. That was before
> They murdered the ice-cream man on the Lisburn Road
> And you bought carnations to lay outside his shop.
> I named for you all the wild flowers of the Burren
> I had seen in one day: thyme, valerian, loosestrife,
> Meadowsweet, tway blade, crowsfoot, ling, angelica,
> Herb robert, marjoram, cow parsley, sundew, vetch,
> Mountain avens, wood sage, ragged robin, stitchwort,
> Yarrow, lady's bedstraw, bindweed, bog pimpernel.

This is a little triumph of its kind, a *tour de force* which paradoxically calls no attention to itself, but only to its object. If Edward Thomas's sponsorship is somewhere behind this, the poem reminds us too that the naming of wildflowers goes a long way further back than Thomas in English poetry, since it is not with Thomas but with Milton and Shakespeare that these lines connect more immediately: the Milton of the elegiac strewing of flowers in 'Lycidas', and the Shakespeare of Ophelia's last appearance in *Hamlet*, 'larded all with sweet flowers', and of Perdita's catalogue of flowers in *The Winter's Tale*. The persistence suggests Longley's resourcefulness as the discoverer of potential in a long English tradition of the melancholy collocation of human death and botanical life.

This does not, however, detract from the originality of this poem, which is almost purely catalogue, but very artfully managed catalogue. The list of ice-cream flavours in the first line culminates in a flavour – peach – which is also a plant: so the poet's recitation of the names of the wild flowers of the Burren seems doubly continuous with the daily recitation made in the ice-cream man's shop by the poem's addressee. This continuity between the activity of the shop and the activity of the poem is enforced by the way the recitation in the shop is defined as a 'rhyming', where the colloquialism is at once conventional and inflected with regard. It is probably heavy-handed to point this out, but the word makes of the activity of the ice-cream shop a kind of poetry too and, in doing so, indicates something entirely distinctive in Longley: an aesthetic unpresumptuousness in which other – it may seem, more

mundane – activities are accorded a properly generous appreciation. This implies, too, something else generally true of his work:
its tactful hesitation about any consolation poems might offer for
human suffering, and its deep unease about the legitimacy of
making poems from violent deaths.

These elements of this poem's behaviour – its good behaviour –
are enhanced also by the way the poem is an address to another who
has been distressed by the murder. That person's testimonial – the
wreath of carnations laid outside the shop – is a gesture of affection
and helplessness, as all such gestures are; but behind the poem's
catalogue there is presumably a conversation in which distress and
helplessness have been articulated. To offer consolation for, or
palliation of, these feelings is manifestly impossible, since there is
none, and behind this poem too there may therefore be the accurate
cliché that 'there are no words'. The poem offers, therefore, no
words at all of the conventionally consolatory or analytical kind;
but it does nevertheless offer words: the names of wild flowers,
which are offered as if they are themselves a wreath, to join the
wreath of carnations. This is a wreath now offered not to the ice-
cream man himself, but to this other, the poem's addressee, in his or
her grief. The list proposes, I suppose, the fact of botanical
persistence, the wonderful rich profusion and variety of the natural
world, even in the face of the grotesque damage done by human
atrocity; but it also, beyond that, offers to helplessness the resistance
that is the act of naming itself, the patient onomastics of recital in
which rhyming and naming, however tentatively and pitifully,
bravely encounter and resist that other verb prominent in 'The Ice-
Cream Man', 'murdering'. There is a Rilkean vigour and defiance in
this, that luminous defiance of the *Duino Elegies*, in which Rilke
discovers that what we are here for is naming – 'such saying as never
the things themselves / hoped so intensely to be'.[6] In this context, 'I
named for you' is the most that can be done for anyone in distress,
and the verb 'named' accrues a newly active strength from the
patient punctiliousness of the itemization that succeeds it.

III

So botany is what it is in Longley, the thing and the name of the
thing; but 'The Ice-Cream Man' also suggests something of the

way in which it is intertwined with themes of identity, death and political history. The self in Longley's poetry, the manifestation of subjectivity, is recorded but also rendered oblique or, as it were, hesitated before; and the way this hesitation is often profoundly involved in the botanical is clear from the poem 'Alibis', in *An Exploded View*. In a mode continuous with such metamorphic fantasias of Derek Mahon's as 'Lives', this poem's lyric first person wanders in and out of a set of variant selves: he is a saxophonist on the Souza Band's Grand Tour of the World, diarist, music teacher, the drafter of appendices to lost musical manuscripts, the saviour of damaged birds, the author of an *Apologia Pro Vita Mea*, and so on. Before any of these things, however, he identifies himself in the poem's opening stanza as a botanist:

> My botanical studies took me among
> Those whom I now consider my ancestors.
> I used to appear to them at odd moments –
> With buckets of water in the distance, or
> At the campfire, my arms full of snowy sticks.
> Beech mast, hedgehogs, cresses were my diet,
> My medicaments badger grease and dock leaves.
> A hard life. Nevertheless, they named after me
> A clover that flourished on the distant slopes.

The humoresque of this poem, its lighthearted buoyancy and flourish, keep the matter of identity in play as itself a form of play, a feinting at, and wavering among, possibilities or 'alibis'. The poem is the place where you do not keep yourself to yourself, the place where you are always elsewhere, but where you do indeed find an answer to the far from simple question, as 'Alibis' puts it, 'Of being in two places at the one time'.

The ways in which the botanical alibi may articulate historical attitude or veiled biography under the forms of natural history are suggested by many other poems of Longley's. The elegantly fluent little poem 'Flora', in *Man Lying on a Wall* (1976), virtually defines this kind of simultaneity when it imagines a flower, which has been used as a bookmark, staining photographs of the poet. The whole poem may be read as a kind of unravelling of the pun on the word 'leaves' which ends its first line: the leaves, that is, of both plant and book, which is the pun that Joyce uses at the close, or recommencement, of *Finnegans Wake* ('my leaves have fallen from me. But one clings still'); and, indeed, the entire botanical element in Longley is coincident with the fact that the Greek word from which 'anthology' derives means a collection of flowers: 'flora' in Longley are, you might say, flowers and poems too. Frequently, therefore, Longley poses the persona of his poems, as Nicholas Hilliard, that other miniaturist, poses his subjects, intertwined with flora, or at nest or ease in a vegetable world. When, in 'Watercolour', for instance, he offers a poetic version of his portrait by Jeffrey Morgan, he notes that his shirt is 'a running / Together of earth-colours, wintry grasses, bracken'; but it is the third part of 'Spring Tide' in *The Echo Gate* that seems almost paradigmatic in this respect:

> The spring tide has ferried jelly fish
> To the end of the lane, pinks, purples,
> Wet flowers beside the floating cow-pats.
> The zig-zags I make take me among
> White cresses and brookweed, lousewort,
> Water plantain and grass of parnassus
> With engraved capillaries, ivory sheen:
> By a dry-stone wall in the dune slack
> The greenish sepals, the hidden blush
> And a lip's red veins and yellow spots –
> Marsh helleborine waiting for me
> To come and go with the spring tide.

The minute particularity of this suggests an affinity between Longley and the botanical psychodrama to be found in the work of Theodore Roethke, which was very influential during the 1950s and early 1960s (on Sylvia Plath, amongst others) but is, I think, not much read now. Utterly unlike Roethke, however, it has a poised, lucid calm; and if we are to read psychic distress into these lines, it is only the generalized distress which realizes that the psyche – human consciousness itself – is intrusive in the botanical realm. The line-break and the cumulative syntactical sway of the penultimate line dramatize both longing and disappointment: that almost erotically evoked 'Marsh helleborine' is not 'waiting for me', alas, but is 'waiting for me / To come and go with the spring tide'. The helleborine will persist, as this personification or psychologizing of the plant proposes, whereas the poet's intrusive subjectivity will not: so that botany becomes *memento mori*, as it does more than once elsewhere in Longley too. There is a range of poems in his work in which, with great delicacy, botany and psychology interpenetrate in a way that seems almost to constitute identity as evanescence; a lyric subjectivity discovers itself only in the act of witnessing or recording its own vanishing. This occasionally runs the risk of the over-exquisite or the exiguous, and its reticences and hesitations, its decorums of diction and rhythm, sometimes come close to what Gerard Manley Hopkins called the 'Parnassian', a term used to distinguish 'the language of inspiration' from a language which 'can only be spoken by poets, but is not in the highest sense poetry'.[7] These may, however, be regarded as necessary risks for a poetry so devoid of the will to self-aggrandisement, so little preoccupied with making a show or cutting a figure; and all this, I hope it is not nugatory to remark, in the context of modern and contemporary poetry written by Irish men, where the firm inscription of characteristically identifiable signature is virtually taken as normative.

If 'Spring Tide' does not register distress, however, there is at least one poem in Longley's *oeuvre*, 'Eurycleia', from *Gorse Fires*, in which some more immediate psychic disturbance does seem to be addressed, and in a way which to some extent refocuses all those poems in which the lyric self is present at the centre of a botanical realm. One of a significant number of Longley's later poems in which personal experience or feeling is refracted through parallels in other writing, notably the texts of Homer and Ovid, 'Eurycleia' revisits that moment in the *Odyssey* when Odysseus' old nursemaid, while washing his feet on his return to Ithaca, recognizes him when she sees the scar of a wound inflicted by a boar during his youth. Longley's version of the recognition scene composes the first part of the poem. This is the second, which accompanies it:

> I began like Odysseus by loving the wrong woman
> Who has disappeared among the skyscapers of New York
> After wandering for thousands of years from Ithaca.
> She alone remembers the coppice, dense and overgrown,
> Where in a compost of dead leaves the boar conceals
> Its bristling spine and fire-red eyes and white tusks.

The story of Longley's relationship with his own nursemaid, and of his difficult relationship with his mother, is one he has told in his autobiographical prose piece *Tuppenny Stung*.[8] In the mythologizing parallel of the poem 'Eurycleia', the psychic pain is read as an Odyssean scar: a mark of secret recognition, certainly, but also of permanent damage done. The poem 'remembers' the coppice, dense and overgrown too, where the damage is inflicted; but that compost of dead leaves may well be the germinant source of a great deal of the botany in the poetic compositions of Michael Longley.

If these have their Marvellian elegance, wit and grace, making this poet too, sometimes, as Marvell describes himself in 'Upon Appleton House', an 'easie philosopher, / Among the birds and trees confer[ing]', they also have their darker side, where botany names distress and is sought for succour. Frequently, the lyric self or poetic persona is situated in womb-like, protective covering: in 'In Aillwee Cave', in *Gorse Fires,* he is wombed below the botanical stratum but also between it and what seems a kind of Hades: 'Darkness above the darkness of the seepage of souls'; in 'The White Garden', in *The Ghost Orchid,* he disappears into the garden's white 'lace and veils', at the still centre of a kind of white nowhere which is the origin of writing, the place where words begin, mysteriously, to emerge; and in the same book's light-hearted pastiche sequence 'Chinese Occasions', 'I fall into the flowerbed (drink taken), / Soil and sky my eiderdown and pillow.' This longing for the security of a botanical space as a psychic shelter is finely figured too, and most memorably, in another Odyssean parallel poem, 'A Bed of Leaves', in *The Ghost Orchid*, where Odysseus beds himself down into a 'mattress of leaves, / An eiderdown of leaves' – 'So was his body in the bed of leaves its own kindling / And sleep settled on him like ashes and closed his eyelids.' In the context of these linkages between botany and psychology it is unsurprising – although this is the only unsurprising thing about this strangely unsettling poem – to discover a botanical relation too when, in 'X-Ray', in *Gorse Fires*, Longley contemplates the womb in which he was actually gestated. He has written in prose, in *Tuppenny Stung*, about this experience too, that of scrutinizing an X-ray photograph of his mother's womb while she was pregnant with himself and his twin brother.[9] The poem appears to contain distress or even rage, when its first person wants the mother to 'eat the world, giblets, marrow, / Tripes and offal, birds, fields of grain'; but subsequently this language of rapacity and engorgement dissolves into the language of forgiveness and retrospective assuagement, a medicinal healing in which the lyric self prescribes 'in the dark a salad of landcress, / Fennel like hair, the sky-blue of borage flowers'. That curative capacity, the capacity to make whole again what has been wounded or broken, is the deepest element of the botanical interest in Longley.

IV

It is not only personal history, however, that Longley's botanical poems plot into their figures and forms: it is also public, political history, as we have seen already in 'The Ice-Cream Man'. The poem 'Finding a Remedy', from the sequence 'Lore' in *The Echo Gate,* has the same quality of desired reparation as the conclusion of 'X-Ray', but, in this volume, published in 1979, the desire is manifestly turned out towards the public life of its time more than it is turned inwards to personal distress. This poem too is a herbal prescription, containing an instruction in its use:

> Sprinkle the dust from a mushroom or chew
> The white end of a rush, apply the juice
> From fern roots, stems of burdock, dandelions,
>
> Then cover the wound with cuckoo-sorrel
> Or sphagnum moss, bringing together verse
> And herb, plant and prayer to stop the bleeding.

This is reticent about the actual source of the bleeding, but, in a poem from Northern Ireland in the 1970s, there is obviously a political subtext. The concept of the poem as a spell, as a careful and patient instruction in a healing ritual, as a measured contemplation of desperation: all are implicit in the botany of 'Finding a Remedy'. The scrupulous hesitation of this way of addressing the Troubles – where 'addressing' is altogether too emphatic a word – is continuous with Longley's stated unease in *Tuppenny Stung*: 'I find offensive the notion that what we inadequately call "the Troubles" might provide inspiration for artists; and that in some weird *quid pro quo* the arts might provide solace for grief and anguish'; and again, 'In the context of political violence the deployment of words at their most precise and most suggestive remains one of the few antidotes to death-dealing dishonesty.'[10] This is a view consistent with all the poems in which the Troubles figure at some level in Longley; and I have myself written elsewhere about the pains he takes to 'establish credentials' in these poems, the way he manages 'an authenticating relationship between public and private'.[11]

A further mode of authentication is the way, occasionally and obliquely, the Troubles are caught up into Longley's permanent botanical poetic. His poem 'Peace', after Tibullus, in *The Echo Gate*, is one such case, when its version of the Latin elegist concludes in a dream of alterity, where Peace is figured as feminized, maternal, erotic and botanical all at once, in what we might think of as a kind of sudden Arcimboldo effect in language: 'As for me, I want a woman / To come and fondle my ears of wheat and let apples / Overflow between her breasts.' John Kerrigan has written perceptively about the way this poem secretes, in its reference to a statue carved out of bog-oak, a reclamation of a harmless household god from the always ominous bogland territory of Seamus Heaney's poems; and it would be possible to write at some length about the variant uses of the bog in early Longley and Heaney, where it is very much common ground trodden with a difference.[12] Such a comparison might also have 'as much political significance as we want to assign it'. What I want to do in this context, however, is to offer a reading of the poem in which Longley does signally bring together herb, plant and prayer, and bogland too – 'Bog Cotton' from *The Echo Gate*:

> Let me make room for bog cotton, a desert flower –
> Keith Douglas, I nearly repeat what you were saying
> When you apostrophised the poppies of Flanders
> And the death of poetry there: that was in Egypt
> Among the sandy soldiers of another war.
>
> (It hangs on by a thread, denser than thistledown,
> Reluctant to fly, a weather vane that traces
> The flow of cloud shadow over monotonous bog –
> And useless too, though it might well bring to mind
> The plumpness of pillows, the staunching of wounds,

Rags torn from a petticoat and soaked in water
And tied to the bushes around some holy well
As though to make a hospital of the landscape –
Cures and medicines as far as the horizon
Which nobody harvests except with the eye.)

You saw that beyond the thirstier desert flowers
There fell hundreds of thousands of poppy petals
Magnified to blood stains by the middle distance
Or through the still unfocused sights of a rifle –
And Isaac Rosenberg wore one behind his ear.

This poem does indeed 'make room' for bog cotton in that it finds a poetic space for this local flower among other kinds of flower already made over into significant poems: Keith Douglas's 'Desert Flowers', a poem of the Middle East in the Second World War, a subtle, fluid poem of turning-points, dissolvings, dreams and transitions, and Isaac Rosenberg's 'Break of Day in the Trenches', that bravely ironic and insouciant poem of the First World War, with its 'Poppies whose roots are in men's veins', which ends with an almost dandyish flourish of defiance: 'But mine in my ear is safe – / Just a little white with the dust.'[13]

Longley's poem is, as it were, doubly intertextual not only in that it refers to these two poems, but in that it also mimics Douglas's own reference to Rosenberg, since the second line of 'Desert Flowers' reads: 'Rosenberg, I only repeat what you were saying.' Longley makes space for his flower, then, by bracketing it between other men's flowers, in a system of grateful repetitions; and this makes 'Bog Cotton' implicitly a kind of war poem too. 'Bog Cotton' reads these experiences and previous poems with deference, by opening literal brackets to celebrate its flower; the lunulae of the parenthesis acting as an index of humility before an acknowledged and respected tradition. The brackets, as it were, visibly make room for the flower; they make a room which is within a tradition but to one side of it too. This is a fine tact, I think, and a necessary one, since unlike Douglas and Rosenberg, Longley is not, of course, and has not ever been, a combatant soldier, although he may well be a victim of the general depredations of a province at war for a very long time: naming bog cotton a 'desert flower' may imply precisely that. The parenthesis itself repeats the parenthesis Douglas makes for his acknowledgement of Rosenberg in 'Desert Flowers', an acknowledgement of his own anxiety as a latecomer, which is sharpened by those prose statements in which he has no illusions about the fact that the great war poems have all, long since, been written. This is, I assume, one of the implications of the concluding stanza of Longley's poem too, where the address to Douglas has him seeing beyond the desert flowers of the Second World War to the 'hundreds of thousands of poppy petals' of the First. The bog cotton may make room for itself in this tradition, however, because it shares qualities with the already-written desert flowers and poppies. Manifestly, Longley admires in Douglas and Rosenberg strengths which are both poetic and moral, attitudes of irony and self-deflation which make possible the bravery of endurance. 'Desert Flowers' and 'Break of Day in the Trenches' manage their ironies in the face of almost certain death: Douglas knows that 'the body can fill / the hungry flowers', and the roots of Rosenberg's poppies are in men's veins. The bog cotton is less ambivalently ominous a flower than these, but it is certainly an emblem of endurance in place and in function, even if this is an endurance at the very edge of capacity, 'hanging on by a thread'. The cotton is therefore like people compelled to remain in their places or at their posts, whatever the circumstances; but it is also like poetry, 'useless' in that it can offer nothing directly, even if it may well bring a great deal to mind: 'Cures and medicines as far as the horizon / Which nobody harvests except with the eye' – lines which draw once more on the medicinal and prescriptive properties of botany in poems such as 'X-Ray' and 'Finding a Remedy', as we have seen.

Poetry as the curative harvest of the eye is, therefore, a richly beneficent figure informed by the range of Longley's botanical tropes elsewhere; but the lines probably also pick up the conclusion of 'Desert Flowers', where Douglas writes: 'I see men as trees suffering / or confound the detail and the horizon'. Men as trees suffering is a half-allusion to Mark's Gospel 8: 23–6, where Christ cures the blind man: 'And he looked up and said, I see men as trees walking'; and that is, you might say, the harvest of the eye too. So that, if Kerrigan is right to read an intertextual debate with Heaney out of the bog-oak statue of the poem 'Peace', we could claim the same of this poem: that the bog cotton is a reclamation of beneficence from the bogland territory of so many early poems of Heaney's, that territory which so authoritatively provokes images and emblems of terror, punishment, shame and suffering. When, in the sequence 'Kinship' in *North*, 'catkins and bog-cotton tremble', they 'raise up / the cloven oak-limb' of the sacrificial goddess Nerthus; in Longley it is the unsubduable bog cotton itself that is raised up.

V

When Heaney discusses Longley in his essay 'Place and Displacement', it is not as a botanist of history or generalized psychology, but as an erotic botanist whose very eroticism may at times, in poems such as 'The Linen Industry' and 'Self-Heal', be read as analogous with a politics and a history of Northern Ireland. I want to think a little more about the link between botany and eroticism in the poetry and, in doing so, to return this essay to its origin and, I hope, to bring something back. Longley's is a poetry, Heaney says,

> of direct amorous address, its dramatic voice the voice of indolent and occasionally deliquescent reverie, its subject the whole matter of sexual daydream . . . even when the poem is ostensibly about landscape or seascape, about flora and fauna . . . the intonation of the verse is seductive, its melody allaying and cajoling, its typical mood one of tender insinuation and possibility.[14]

It may be that Heaney gives his own tendency to an eroticized critical vocabulary its head here, and the temper of this is itself more seduced and enraptured than the poems themselves seem to me to warrant. Even where an intimacy of erotic address or evocation is being expressed in them, that is to say, they often maintain a classical poise and lucidity which stills the cajolement and insinuation into something different from itself: not at all unlike, indeed, the combination of erotic subject-matter and classical form in the photographs of Robert Mapplethorpe. Heaney is right, however, to have noticed the way botany is, as it were, both the tenor and the vehicle of an erotics in Longley. In some of his poems, the process of metaphorization of the botanical is so complete as to maintain a kind of equivalence.

It is possible to identify several different kinds of erotic botany in Longley. There are those poems such as the sequence actually called 'Botany', in which botanical species are themselves sexualized: duckweed draws in its skirts; the dock may 'blossom into blush or birthmark', and so on. These seem to me in some ways the most conventional of the kind, in which the traditional poetic figuring of women as flowers is given a new configuring and a different perspective or inflection, certainly, but in which the basis of the conceit is an obvious and easily overworked one, and not entirely free of masculinist condescension. The second kind is the obverse of this when, in poems such as 'Sulpicia', 'Martinmas', 'Patchwork', 'Light Behind the Rain' and 'Couplet', the body itself is botanized, so that nipples are read as flowers, lovers are seen as a harvest to be gathered in, the female body is a 'little country' (in a trope continuous with some of John Donne's, of course), and so on. This is a more complex kind because it is more alert to the ways in which it takes its place in what is almost a sub-genre of erotically inflected landscape, more *paysage erotisé* than *moralisé*: in photographers and painters such as Mapplethorpe and O'Keeffe, as we have already seen, but also in the sculpture of Henry Moore, for instance, and in some poems of Seamus Heaney. Then there is the trope – if it is that, precisely – of love-making in the open air, in poems such as 'Mountain Swim', 'On Mweelrea' and 'Autumn Lady's Tresses'; the patron saint of this kind is possibly the 'Sheela Na Gig' in the eponymous poem from *The Ghost Orchid*: at Kilnaboy, 'where the orchids have borrowed her cunty petals . . . / A proper libation would be sperm and rainwater'. The same may be said for the poems that reverse this figure, those in which the landscape enters the bedroom: 'The Linen Industry' is one such, and I shall return to it in a moment, and 'An Amish Rug' is another, where the rug in the lovers' bedroom, to be stepped over as they undress, becomes a 'flower-bed'.

I am unsure whether these categories exhaust the Linnaean taxonomy of Longley's botanical erotics, but it would be exhausting, certainly, to pursue them much further. I offer the catalogue to indicate how deeply the figuration goes in the work, how intimately coterminous it is with an essential kind of poetic energy and address in this poet. There is a classical, primarily – although not exclusively – Ovidian sanction for all of this, which has been picked up on by Kerrigan in his essay 'Ulster Ovids', and which Longley makes explicit in the beautiful poem 'A Flowering', in *The Ghost Orchid*, in which a theme of ageing, sexual desire and timidity is run through glancingly collocated versions of the metamorphoses of Hyacinth and Anemone: 'Ovid's lovely casualties – all that blood / Colouring the grass and changing into flowers'. This reminds us that in the *Metamorphoses* sexual desire is the agent of transformation, but also the agent of violence. The flowerings of Longley's poems are ambivalently inflected with both these qualities, and they make him one of the finest contemporary poets of sexual longing and its possible fulfilment. But they are also, we will remember, a way of being in two places at the one time. They are, that is to say, the opposite of confessional declaration: the poems are turned out towards resolution and clarification, not in upon themselves in any of the customary erotically self-advertising modes of vaunt, exhibition, challenge or depreciation which contemporary poetry has so substantially inherited from mid-century American so-called 'confessional' modes, or the misunderstanding of them. Which is another reason why Heaney's terms, as I instance them above, seem over-heated to me: Longley's finest work has a genuine impersonality and objectivity, of a Gravesian rather than an Eliotic variety; of, in other words, an authentically, rather than a self-deludingly, classicizing kind.

However, now that I have completed what I can offer in the way of taxonomy, let me return to 'The Linen Industry', which is one of the finest distillations of the botanical–erotic essence in Longley:

> Pulling up flax after the blue flowers have fallen
> And laying our handfuls in the peaty water
> To rot those grasses to the bone, or building stooks
> That recall the skirts of an invisible dancer,
>
> We become a part of the linen industry
> And follow its processes to the grubby town
> Where fields are compacted into window-boxes
> And there is little room among the big machines.
>
> But even in our attic under the skylight
> We make love on a bleach green, the whole meadow

Draped with material turning white in the sun
As though snow reluctant to melt were our attire.

What's passion but a battering of stubborn stalks,
Then a gentle combing out of fibres like hair
And a weaving of these into christening robes,
Into garments for a marriage or funeral?

Since it's like a bereavement once the labour's done
To find ourselves last workers in a dying trade,
Let flax be our matchmaker, our undertaker,
The provider of sheets for whatever the bed –

And be shy of your breasts in the presence of death,
Say that you look more beautiful in linen
Wearing white petticoats, the bow on your bodice
A butterfly attending the embroidered flowers.

Heaney reads this emphatically, but tactfully too, as a political allegory, 'the internalisation and affirmation of those feminine powers repressed by man's, and in particular the Ulsterman's, adaptation to conditions in the technological factory world'.[15] This sophisticatedly pulls one thread of this poem's complex interweavings, and suggests how subtle and implicative a poet Longley is at his best. But there are other threads that can be pulled too in this poetic text, which has surely taken into itself the etymology of the word 'text', from the Latin *textus*, 'that which is woven, web, texture'; and I want, of course, to pull the one that most fittingly suits my own purpose here.

'The Linen Industry' may well, as Heaney says, anchor itself in its Northern Irish location, since it is a historical fact that the industry that developed from the availability of flax in the province was the source of Belfast's industrial strength; but the poem also allies itself very strangely and originally with traditions of love-poetry in which the woman's dress and accoutrements are eroticized or even fetishized. The concluding reference to the linen petticoats is a kind of transformation of all those poems of clothing, and the slippage of clothing from the body, in Herrick – poems such as 'Upon Julia's Clothes':

When as in silks my Julia goes,
Then, then (me thinks) how sweetly flowes
That liquefaction of her clothes.

Next, when I cast mine eyes and see
That brave Vibration each way free;
O how that glittering taketh me!

'The Linen Industry', we might say, takes the clothes back to their original liquefaction, when they were flax in the peaty water. In doing so, it offers for account, as Herrick's leisured poems, of course, do not, the industrial basis of pleasure. Latter-day Puritan to Herrick's seventeenth-century Cavalier, Longley uncovers in this poem the labours necessary to delight, and thereby extends the realm of the love-poem: a community as well as a privacy is involved in this act of attic love; despite which, 'The Linen Industry' manages to make privacy contingent in this way without at all courting intrusion. This poem, like all those Longley poems in which the act of love is central, is quite without the disfiguring element of display: 'The Linen Industry' is no encouragement to the voyeur.

If Herrick, or a tradition of erotic lyric that the name Herrick may be taken to represent, is somewhere at the back of 'The Linen Industry', so is Yeats, in a way uncharacteristic of Longley. The rhetorical question 'What's passion but a battering of stubborn stalks . . .?', remembers a Yeatsian rhetoric and cadence ('What's water but the generated soul?', asks 'Coole and Ballylee, 1931'), and the word 'passion' is, of course, an emphatically Yeatsian word. 'The Linen Industry' therefore accommodates Yeats, and the Yeatsian love-lyric (which must, to some degree, shadow any subsequent poet – or, at any rate, any male poet – who writes love poems in Ireland), but accommodates him also to the most typical figures and images of Longley's own poems. This is, I think, managed very deftly here, when the sudden flowering of the Yeatsian tone, with its almost bravado assurance and command, is only the briefest interruption in a poem otherwise so tonally unlike Yeats: not so much a 'battering', indeed, as a 'gentle combing out'. And in that combing-out, what comes clear in the final stanzas of 'The Linen Industry' is the presence of death, the reminder that the linen that makes the white petticoats of love also makes both

swaddling and shroud. The use of the word 'bereavement', and the
presentation of the lovers as 'last workers in a dying trade', run a
submerged pun on sexual consummation as *le petit mort*, and
remind us of that mortuary voluptousness which is also one of the
most peculiar features of Longley's eroticism, in poems such as
'Obsequies', 'Oliver Plunkett' and 'According to Pythagoras'. In
these, he establishes sudden connection with another kind of
seventeenth-century lyric, of which the greatest example is the
charnel eroticism of Marvell's 'To His Coy Mistress', even if his
more immediate source is the conclusion of Louis MacNeice's
poem 'Mayfly' ('But when this summer is over let us die together, / I
want always to be near your breasts'), which Peter McDonald has
shown to be deeply influential on Longley.[16] The unflinching
recognition that the awareness of death is profoundly involved in
the act of love is what steadies 'The Linen Industry' into authority:
it places a serious, concentrated premium on pleasure because it
knows what pleasure must contest. Thinking of seventeenth-
century lyric too, one might say of 'The Linen Industry', finally,
that it is a remarkable contemporary instance of how a little room
may be made an everywhere; since, if there is 'little room among
the big machines', there is, always, this attic room.

VI

I want to end with 'The Ghost Orchid' itself, which brings flower
and poem explicitly together once more in one of Longley's most
delicate lyrical figurings:

> Added to its few remaining sites will be the stanza
> I compose about leaves like flakes of skin, a colour
> Dithering between pink and yellow, and then the root
> That grows like coral among shadows and leaf-litter.
> Just touching the petals bruises them into darkness.

The opening of that may remember the opening of 'Bog Cotton',
where, as we have seen, the poetic act of making room is evoked,
since a stanza is, etymologically, a 'room' too; and the poem
reminds us of the ecology implicit in Longley's whole output and
endeavour. It also, however, in its little hymn to fragility and

ephemerality, compacts into its tiny compass some of the essential elements of the botanical in Longley's poetry. The pun that makes the act of poetic composition continuous with the decomposition of the orchid – which is also a figurative human decomposition, since its leaves are 'like flakes of skin' – is, it might be said, a pun that lies at the very centre of Longley's work. The poet will not bruise his subject here by too persistent a probing or scrutiny, by too emphatic a discovery of significance. What the ghost orchid might be made to mean is almost withdrawn from before it is articulated; but it has to do, as 'The Linen Industry' has, with the inextricability of sexuality and death, of the root that grows in the compost and the petals that bruise into darkness. Longley's poems are one of the few remaining sites where such profound inter-connections can be made with tact, and without sentimentality or melodrama, in contemporary lyric poetry. They form a miniature and permanent perfection.

10

One step forward, two steps back:
Ciaran Carson's *The Irish for No*

I

When Seamus Heaney published *North* in 1975, Ciaran Carson reviewed it in the Belfast *Honest Ulsterman*. The review has been frequently cited in discussions of *North*, since it makes the case for the opposition with memorably caustic incisiveness. Carson castigates Heaney as 'the laureate of violence – a mythmaker, an anthropologist of ritual killing, an apologist for "the situation", in the last resort, a mystifier'. Taking his title from one of Heaney's phrases for himself in the volume's final poem 'Exposure', Carson ironizes it with a query: 'Escaped from the Massacre?'; and answers his own question: 'No one really escapes from the massacre, of course – the only way you can do that is by falsifying issues, by applying wrong notions of history, instead of seeing what's before your eyes.'[1] The criticism has also been pursued by Edna Longley, and implied by Paul Muldoon when, in his *Faber Book of Contemporary Irish Poetry*, he publishes only the dedicatory poems from *North*. While aspects of Heaney's career since *North* may be read as an implicit criticism by the poet himself of some of the procedures he adopts there, these were also, manifestly, an attempt to make a decisive break with the 'well-made poem' that the first generation of Northern poets inherited from the English Movement and other poetry then current in English writing; even if this was in fact only one of several points of origin for them, some others being more indigenously Irish. As Heaney observed at the time, he wanted 'to take the English lyric and make it eat stuff that it has never eaten before . . . and make it still an English lyric'.[2] The publication in 1987 of Ciaran Carson's second full volume of poems, *The Irish for No*, put the criticism into a newly illuminated perspective by emphasizing the extent to which, in challenging Heaney's methods in *North*, Carson was, at the same time, quite as certain as Heaney himself that some disruption of the lyric was essential if the material of Northern

Ireland after 1969 was to be adequately expressed, or at least encountered, in poetry.[3]

The book's title poem contains a veiled or coded reference to Heaney, in something of the way some of Paul Muldoon's poems do too, although Carson is less wryly mischievous and more sharply pertinent. 'The Irish for No' weaves, in an apparently haphazard manner, in and out of several intermittent narratives before it climaxes with the evocation of a blackly almost surreal suicide:

> What's all this to the Belfast business-man who drilled
> Thirteen holes in his head with a Black & Decker? It was just a
>   normal morning
> When they came. The tennis-court shone with dew or frost, a little
>   before dawn.
> The border, it seemed, was not yet crossed: the Milky Way trailed
>   snowy brambles,
> The stars clustered thick as blackberries. They opened the door into
>   the dark:
> *The murmurous haunt of flies on summer eves.* Empty jam-jars.
> Mish-mash. Hotch-potch.

Given that this is a poem which, throughout, almost uninterpretably plays Keats's 'Ode to a Nightingale' across its own wayward surface, it would be too heavy-handed to describe this *bricolage* of reference as straightforwardly satirical at Heaney's expense, but it nevertheless implies a limiting and adverse judgement. The grotesquerie of the Belfast suicide and the unspecific minatory narrative in which 'they' are coming with, presumably, some underhand purpose in mind – murder, kidnapping, extortion – consort oddly with, and must intend some judgement on, the sensory opulence of Heaney's early work. The allusions focus on his second volume, *Door into the Dark*, published in 1969, the second year of the Troubles. The word 'dark' resounds through this book, but it would appear that Carson's poem finds behind the door of Heaney's earlier work not contemporary terror but literature, not the dark of Northern Ireland's nightmare but the luxuriance of Keats's ode; and those jam-jars which are full of frogspawn and blackberries in Heaney's 'Death of a Naturalist' and 'Blackberry-Picking' are, in Carson, ominously empty, the sufferers of a kind of imaginative kenosis. We may infer from the sly allegorizing of

'The Irish for No', therefore, that, in the dark of contemporary social and political attrition, Heaney's poetic of late Romantic expansiveness is found wanting.

Carson's review of *North* is continuous with this subversive interlude, suggesting a deep suspicion of the yearning for imaginative plenitude which may be read out of Heaney's mythical structures, in which the poetic imagination responds to present depredation by inviting it into the potential assuagement of a form of transcendence. If these are 'wrong ideas of history', since, in Carson's view, they translate all sense of political consequence into the 'realm of inevitability', they are also, presumably, wrong ideas of literature, deriving too calculatedly from the traditions of Romanticism and High Modernism. The structures of *North*, even if they are ironized by the book's self-division, may be read as intimately continuous with what Eliot, reading *Ulysses*, famously christened the 'mythical method'.[4] In the philosophy and literary theory of postmodernism, the will to such mythical, transhistorical coherence is castigated as an ideologically fraught 'master narrative' or 'metanarrative', a tale of suspect plenary interpretation. An 'incredulity toward metanarratives' is, for Fredric Jameson, the simplest definition of the postmodern;[5] and, in the book Jameson is introducing when he makes this remark, Jean-François Lyotard declares that the signal of the postmodern is not merely the lack of credibility of the grand narrative, but the end of the 'period of mourning' for it.[6]

In the challenge to the earlier phase of Heaney's work represented by Carson's review, it is possible to see the ground of a Northern Irish poetry of the postmodern beginning to prepare itself; and it is tempting to view his ten-year poetic withdrawal after the publication of his well-received first book, *The New Estate*, in 1976, as, at least in part, the result of his personal search, in the cunning of a stay-at-home silence, for a way of registering in his own writing the full shock of the challenge to recognized modes and forms represented by the realities of post-1968 Northern Ireland, and more particularly by post-1968 Belfast. Carson's work is inextricably meshed into the city in which he has spent his entire life. A resolutely urban poet, even when he strays into the Irish *rus* it is discovered as a squalidly depleted one: the Donegal-derelict rather than the Derry-lush of early Heaney, or the Armagh-deciduous of Muldoon. His

Northern postmodernism has its origin here: he is, pre-eminently, the poet of Belfast in its contemporary disintegration. A response to that city in this time has provoked, or even demanded, the construction of his radically individual forms. In rejecting the metanarrative of myth, Carson creates a narrative poetry of his own: *The Irish for No*, like the books which have followed it in rapid succession – *Belfast Confetti* (1990), *First Language* (1993), *Opera et Cetera* (1996) and *The Twelfth of Never* (1998) – is a powerfully original contribution to the combinations of lyric and narrative characteristic of some of the most interesting British and Irish poetry of the 1980s and 1990s. Carson's narratives are not the clipped, staccato abruptions of Tom Paulin or the 'deconstructed' sonnets of Paul Muldoon, with their inbuilt interruptions in the flow of narrative current; his are, rather, exfoliations, turnings and returnings, digressions and parentheses, lapses and dissolvings, mazes of the seemingly aleatory and circuitous. I want to try to define here the contours of the narratives of *The Irish for No*, which seems to me the most perfectly constructed and articulated of his books, and to suggest the ways in which an alignment of them with some theories of the postmodern may be both analytically useful and culturally suggestive. I do not intend to press the word 'postmodern' upon the poems with too insistent a diagnostic rigour, however; but to read the most knowledgeable synthesizing interpreters of postmodernism is to recognize a discourse, and a range of categories, appropriate to the striking originality of Carson's poems, and to their intense inwardness with a particular phase of the culture.

II

The Irish language has no word for no: there is no Irish for no. In the poem 'The Irish for No', it is made plain that there is, nevertheless, an Ulster English for no: *Ulster Says No* is scrawled in huge letters on the side of a 'power-block' (*sic*). The presence of the other language of Irish can be glimpsed several times through the English of *The Irish for No*; and the book's title, with its signals of alterity, impossibility and negativity, is profoundly appropriate to its poems. These are difficult to describe in any available prosodic terms, but formally they may be said to join together two widely divergent kinds of structure: the very long line which Carson derives primarily from the American poet C. K. Williams, and the oral forms of Irish traditional story-telling and even Irish traditional music.[7] The book is scrupulous in acknowledging 'John Campbell of Mullaghbawn whose storytelling suggested some of the narrative procedures of some of these poems'; and in letters to me Carson has illuminatingly outlined his conception of an experimentally individualized prosody developed from an intertwining of various kinds of otherness:

> Storytelling is there; the line breaks are points of suspense, where you want to see what happens next. The length of line is a story-teller's deliberate fast-paced gabble. It's also based around *haiku*'s seventeen syllables, and the intention is to have a kind of *haiku* clarity within the line – stumbling-blocks of word-clusters, piling up adjectives, etc. And it's not unlike Irish (seán-nos) singing. The traditional dance form known as a reel is there too – the line and rhythm of a reel is always in my ear, the way you extend notes beyond ostensible bar lines, or cut them short: going against the form all the time, but observing it; knowing that it's always there, 'in back', as they say in the States. It's supposed to tease the reader a little, or to keep him on the edge of the seat. I hope the humour of this comes across.[8]

Some of this is probably a bit fanciful, but the humour of the writing does indeed come across – it is the keenest first impression the reader takes from a Carson poem – and *Belfast Confetti* goes on, perhaps a little too self-consciously, to use actual *haiku* form. The passage also manifestly registers an affiliation based on passionate knowledge and affection. Although he was born in Belfast, Carson's first language is Irish, and he was for many years Traditional Arts Officer for the Arts Council of Northern Ireland, a job which involved the playing and collecting of Irish stories and music; he himself plays the flute and has published a guide to Irish traditional music and, in *Last Night's Fun* (1996), a richly inventive series of prose meditations on, and from, the life of a musician.[9] He insists that this work for a long time made the writing of poetry seem, by comparison, 'remote, alien, artificial, unattached to ordinary speech. The music, singing and yarn-spinning seemed much more vital.' Playing the oral against the literary, the long lines of his poems have something of the sustained, improvisatory panache of the Irish story-teller or *seanachie*, always aping the movement of the speaking voice in an address that is self-involved, certainly, but, at the same time, aware of an audience: the poems are repetitive, self-corrective, elliptical. They also, in their sustained syntactical ebb and flow, maintain a degree of control with an uncommonly sophisticated writerly resourcefulness. With an ear attuned to the oral energies of Irish speech and song and an intelligence, as well as an ear, alert to a range of contemporary American models – John Ashbery is probably there too, at some level – Carson has found a means of constructing a fertile poetic resource, one that allows him the possibility of writing a poetry of the Northern Irish present which is fraught with the urgency and terror of its moment, but which is also vigilantly resistant to the potentially seductive and glamorizing modes offered by some influential elements of a modern literary tradition.

The sinuous shapeliness of the line in *The Irish for No* is writ large in the shapeliness of the book's structure. It has three sections, the first and last of which each contain four separate long narratives; and the central section contains sixteen short poems on Belfast which employ a similar long line but have in common nine lines, divided into two stanzas of five and four lines respectively. In the Wake Forest and Bloodaxe editions – but not in the original from Gallery Press – the whole is prefaced by a further short poem of this kind called 'Turn Again'. The book therefore combines a high degree of well-shaped formality with the apparently wanderingly digressive thread of its actual narrative structures, as indeed its individual poems do too. This suavely sophisticated playing of control against licence is the crucial element in their delicate manipulation of tone. These are shapes which can accommodate the blackly humorous, the wry, the witty, the intensely nostalgic, the murderously brutal, and the near-slapstick, all in the same poem-space. They can, as it were, hesitate across their line-breaks between such variant tones, moving always with a buoyancy whose apparent confidence may at any moment collapse into a chasm of poignancy, regret, misgiving or hopelessness.

In 'Dresden', for instance, the variations are orchestrated with a consummate poetic tact which is also a kind of ethical and political tact: it is a poem which, inventing a postmodern form for itself, also invents a new register for the neo-classical virtue of decorum. It opens with a good joke about the dubious naming of its main protagonist:

Horse Boyle was called Horse Boyle because of his brother Mule;
Though why Mule was called Mule is anybody's guess.

Anybody's guess is nobody's certainty, least of all this insouciant
but interestedly sympathetic narrator's: so the joke about how
Horse second-handedly derived his name is also an indication of
narrative undecidability, a sort of *mise-en-abîme* opening as the
poem itself opens. But Horse's second-hand name, and perhaps
the way his narrative is conveyed to us by a proxy (or second-hand)
narrator, are an appropriate introduction and response to the fact
that Horse's tale is, in the end, one of second-handedness and
subjection, like the tales of many of the characters in *The Irish for
No*. This narrative initiated by a joke stays a humorous narrative,
just about, but grows in tonal complexity, as it grows in social
implication, during its recounting. It accommodates the almost
stage-Irish, Flann O'Brien-like farce of Horse's tale of Flynn, who
carries a bomb on a bus across the border for the IRA and
immediately guiltily confesses to a policeman, who has in fact
boarded the bus only because his bicycle has a puncture. This is a
tale, however, whose farce is transformed into something quite
different when, during his consequent seven years' imprisonment,
Flynn learns to speak 'the best of Irish': 'He had thirteen words
for a cow in heat; / A word for the third thwart in a boat, the wake
of a boat on the ebb tide': the pathetically confined spirit of Irish
nationalism meeting the beautiful, antique redundancies of the
Irish language. The narrative also includes the much less attractive
Irishism, of Horse's story of the schoolmaster McGinty, which
anatomizes the stonily mean-spirited and ill-natured parish of
Carrowkeel, 'so mean and crabbed . . . men were known to eat
their dinner from a drawer. / Which they'd slide shut the minute
you'd walk in', where the line-break reveals excellent comic
timing. Such tales-within-the-tale accumulate towards a revelation
of the nature and kind not only of the individual, Horse Boyle,
but of the depleted and demeaning social, cultural and political
context in which he survives resourcefully.

The full revelation comes only at the end of the poem, where the
reason for its title becomes clear at last. This is probably a matter
of some frustrating delay for the first-time reader, eagerly nosing
forward into the narrative for some way of attaching it to such a
significant name: titles too play their part in the heuristic

recessiveness of these poems. In his youth Horse has, in another representatively Irish mode of subjection, been an unwilling emigrant to England and been so bored by his work in Manchester ('Something to do with scrap') that he enlists in the RAF during the war, flying as a rear-gunner over Dresden. The poem releases its epiphanic climax as Horse remembers this mission which 'broke his heart':

> As he remembered it, long afterwards, he could hear, or almost hear
> Between the rapid desultory thunderclaps, a thousand tinkling
>   echoes –
> All across the map of Dresden, store-rooms full of china shivered,
>   teetered
> And collapsed, an avalanche of porcelain, slushing and cascading:
>   cherubs,
> Shepherdesses, figurines of Hope and Peace and Victory, delicate
>   bone fragments.
> He recalled in particular a figure from his childhood, a milkmaid
> Standing on the mantelpiece. Each night as they knelt down for the
>   rosary,
> His eyes would wander up to where she seemed to beckon to him,
>   smiling,
> Offering him, eternally, her pitcher of milk, her mouth of rose and
>   cream.

This is itself heartbreaking poetry, as the *kitsch* statue remembered from Horse's childhood serves as his sad, quasi-religious benediction for the diminishments of his own life, and for those of the Irish and European history he has lived through. Its femininity is an erotic substitute for the Marian-virginal piety of the rosary, an eroticism in which the 'eternal' promise and solace is a sexual, not a religious, one. Beckoning, smiling and offering him her pitcher and her mouth, she is set over against the apparently quite womanless and sexless, and, it is implied, alcoholic world Horse shares with his brother. The end of the poem lets us know that Horse eventually dropped the statue, 'reaching up to hold her yet again', and that her remains (the hand and pitcher) now share a biscuit tin with pencils, snuff, tobacco, his war medals and a 'broken rosary': which would make this, in the pathos and nostalgia of its assemblage, almost a kind of Joseph Cornell box, one of those mysteriously suggestive artefacts by the American sculptor which have been vividly characterized as 'star-maps of a private universe'.[10] Compacted in Horse's memory into his experience of bombing Dresden, the statue acts, therefore, as a radiant but for ever lost metonym for all the lives broken there along with the china; since those 'delicate bone fragments' are presumably to be read as the remains of human bodies as well as of expensive porcelain.

The 'thousand tinkling echoes' of the breaking china which Horse imagines he can hear over Dresden may also metonymically summarize or include all those other noises which this poem so prominently contains: the collapsing 'baroque pyramids of empty baked bean tins' which surround – 'good as a watchdog' – the caravan that Horse shares with Mule; the tinkling of the shop bell which this noise recalls to the poem's unnamed narrator; the 'grate and scrape' of a spade digging into the miserably poor ground of Carrick, which reminds Horse of the noise of digging a tip of broken delft and crockery and of the squeaking of chalk on a blackboard. These noises – mnemonic, associative, setting the memory on edge in the way the teeth are set on edge by squeaking chalk on a blackboard – chime together in the peculiar atonal harmony of 'Dresden'. Doing so, they draw the narrative's different stories together too, making out of Horse Boyle's life not only a tale, but an emblem of diminishment and depredation. Permanently maimed by the act to which he was led by his own subjection – the act of placing others under the ultimate subjection of death by bombing in Dresden – Horse is a mule too, doing for England to beautiful, strategically insignificant Dresden what poor farcical Flynn would do to England for his idea of Ireland and for the IRA. For all its noises of lighter timbre, the noise that this poem called 'Dresden' actually echoes with is the noise of exploding bombs, those almost oxymoronic 'rapid desultory thunderclaps'.

III

Despite all the deadpan humour in Carson's narrative poems, and the grace and delicacy of their procedures, they almost always reveal, even if only in the end – like 'Dresden' – stories of depredation. Their characters and narrators are the rundown, the supernumerary, the pathetic. They are mentally ill or subnormal, like the Johnny Mickey of 'Judgement', who is on his way into the care of 'two attendants', and like the Uncle John of 'Asylum' with his 'babbling, stammering' tale; they are the loonies, winos, down-and-outs, tinkers and murder victims of the working-class Belfast of Part II. The subjects of their own narratives, they are themselves subjected by the narratives of history and politics into which they are written. In the passage from 'Dresden' which I quote above, Carson's trope for this imprisoning narrative of history is the map: Horse in his bomber-plane imagines the china breaking 'all across the map of Dresden'. Human lives are being broken because they happen where they are target points on an already written chart: people's lives are taken out of their hands by the alien map-makers and map-readers of their destinies.

The map is prominently a figure for such entrapment throughout *The Irish for No*, inheriting a significance from its prominent role in a colonial history; and the first, Gallery Press edition of the book featured a street-map of Belfast as its cover design. The prefatory poem, 'Turn Again', initiates the trope in its opening line, referring to a Belfast map which does not exist, citing a collapsed bridge, non-existent streets, gaols which 'cannot be shown for security reasons':

> The linen backing is falling apart – the Falls Road hangs by a thread.
> When someone asks me where I live, I remember where I used to live.
> Someone asks me for directions, and I think again. I turn into
> A side-street to try to throw off my shadow, and history is changed.

Everywhere in Carson metaphor and figure tend to be themselves dense with a social and cultural history: here the 'linen' backs the Belfast map because Belfast's economic development through the late eighteenth and the nineteenth century was largely dependent on the linen trade. In 'Turn Again', the figure of the map follows Belfast's social history into the present moment, however, with its implications of disintegration, directionlessness and pursuit. The 'other' Belfast represented by the non-existent map remains a haunting shadow, the ghost of a never-realized possibility. The nature of the exclusion is plain when the meticulously itemized street-names of Belfast map their Irish streets with British imperial names (Raglan, Inkerman, Odessa, and so on); and the map as a trope of cultural and political inscription, as imprisoning maze and labyrinth, is made explicit in 'Smithfield Market', where the burned-out old market of Belfast harbours a secret, unidentifiable beast:

> Since everything went up in smoke, no entrances, no exits.
> But as the charred beams hissed and flickered, I glimpsed a map of Belfast
> In the ruins: obliterated streets, the faint impression of a key.
> Something many-toothed, elaborate, stirred briefly in the labyrinth.

The city as a labyrinth is a staple modern and postmodern figure, in painting as well as writing; and Carson renders it here with an almost gothic *frisson* by raising the ghost of the labyrinth's original inhabitant. In a complex, punning and wittily dark conceit, the 'key' to this burning map has many teeth, like a house key, but they are teeth which may bite, like the teeth of a mythical wild beast or Minotaur, fed on human flesh in the Cretan labyrinth. The key to the map of Belfast may offer not a way out, but only a way further into the ungovernable source of its own conflagration. Always out of date, as explosions and demolitions eat away the city's fabric, and even when burning, the map of Belfast secretes within itself the most minatory of possibilities: since bombs, like Minotaurs, feed on human flesh.

If human subjects are dispersed along the labyrinthine grid of a map in *The Irish for No*, however, suffering the history they are plotted into, they are markedly dispersed into other kinds of inscription in the volume too: in particular, into brand name, advertising slogan, and list or catalogue. The book contains a remarkable number of brand names, often themselves occurring in lists. The following is my own selective listing, from the book's twenty-four poems (I italicize where Carson does): Gold Leaf, the *Dundalk Democrat*, Gold Label, Cointreau, Blue Grass, Calvin Klein's *Obsession*, Andy Warhol (a brand name of a kind, after all), Brylcreem, *Phoenix* beer, Guerlain's *Sous le Vent*, Saravel's *White Christmas*, Corday's *Voyage à Paris*, *Rhythm*, Boots's *Buttermilk and Clover* soap, Saracen, Kremlin–2 mesh, Makrolon face-shields, Sellotape, Blu-Tack, *Contact*, *Men Only*, Porta-kabins, Telstar Taxis, Durex, Drawbridge British Wine, Black & Decker, Jabberwocks, Angels' Wings, Widows' Kisses, Corpse

Revivers, *Pampers*, HP Sauce, Heinz Baked Beans, Crosse &
Blackwell's Cock-a-Leekie, Ford Zephyr, Audi Quattro, Red Heart
Stout, Park Drive cigarettes, Dunville's whisky, *Guinness*, *Peter Pan
loaf*, Harp, Paddy whiskies, Lucozade, Polaroids, baby Power's.
Brand names can be affectionately or nostalgically evocative of
particular times and places, as they are in those most quintessen-
tially English poets, John Betjeman and Craig Raine, for instance,
but as they are also in Louis MacNeice; and Carson is a superb
poet of evocation, of the moods and atmospheres conjured by
retrospect and recall. The brand names label the moment, freeze
the frame of history; and nowhere more vividly than in 'Patchwork', where somebody buys a bottle of Lucozade in a pub:

> the baby
> Version, not the ones you get in hospital, wrapped in crackling see-
> through
> Cellophane. You remember how you held it to the light, and light
> shone through?
> The opposite of Polaroids, really, the world filmed in dazzling
> sunshine:
> A quite unremarkable day of mist and drizzle.

When the word 'Lucozade' is used, who does not remember such
bedridden transformations of reality, the *ersatz* orange dazzle of
the Lucozade cellophane harmonizing with your drugged or
fevered state? Carson is full of such moments when the almost
forgotten and the almost inconsequential are given their accurate
names.

But brand names can also appear eerily dominating when used in
such profusion: they may then come to suggest the ways in which
human subjects are subject to, precisely, the manipulative man-
oeuvres of the market-place. If the market-place in question is the
streets of Belfast (and it is, after all, Smithfield *market* that has gone
up in smoke), then the agents of domination and control may hide
themselves in the glitter of packaging and product as easily as they
reveal themselves in the obviousness of military surveillance. In
streets patrolled by armoured personnel carriers branded 'Saracen,
Kremlin–2 mesh', all other brand names are likely to seem less
innocent too, more malevolently or ironically elements in a system of signification which is also a system of subjugation: human

beings, wandering in the interstices of such names, may themselves appear all too easily commodifiable. In *The Irish for No*, named commodities have a habit of refusing their proper function, of rebelling against the uses for which they are advertised. A pornographic magazine called *Contact*, when read by a lonely British soldier in his Belfast barracks, reminds us that soldiers make 'contact' with the enemy as well as with sexual partners and, indeed, that in Belfast they do the former where they dare not do the latter. Durex is used for making bombs as well as for making love. A Black & Decker drill may be employed for the novel DIY job of putting terrified suicidal holes in your own head; and when you have become the half-forgotten data of someone's cocktail-bar reminiscence, the names of the cocktails ('Widows' Kisses', 'Corpse Revivers') will grotesquely ironize your death and the consequences for your family. If you are Horse Boyle, Heinz baked bean tins will be the only watchdog you can afford, but you will need a watchdog.

The itemizations in the volume are also, however, manifestly Carson's attempt to keep a tally of Belfast as it disappears; and in this, brand names join street names and other kinds of list, some of them intense little mnemonic poems-within-poems (the itemization of smells at the opening of 'Calvin Klein's *Obsession*', for instance). Such acts of poetic reclamation may be acts of love, but they may also be preparatory to acts of vengeance, as the end of 'Slate Street School', the final shorter poem of Part II, makes plain. The poet remembers returning to his primary school at the beginning of a new term and chanting once again the mnemonic lists of rote-learning which once constituted the essence of primary-school education for children in the British Isles: distances, weights and measures, the multiplication tables. When the Belfast snow begins to fall, an anonymous voice (the teacher's, a priest's or some religious manual's?) uses the snowflakes as an opportunity for catechetical instruction:

> *These are the countless souls of purgatory, whose numbers constantly diminish*
> *And increase: each flake as it brushes to the ground is yet another soul released.*
> And I am the avenging Archangel, stooping over mills and factories and barracks.
> I will bury the dark city of Belfast forever under snow: inches, feet, yards, chains, miles.

The prophetic, Blakean savagery of the denunciation here is a note struck only this once in the book, but it is given its licence and authentication by the tally kept in the rest of the volume. That computation indicates that Slate Street School has made a poet: mnemonic itemizations chanted in rhythm may be the origin of those others chanted in these poems by the poet who here remembers the child he was. The Belfast classroom, however, is also the origin of a tally of the depredations which must be avenged, as well as remembered. 'Avenging' is a dangerous adjective to use in a poem about Belfast, although it goes without saying that no serious poem about the politics of Belfast can afford to ignore the palpably motivating effect of the emotions generated by the desire for retribution. 'Slate Street School' confronts such emotions within the child/poet himself, but retains a probity in relation to them. The lines originate in pity, implying that the city of Belfast is the true purgatory for those 'countless souls' longing for release, and thereby giving *The Irish for No* probably its single most memorable figure of entrapment, significantly but understatedly drawn from religious instruction. The poet/archangel/avenger then promises to exact vengeance not on faction or person, not on organization or tribe or side, but on the city itself, making the poem for once (from a depth of quite unironized anger) not a retrieval system, but a grave: calling up, itemizing, evoking with a view to burying in language what has become insupportable in place, eradicating in its own linguistic space those sites of repression and subjugation, 'mills and factories and barracks' which form the chosen ground of Carson's imagination, just as the labyrinth of the Falls Road was the given ground of his childhood.

IV

When Carson reviewed Heaney's *Sweeney Astray*, his translation of the early medieval Irish poem *Buile Suibhne*, in the *Honest Ulsterman* in 1984, he remarked on the way in which that narrative poem seems always written over, or written into, by the hero Sweeney's prophesied death:

> He is the chronicle of a death foretold; he is living out the knowledge of a prophecy. The intricate circularity of purpose is mirrored in the

rule of the Irish verse forms, that they must begin and end on the same word; the effect, at times, is like taking one step forward and two steps back.[11]

Repeated readings of the poem, consequently, make Carson's mind, he tells us, feel 'a bit like Sweeney's, reeling and frantic'. This is the effect of some of Carson's own poems on the reader too, it seems to me; and the dance simile used of the forms of *Sweeney Astray* ('one step forward and two steps back') occurs also in 'Calvin Klein's *Obsession*'. The poem's erotic reverie free-floats over a love affair in early adolescence, which is remembered in tandem with a pop song of the time, Frank Ifield's intensely nostalgic 'I Remember You':

> It was April, a time
> Of fits and starts; fresh leaves blustered at the window, strips and
>   fronds
> Of fish and water-lilies sloughed off round my feet. A Frank Ifield
>   song
> From 1963, I think, kept coming back to me: *I remember you –*
>   *you're the one*
> *Who made my dreams come true – just a few kisses ago*. I'm taking
> One step forward, two steps back, trying to establish what it was
>   about her
> That made me fall in love with her, if that's what it was . . .

Carson writes his own characteristic signature into the self-reflexivity of contemporary lyric narrative by letting the reflexes cluster and collide almost exhilaratedly; and this is a character-istically self-reflexive passage. The time of fits and starts is the time of the poem as well as the time of the year, as its memories stagger forwards and backwards in the discontinuities and intermit-tences of personal voluntary and involuntary memory; the song remembered and associated with a remembered love-affair is a song about a remembered love affair; as soon as 'love' is men-tioned, it is placed under suspicion, scrutinized by the undermining scepticism of a past conditional. The passage, that is to say, is itself a demonstration of moving in the stately, obsessive and slightly absurd waltz or pavanne of 'one step forward, two steps back'.

Movement by digression, the characteristic movement of all the longer poems in the book, is the movement of one step forward, two steps back too: these poems, as they unwind, get not exactly forward but back in upon themselves. In their intricate circularity of purpose, they too plot prophecies of foretelling and prefiguring and maps of dislocation, erasure and derangement: the title of one poem, 'Serial', and its vertiginous realization of the impression of *déjà vu*, may be regarded as paradigmatic. This is as true of the poems of the personal and creative life as it is of the more outwardly turned and social poems. Indeed, it is 'Calvin Klein's *Obsession*' that gives this structure an implicit figure for itself when it remembers Boots's *Buttermilk and Clover* soap 'Slipping and slipping from my grasp, clunking softly downwards through / The greying water; I have drowsed off into something else.' The narrative of past time in this poem, its *recherche du temps perdu*, is a slow, expansive drowse through the processes of memory and sensation provoked by the Proustian mnemonic spurs of taste and smell. His glass of beer reminds him of the Ulster brewery, which reminds him of the perfume *Blue Grass*, which reminds him of the fur worn by an early girlfriend, which reminds him of candy apples, which remind him of buying snuff for his grandmother; and so on, in a gradual drift of apparently free association. The drift, however, is in fact cunningly plotted into a wistful, rueful account of the haunting of one's present by one's past, of the temptations to sentimentality and nostalgia, and of the tricks and turns of a fictionalizing memory. The drowsing digressions, the artful somnambulisms of 'Calvin Klein's *Obsession*', point ultimately into another black hole or *mise-en-abîme*: in its final line, memory and perhaps language itself are conjured in all their recessive duplicity, as products without origin and names without substance, when they disappear into a suspicious association with a perfume manufacturer's dream of the ultimately skilful piece of marketing: '*Or maybe it's the name you buy, and not the thing itself*'.

That line is a kind of pseudo-quotation: it represents the drifting into consciousness of a suddenly new appropriateness for the cliché that 'you're only paying for the name'. This kind of citation is typical of *The Irish for No*, whose intertexts are frequently those of popular culture, Irish ballad, advertising and, as I have already noted, street-maps. Early on in 'Calvin Klein's *Obsession*', however, Carson quotes (or actually slightly misquotes) Edward Thomas's poem on memory and association, 'Old

Man': '*I sniff and sniff again, and try to think of what it is I am
remembering.*'[12] 'I think that's how it goes,' he says, 'like Andy
Warhol's calendar of perfumes', and he is immediately into the
next association. In that casual, imprecise and almost languid 'I
think that's how it goes' (which could as appropriately be said of,
say, a Frank Ifield song), there is a marked lack of respect for the
products of high art. Where Heaney is sometimes almost reveren-
tial and entranced in his literary allusiveness, and Muldoon is, for
all the slyness and obliquity with which he manages it, endlessly
and insouciantly allusive to the texts of high literary culture
(along with many other kinds of text too, of course), Carson's
literary allusions are notably not a major feature of the nevertheless extremely sophisticated play of his poems. And when he is
allusive, he is almost uninterpretably so: not pointed, ironic,
context-creating or self-displaying in any of the usual ways. The
poem in which this is at its clearest is 'Whatever Sleep It Is'; and,
since this is also the poem in *The Irish for No* most manifestly
itself about the processes of creativity, I want to discuss it here in
some detail.

The poem is a painter's account of making an apparently
relatively representational canvas; which is, it appears, a process of
continuous erasure and substitution. The problematic leg of a spy
or a pilot is changed into a flight of stairs, which then, punningly,
'leads to' a skylight; the skylight is eventually given a broken pane,
and the painter imagines that it has been broken by the figure just
painted out. This figure is in love with a woman who is quickly
painted in, behind a rather corny Chianti bottle with a candle.
Then, suddenly, the painting's final narrative realizes itself, although perhaps only as imaginative possibility rather than canvas
actuality since, as in several of Carson's most stunning effects, the
syntax is fluidly irresolvable, and there is a slippage between the
tenor and the vehicle of metaphor. The erased figure ('Mr
Natural, / As we'll call him': he who is anything but natural, this
abandoned product of imaginative artifice) turns out to be an
angel, and the painting – apparently without the painter's conscious decision or manipulation – becomes a kind of contemporary Annunciation:

> I see it is an angel, not a man, who has
> Descended, looking faintly puzzled at the poor response of the girl

To whatever important announcement he has just made. She is, in
    fact, asleep,
Oblivious also to the clink and hum of the electric milk float
Which has just pulled up outside. And the milkman looks up,
    momentarily
Amazed at curtains, wings, gusting from the attic window. He rubs
    his eyes;
He is still drowsy with these six days out of seven. Tomorrow
    yawns ahead
With routine promises; tomorrow, after all, he will be free.

The milkman's amazement apes the reader's at the successive
metamorphoses of this painting (and this poem). An allegory of
its own process of creation or construction, of the one-step-
forward, two-steps-back kind of accident, trial and error that
make all paintings and poems, 'Whatever Sleep It Is' noses out its
own narrative in a ritual of self-cancellation, discovering itself
only – in the memorable Derridean phrase – by 'letting go of the
pen', just as this painting's narrative discovers itself in the series of
controlled accidents produced by letting go of the brush.[13] To
paint an Annunciation, of all things, by accident, and only *faute
de mieux*, seems a destabilizingly postmodern recognition of the
artist's or poet's lack of rational control over the processes of his
or her own creativity. This angel has indeed descended – come
down – a long way in the world since the orthodox angels of
Biblical tradition, the painted angels of Renaissance iconography
and, indeed, the imaginative angels of modern literary tradition;
he would clearly feel more at home in Wim Wenders's movie
Wings of Desire than in Rilke's *Duino Elegies* or Wallace Stevens's
'Angel Surrounded by Paysans'. And yet this coming-down, this
bathos, is a kind of epiphany too, if not for the sleeping Virgin,
then at least for the milkman, rapt from his routine.

This is what appears to happen in 'Whatever Sleep It Is'; this
seems to me the story that takes shape within the story this
painter–narrator tells. It is a story, however, that happens virtually
independently of the poem's nevertheless heavily foregrounded
allusiveness. The poem takes its title from a phrase in one of
Robert Frost's best-known poems, the endlessly surprising 'After
Apple-Picking', even though the phrase does not itself actually
appear in Carson's poem: so that the title's allusion in effect, and

on its own, points almost nowhere as far as an interpretation of
the poem is concerned – unlike, say, such allusively entitled poems
as 'Singing School' by Seamus Heaney, or 'Good Friday, 1971.
Driving Westward' by Paul Muldoon. 'After Apple-Picking' is
cited, however, as part of an almost arch literary joke, towards the
poem's conclusion. The woman in the painting has 'a bowl of
apples at her elbow':

> Meanwhile Mr Natural,
> As we'll call him, has climbed on to the roof, and, with his feet
>   lodged
> In the guttering, is staring through the hole at her. *The pane of glass*
> *I skimmed this morning from the drinking-trough*, he whispers to
>   himself,
> *Melted, and I let it fall and break.* Early frost: the stars are blazing
> Now like snowflakes – stem end and blossom end
>
> Swelling and dimming over the black Alp of the roof.

The presence of Frost's poem here seems peculiarly supernumerary, like the presence of Keats's 'Ode to a Nightingale' and
Heaney's *Door into the Dark* in 'The Irish for No', and like
Edward Thomas's 'Old Man' in 'Calvin Klein's *Obsession*'. Apparently instances of frail but poised coincidence, rather than of
the more vibrant energy and tension usually evident in complex
and sophisticated intertextuality, they have their clear local point,
but they lack defining context. In the Carson poems, that is to say,
the allusions seem themselves parenthetical, digressive, in no sense
an inevitable element of the structure, suspended in an air of
almost irretrievable connections ('I think that's how it goes'). They
seem therefore not easily recuperable by the will to interpret and
explain. What is the point of the Frost poem here? To frame the
narrative? To ironize the possibility of 'naturalness' in a work of
art? To suggest to the reader who knows the anxiety, or even
death-inflectedness, of Frost's poem that this poem of Carson's is
the 'trouble' that must disturb an artist's sleep? Or that paintings
and poems are, always, the forms given to dreams? Or that they
offer a world transformed in the way it might seem if looked at
through a pane of ice? To act merely as decoration? Simply to
provide the opportunity, in the 'early frost' joke, for a moment of

pawky self-congratulation for the literary reader? Or to make that joke, in its possibly preening self-regard, the vehicle for a criticism of exactly such opportunities afforded by allusion in modern poetry, a poetry written and read almost exclusively by people trained in the English departments of institutions of higher education? Or just to supply the chance for that lovely, glancing and zany comparison of Frost's apples to the painting's stars?

All these things, perhaps, but none of them of necessity. The poem does not explore or explicate the allusion in a way that would allow readerly certainty: it retains a heuristic secrecy and patience. It is as if the literary reference takes its place as just another element in the poem's patchwork fabric, another piece happening to hand, but one which makes 'Whatever Sleep It Is' the tracing of an acknowledgement, a deference as well as a difference. Given that apple-trees are in question here, it may not be beside the point to adduce Jacques Derrida's phrase for Mallarmé's *Mimique*: it is, he says, 'grafted onto the efflorescence of another text'.[14] The graft gets by on its own, however, independent of origin. The allusion to Frost in 'Whatever Sleep It Is' appears actually to lighten the burden of what the writer must drag behind him, asserting no system of hierarchy or patrimony. In this, it manifestly divorces itself from the sanctity of any Eliotic conception of tradition and from the impassioned anguish and rhetorical gusto of any Bloomian struggle and swerve. As such, it might well be regarded as the turning to profit of a genuinely postmodern sense of the intertextual: a kenotic one in which hierarchy is emptied into equivalence.

The way Carson uses past literature, indeed, may imply that literature is almost what his poems aspire not to be. Tall tales, ballads, songs, fiddle tunes and flute tunes, reportage and annotation: these seem much more what they would wish to be, given the chance. Literature is too full for them. If the poems of *The Irish for No* are full, they are full of holes too, emptying themselves out into gap, fissure and the other story that they always seem aware they might be telling. The painting in 'Whatever Sleep It Is' has 'everything as full of holes as a Swiss cheese', and in 'Snowball', 'Like a fish-net stocking, everything is full of holes.' The poems' own interpretative holes, their irresolvable abysms and aporias, are the register of a scepticism, even a guilt, about the relationship between poem or 'story' and the matter it must handle in contemporary Belfast which is probably their profoundest principle of form. It is a scepticism, it should be said, which is given a more than merely figurative authority by Carson's long poetic silence, but it finds its most perfect figure in *The Irish for No* at the end of 'Snowball', where a postman is at work in the Tomb Street GPO in Belfast at Christmas time:

> Arse-about-face, night-shift and the Christmas rush, perfume
>   oozing from
> Crushed packets – *Blue Grass, Obsession* – and, once, in a
>   forgotten pigeon-hole,
> I woke up to this card stamped 9 August 1910: *Meet me usual place
>   and time*
> *Tomorrow – What I have to tell you might not wait – Yours –*
> *Forever – B.*

A card in a hole in a Tomb: a very dead letter indeed, undelivered for decades, its written urgency and desire ironically poignant and finite where they wished to be eternally enduring. This seems the aptest of emblems for the well-directed but anxious book *The Irish for No* (written, as some poems in *The New Estate* and *Belfast Confetti* make clear, by a postman's son). The emblem has its interesting correspondences with Derrida's fascination with the postcard in his extraordinary book *The Post Card: From Socrates to Freud and Beyond,* and his sense there that, once committed to the post, there is always the risk that the letter will be lost or disseminated.[15] Those oozing perfumes, too, which reappear from 'Calvin Klein's *Obsession*', perhaps also figure a scepticism about how much can be made to cohere in any organization of poetic language, a consciousness of how much may ooze and slip and spill. This is a very long way from the claims implicit in mythical methods: more disillusioned, more jaded, later. If such scepticism has its affinities with postmodern theory, its formal expression in Carson's poems is also peculiarly appropriate to a poetry of the contemporary fate of Northern Ireland. Narratives wander duplicitously or digressively, taking wrong turnings, turning again; language may well not mean at all what it seems to say, or it may be read quite differently from the intention behind its writing; messages may not be delivered for eighty years. If you take one step forward, you may well take two steps back. But there is no Irish for no.

Notes

Notes to Chapter 1: Architectures of Yeats: perspectives on
The Winding Stair

1   C. L. Innes, *Woman and Nation in Irish Literature and Society, 1880–1935* (Harvester Wheatsheaf, 1993), 94.
2   This came about because the volume in fact combines two earlier, interim books, *The Winding Stair* (1929) and *Words for Music Perhaps and Other Poems* (1932), to which are added the poems 'Swift's Epitaph' and 'Crazy Jane Talks with the Bishop'.
3   Terry Eagleton, *Crazy John and the Bishop and Other Essays on Irish Culture* (Cork University Press, 1998), 290.
4   Louis MacNeice, *The Poetry of W. B. Yeats* (1941; Faber & Faber, 1967), ch. vii.
5   W. J. McCormack, *From Burke to Beckett: Ascendancy, Tradition and Betrayal in Literary History* (Cork University Press, 1994), 123–8, 393.
6   Louis MacNeice, *The Poetry of W. B. Yeats*, with a foreword by Richard Ellmann (1941; Faber & Faber, 1967), 197.
7   Seamus Heaney, *The Redress of Poetry: Oxford Lectures* (Faber & Faber, 1995), 146–63. In private conversation with me, one eminent scholar of Yeats has wondered whether the line 'Man has created death' implies a reference to Cain and Abel: Cain was, of course, the first human being to create death by killing his brother. But Abel would die in any case, eventually, and so will Cain, and so will we all, as the consequence of 'our' expulsion from Eden. What Cain has in fact created is not death, but murder; and it is of course arguable that, in the Genesis myth, it is God who has created death: witness how hard it is for Milton to make it seem otherwise in *Paradise Lost*.
8   J. L. Austin, *How to Do Things with Words*, ed. J. O. Urmson and Marina Stisà (Oxford University Press, 1975), 6.
9   See McCormack, *From Burke to Beckett*; and 'The Literary Myths of the Revival', in Seamus Deane, *Celtic Revivals: Essays in Modern Irish Literature 1880–1980* (Faber & Faber, 1985).
10   Daniel Albright (ed.), *W. B. Yeats: The Poems* (Dent, 1990), 694.
11   I am grateful for this point to Professor Terence Brown.
12   Deane, 'Literary Myths', 28.
13   Daniel A. Harris, *Yeats, Coole Park and Ballylee* (Johns Hopkins University Press, 1974), 229.

14 Stan Smith, *The Origins of Modernism: Eliot, Pound, Yeats and the Rhetorics of Renewal* (Harvester Wheatsheaf, 1994), 233.

15 See Elizabeth Butler Cullingford, *Gender and History in Yeats's Love Poetry* (Cambridge University Press, 1993), 227–44.

16 Harold Bloom, *Yeats* (Oxford University Press, 1970), 403. It is also conceivable, although I have not come across this interpretation of the lines in published criticism of Yeats, that something other than priority or contiguity is being insinuated here: that is, the identity of the excremental and the genital functions which would occur in anal sex. This might well be thought in tune with such disparate interests of Yeats's as satanism, Baudelairean decadence and the D. H. Lawrence of *Lady Chatterley's Lover*.

17 MacNeice, *The Poetry of W. B. Yeats*, 122.

Notes to Chapter 2: The blessings of Onan: Austin Clarke's 'Mnemosyne Lay in Dust'

1 'Austin Clarke', in Denis Donoghue, *We Irish: Essays on Irish Literature and Society* (University of California Press, 1986), 243.

2 *Selected Poems*, ed. Thomas Kinsella (Dolmen Press, 1976); *Selected Poems*, ed. Hugh Maxton (Lilliput Press, 1991), subsequently published by Penguin Books. The *Collected Poems* was beautifully edited and designed by Liam Miller (Dolmen Press, 1974).

3 Austin Clarke, 'The Gate', with a commentary by Dardis Clarke, in W. J. McCormack (ed.), *In the Prison of his Days: A Miscellany for Nelson Mandela* (Lilliput Press, 1988), 72–5.

4 These remarks are made in Kinsella's introduction to his edition of Clarke's *Selected Poems*.

5 Austin Clarke, 'Scalping the Muse', *Irish Times*, 30 Sept. 1950, 7.

6 *Quarterly Review of Literature*, 14: 1/2 (1966), 116–40.

7 Terence Brown writes very interestingly about the characteristic presence of 'secretions of various kinds' even in Clarke's erotic poems; and the somatic nature of human being is, indeed, what often gives the work its individuality, making it ripe for a Bakhtinian reassessment. See 'Austin Clarke: Satirist', in *Ireland's Literature* (Lilliput Press, 1988), 127–40. John Donne is the only other poet I know in whom eroticism and secretion are similarly combined; and, although this is managed quite differently in Donne, a comparison with Clarke might prove a fruitful one.

8 Austin Clarke, *Twice Round the Black Church* (Routledge & Kegan Paul, 1962), 142.

9 Nuala Ní Dhomhnaill, *Pharaoh's Daughter* (Gallery Press, 1990), 33–5.

10 W. J. McCormack writes illuminatingly on the sense of being looked at in the poem, and suggests how useful a Foulcauldian reading of

Clarke might prove, particularly in the context of the Irish literature
of mental illness. See 'Austin Clarke: The Poet as Scapegoat of
Modernism', in Patricia Coughlan and Alex Davis (eds.), *Modernism
and Ireland: The Poetry of the 1930s* (Cork University Press, 1995),
75–102.

11 Donald Davie, 'Austin Clarke and Padraic Fallon', in Douglas Dunn
(ed.), *Two Decades of Irish Writing* (Carcanet, 1975), 38.

12 In ' "Stephen Dedalus": The Author of *Ulysses*' (1924), Clarke,
recalling a meeting with Joyce in Paris, says that the *Portrait* 'had long
since become confused with my own memories or had completed
them'. The article, originally published in the *New Statesman*, is
reprinted in Gregory A. Schirmer (ed.), *Reviews and Essays of Austin
Clarke* (Colin Smythe, 1995), 43–5.

13 Hugh Maxton's annotation of the poem instances particularly the
death by hunger-strike in Brixton Prison of Terence MacSwiney, Lord
Mayor of Cork, on 25 October 1920. See Clarke's *Selected Poems*, ed.
Maxton, 251.

14 McCormack, 'Austin Clarke', 98, however, thinks that the mother
here 'should surely be interpreted as an allusion to Mnemosyne,
mother of poetry'. My own view is that the actual mother accords
with the pattern of mythopoeic collapse I am describing here, in
something of the way, it may be, in which Stephen's mother appears
at the end of the *Portrait* 'putting [his] new secondhand clothes in
order' in a gesture – heavy with ironic, gendered significance – which
undermines the vaunt of the hero's final mythical prayer to Daedalus
as 'old father, old artificer'.

15 Clarke's *Selected Poems*, ed. Maxton, 251; and note also his information: 'As a domestic union, the marriage [to Geraldine (Lia)
Cumming], which was unconsummated, lasted ten days.'

16 Martin Dodsworth, 'To Forge the Irish Conscience', *Times Literary
Supplement*, 13 Dec. 1974, 1406.

17 Clarke's *Selected Poems*, ed. Kinsella, x.

*Notes to Chapter 3: Makeshift monologue: the poetry of
Padraic Fallon*

1 In Seamus Deane (ed.), *The Field Day Anthology of Irish Writing*, 3
vols. (Field Day Publications, 1991), 1309.

2 See Declan Kiberd, *Inventing Ireland* (Jonathan Cape, 1995).

3 Seamus Heaney, 'Introduction' to Padraic Fallon, *Collected Poems*
(Carcanet/Gallery, 1990), 12.

4 Ibid.

5 Seamus Heaney, *Preoccupations: Selected Prose 1968–1978* (Faber &
Faber, 1980), 37.

6 Heaney, 'Introduction', loc. cit., 17.

7 Donald Davie, 'Austin Clarke and Padraic Fallon', in Douglas Dunn (ed.), *Two Decades of Irish Writing: A Critical Survey* (Carcanet, 1975), 54.

8 Robert F. Garratt, in *Modern Irish Poetry: Tradition and Continuity from Yeats to Heaney* (University of California Press, 1986), 70–7, reads in these poems only Fallon's 'capitulation' to Yeats. It will be clear from what I have written here that I find this a serious misreading, and one that undermines the whole enterprise undertaken in Fallon's work. Garratt did not, of course, have the benefit of the full extent of the poetry made available in the *Collected Poems*.

9 Elizabeth Bowen, *The Mulberry Tree*, ed. Hermione Lee (Virago, 1986), 26.

10 Peter Sirr's 'Some Distinction: Padraic Fallon's Athenry', *Eire-Ireland* (Fall, 1985), 93–108, one of the very few extended treatments of Fallon, is illuminating on the place of Athenry in poems such as this; and he dates the poem to 1965.

11 See Leo Steinberg, *The Sexuality of Christ in Renaissance Art and in Modern Oblivion* (Faber & Faber, 1983).

12 Davie, 'Austin Clarke and Padraic Fallon', 57.

13 Anthony Julius brilliantly decodes the collusion between Eliot's misogyny and his anti-Semitism in these poems in *T. S. Eliot, Anti-Semitism and Literary Form* (Cambridge University Press, 1995).

Notes to Chapter 4: Keeping the colours new:
Louis MacNeice in the contemporary poetry of Northern Ireland

1 Stan Smith, *W. H. Auden* (Basil Blackwell, 1985), 2–4, 23–5.

2 'Introduction: Revising Irish Literature', in Edna Longley, *The Living Stream: Literature and Revisionism in Ireland* (Bloodaxe Books, 1994), 51.

3 Derek Mahon, *Journalism: Selected Prose 1970–1995*, ed. Terence Brown (Gallery Books, 1996), 25.

4 Ibid., 30–1.

5 Professor Terence Brown points out to me, however, that the Belfast of Mahon's (and his own) childhood was then too a 'bombed-out town' as a result of German air-raids during the war.

6 Tom Paulin, 'Letters from Iceland: Going North', in John Lucas (ed.), *The 1930s: A Challenge to Orthodoxy* (Harvester Press, 1978), 59. The essay was published earlier, in 1976, in the journal *Renaissance and Modern Studies*.

7 Michael Longley, 'The Neolithic Night: A Note on the Irishness of Louis MacNeice', in Douglas Dunn (ed.), *Two Decades of Irish Writing* (Carcanet, 1975), 104.

8   Michael Longley (ed.), *Louis MacNeice: Selected Poems* (Faber & Faber, 1988), xxiii.

9   'The Placeless Heaven: Another Look at Kavanagh', in Seamus Heaney, *The Government of the Tongue: The 1986 T. S. Eliot Memorial Lectures and Other Critical Writings* (Faber & Faber, 1988), 8.

10   Seamus Heaney, 'From Monaghan to the Grand Canal: The Poetry of Patrick Kavanagh', in *Preoccupations: Selected Prose 1968–1978* (Faber & Faber, 1980), 116.

11   Heaney, *The Government of the Tongue*, 8.

12   Seamus Heaney, *The Place of Writing* (Scolars Press, n.d. [lectures delivered 1988]), 43.

13   The poem was first published in John Carey (ed.), *William Golding: The Man and His Books* (Faber & Faber, 1986).

14   Heaney, *The Place of Writing*, 44.

15   Seamus Heaney, 'Frontiers of Writing', *Bullaun: An Irish Studies Journal*, 1: 1 (1994), 11–14. The lecture was subsequently published, in revised form, in *The Redress of Poetry: Oxford Lectures* (Faber & Faber, 1995). The figure of the quincunx is derived from Sir Thomas Browne's *The Garden of Cyrus*.

16   I do take up some of the implications in *The Poetry of Seamus Heaney: A Critical Study* (Faber & Faber, 1998), ch. 9. See also Peter McDonald, *Mistaken Identities: Poetry and Northern Ireland* (Clarendon Press, 1997), ch. 1.

17   'The Man from No Part', in Tom Paulin, *Ireland and the English Crisis* (Bloodaxe Books, 1984), 76.

18   Hedli MacNeice, 'The Story of the House that Louis Built', in Jacqueline Genet and Wynne Hellegouarch (eds.), *Studies on Louis MacNeice* (Centre de Publications de l'Université de Caen, 1988), 9.

19   Cited in Seamus Heaney, *The Place of Writing*, 37.

20   See Louis MacNeice, *The Poetry of W. B. Yeats* (1941; Faber & Faber, 1967), 142, 152, 183.

21   Heaney, *The Place of Writing*, 53.

22   It did in fact include, Carpenter tells us, a trained chimpanzee and also someone who specialized in inserting a cigarette in his anus and puffing out smoke. I have always thought it odd that a poem by Paul Muldoon finds no room for them. See Humphrey Carpenter, *W. H. Auden: A Biography* (Allen & Unwin, 1981), 304.

23   See John Kerrigan, 'Ulster Ovids', in Neil Corcoran (ed.), *The Chosen Ground: Essays on the Contemporary Poetry of Northern Ireland* (Seren Books, 1992), 237–69.

24   Ibid., 252.

25   L. C. Martin (ed.), *The Poetical Works of Robert Herrick* (Clarendon Press, 1956), 28.

26   Louis MacNeice, *Selected Literary Criticism*, ed. Alan Heuser (Clarendon Press, 1987), 155.

27 MacNeice, *The Poetry of W. B. Yeats*, 146.
28 John Haffenden, *Viewpoints: Poets in Conversation* (Faber & Faber, 1981), 141.
29 'The Room Where MacNeice Wrote Snow', in Longley, *The Living Stream*, 265.
30 Daniel Albright (ed.), *W. B. Yeats: The Poems* (Dent, 1990), 839.
31 Cited in A. Norman Jeffares, *A Commentary on the Collected Poems of W. B. Yeats* (Macmillan, 1968), 512.
32 MacNeice, *The Poetry of W. B. Yeats*, 192.
33 'Yeats's Epitaph: *Last Poems and Plays*, by W. B. Yeats', in MacNeice, *Selected Literary Criticism*, 119.
34 John Berryman, 'Despondency and Madness: On Lowell's "Skunk Hour" ', in *The Freedom of the Poet* (Farrar, Straus & Giroux, 1976), 316.
35 Christopher Ricks, *Beckett's Dying Words* (Clarendon Press, 1993), 133–4.
36 Kerrigan, 'Ulster Ovids', 253.
37 Haffenden, *Viewpoints*, 140.

Notes to Chapter 5: Strange letters: reading and writing in contemporary Northern Irish poetry

1 Frances Yates, *Giordano Bruno and the Hermetic Tradition* (Routledge & Kegan Paul, 1964), 75.
2 Ibid., 75–6.
3 For *ostranenie*, see Lee T. Lemon and Marion J. Reis (eds.), *Russian Formalist Criticism: Four Essays* (University of Nebraska Press, 1965). Heaney's fascination with the figure of the bricklayer is reinforced by the classical example he makes of him in 'Damson' in *The Spirit Level* (1996).
4 Jacques Derrida, 'Two Words for Joyce', in Derek Attridge and Daniel Ferrer (eds.), *Post-Structuralist Joyce: Essays from the French* (Cambridge University Press, 1984), 146.
5 Pat Adams (ed.), *With a Poet's Eye: A Tate Gallery Anthology* (Tate Gallery Publications, 1986). Muldoon's poem and the *en face* Klee painting appear on pp. 96–7. For an excellent account of the tradition of ekphrasis, see James A. W. Heffernan, *Museum of Words: The Poetics of Ekphrasis from Homer to Ashbery* (University of Chicago Press, 1993).
6 Cited in Will Grohmann, *Paul Klee* (Harry N. Abrams, n.d.), 20, 21, 48.
7 See Walter Benjamin, 'The Work of Art in the Age of Mechanical Reproduction', in *Illuminations* (1970; Fontana 1973), 219–53.

8 Ciaran Carson's volume *The Irish for No*, and notably its title poem, also scrutinize such large Ulster negatives, as I show in ch. 10 below.

9 See Alistair Rowan, *The Buildings of Ireland: North-West Ulster* (Penguin Books, 1979). Paulin is adapting a passage on p. 297, and I am grateful to him for pointing this out to me.

10 See C. I. Macafee, *A Concise Ulster Dictionary* (Oxford University Press, 1996), 271.

11 See 'Paisley's Progress', in Tom Paulin, *Writing to the Moment: Selected Critical Essays 1980–1996* (Faber & Faber, 1996), 28–47, reprinted from *Ireland and the English Crisis* (Bloodaxe Books, 1984).

Notes to Chapter 6: Examples of Heaney

1 Seamus Heaney, *Preoccupations: Selected Prose 1968–1978* (Faber & Faber, 1980), 98–114.

2 'A Tale of Two Islands: Reflections on the Irish Literary Revival', in P. J. Drudy (ed.), *Irish Studies 1* (Cambridge University Press, 1980), 1–20.

3 Heaney, *Preoccupations*, 220.

4 Ibid., 221.

5 Seamus Heaney, *Among Schoolchildren: A Lecture Dedicated to the Memory of John Malone* (John Malone Memorial Committee, 1983), 11.

6 Seamus Heaney, 'Envies and Identifications: Dante and the Modern Poet', in *Irish University Review*, 15: 1 (1985), 5–19, 11.

7 Heaney, *Preoccupations*, 13.

8 *Poetry Book Society Bulletin* (Autumn 1979).

9 Seamus Heaney, *Robert Lowell: A Memorial Address and An Elegy* (Faber and & Faber, privately printed, 1978), 9.

10 *Crane Bag*, 1: 1 (1977), 61–4, 64. The interview was reprinted in M. P. Hederman and Richard Kearney (eds.), *The Crane Bag Book of Irish Studies* (Colin Smythe, 1983).

11 All quotations are from Seamus Deane, *Celtic Revivals: Essays in Modern Irish Literature 1880–1980* (Faber & Faber, 1985).

12 For an excellent account of this see, in particular, Marilynn J. Richtarik's *Acting Between the Lines: The Field Day Theatre Company and Irish Cultural Politics 1980–1984* (Clarendon Press, 1994).

13 See, in particular, '"Inner Emigré" or "Artful Voyeur"? Seamus Heaney's *North*', in Edna Longley, *Poetry in the Wars* (Bloodaxe, 1986).

14 Heaney uses the word 'declarative' of these poems in an interview. See John Haffenden, *Viewpoints: Poets in Conversation* (Faber & Faber, 1981), 57–75.

15 See Ferdia MacAnna, 'The Dublin Renaissance', *Irish Review*, 10 (Spring 1991), 14–30.

16 *Irish University Review*, 15: 1 (1985), 5–19.

17 Denis Donoghue, *We Irish: Essays on Irish Literature and Society* (University of California Press, 1986), 12.

18 Heaney significantly revises the Joycean passage in the version of the poem he publishes in his *New Selected Poems 1966–1987* (Faber & Faber, 1990), in a way that suggests a continued uncertainty about the degree of self-aggrandisement that may be read into the encounter.

19 James Joyce, *A Portrait of the Artist as a Young Man*, ed. Seamus Deane (Penguin Books, 1992), 274.

20 Ibid., 205.

21 James Joyce, *Ulysses*, ed. Seamus Deane (Penguin Books, 1992), 430.

22 Seamus Heaney, 'The Poet as a Christian', *Furrow*, 29: 10 (1978), 603–6.

23 Seamus Deane, *A Short History of Irish Literature* (Hutchinson, 1986), 112.

24 Helen Gardner, *The Composition of 'Four Quartets'* (Faber & Faber, 1978), 187.

25 T. S. Eliot, *On Poetry and Poets* (Faber & Faber, 1957), 256.

Notes to Chapter 7: A languorous cutting edge: Muldoon versus Heaney?

1 Medbh McGuckian and Nuala Ní Dhomnaill, 'Comhrá, with a Foreword and Afterword by Laura O'Connor', *Southern Review*, 31: 3 (1995), 592.

2 Paul Muldoon, 'Caprice des Dieux', *Times Literary Supplement*, 11 May 1984, 516.

3 Edna Longley, *Poetry in the Wars* (Bloodaxe Books, 1986), 206.

4 Seamus Heaney, *The Place of Writing* (Scolars Press, n.d. [lectures delivered in 1988]), 52.

5 The apparent arrogance of this latter instance, if it is not just Longley's fantasy of the poem, is breathtaking. Where Muldoon is Coleridge, surely Heaney would have to be Wordsworth, not Southey? Is it significant that Wordsworth is the one major Romantic missing from 'Madoc', even though the other non-pantisocrat, Byron, is prominently present, usually criticizing Southey? Wordsworth would then become what Bob Dylan, in 'Lily, Rosemary and the Jack of Hearts', memorably characterizes as 'the only person on the scene / missing'. My sense that this probably is significant, but at such a hermetic level as to be virtually undiscoverable, and then uninterpretable, constitutes one of several objections I have to Muldoon's procedures in this sometimes altogether baffling poem.

6   Longley, *Poetry in the Wars*, 169.
7   Seamus Heaney, *Place and Displacement: Recent Poetry of Northern Ireland* (Trustees of Dove Cottage, 1985). This is reprinted in Elmer Andrews (ed.), *Contemporary Irish Poetry* (Macmillan, 1992), 124–44.
8   Ibid., 16.
9   John Carey, 'The Stain of Words', *Sunday Times*, 21 June 1987, 56.
10 Seamus Heaney, 'Anglo-Irish Occasions', *London Review of Books*, 5 May 1988, 9.
11 The letter is reprinted in Robert Lowell, *Collected Prose* (Faber & Faber, 1987), 370–1.
12 See Neil Corcoran, *The Poetry of Seamus Heaney: A Critical Study* (Faber & Faber, 1998), ch. 5.
13 Paul Muldoon, 'Sweaney Peregraine', *London Review of Books*, 1 Nov. 1984, 20–2.
14 I do so myself in *The Poetry of Seamus Heaney*, ch. 9.
15 Edna Longley, 'Derek Mahon: Extreme Religion of Art', in Michael Kenneally (ed.), *Poetry in Contemporary Irish Literature* (Colin Smythe, 1995), 280. She makes some use of a Bloomian terminology, while still pursuing her critique of his method, in ' "It is time that I wrote my will" ': Anxieties of Influence and Succession', in Warwick Gould and Edna Longley (eds.), *Yeats Annual No. 12 (That Accusing Eye: Yeats and his Irish Readers)* (Macmillan, 1996), 117–62.
16 Neil Corcoran, *English Poetry since 1940* (Longman, 1993), xv.
17 Lynn Keller, 'An Interview with Paul Muldoon', *Contemporary Literature*, 35: 1 (Spring 1994), 16.
18 Tim Kendall, *Paul Muldoon* (Seren Books, 1996), 153.
19 Michael Allen, 'The Parish and the Dream: Heaney and America, 1969–1987', *Southern Review*, 31: 3 (1995), 726–38.
20 Harold Bloom, *The Anxiety of Influence* (Oxford University Press, 1973), 16.
21 Seamus Heaney, 'An Interview' [conducted by Rand Brandes], *Salmagundi*, 80 (1988), 17.
22 Seamus Heaney, *Preoccupations: Selected Prose 1968–1978* (Faber & Faber, 1980), 65.
23 Paul Muldoon (ed.), *The Essential Byron* (Ecco Press, 1989), 4.

Notes to Chapter 8: Resident alien: America in the poetry of Derek Mahon

1   John Kerrigan, 'Ulster Ovids', in Neil Corcoran (ed.), *The Chosen Ground: Essays on the Contemporary Poetry of Northern Ireland* (Seren Books, 1992), 261.

2   Seamus Deane, *Celtic Revivals* (Faber & Faber, 1985), 156.

3   Peter Denman, 'Know the One? Insolent Ontology and Mahon's Revisions', *Irish University Review*, 24: 1 (1994), 34. Mahon's sometimes extensive revisions to his poems in subsequent printings are discussed illuminatingly in this essay. I myself find them, as many readers do, deeply irritating, and usually disadvantageous. I have, however, thought it necessary to quote in this essay from the versions given in *Selected Poems* (Viking/Gallery, 1991), apart from the instance I particularize in note 15 below. The poems of *The Hudson Letter* are not (yet) affected by Mahon's revisionary mania.

4   Kerrigan, 'Ulster Ovids', 260.

5   Hugh Haughton, ' "Even now there are places where a thought might grow": Place and Displacement in the Poetry of Derek Mahon', in Corcoran (ed.), *The Chosen Ground*, 87–120.

6   Derek Mahon, *Journalism: Selected Prose 1970–1995*, ed. Terence Brown (Gallery Books, 1996), 25. His observation here that, in this sense, 'exile . . . was an option available to Joyce and O'Casey, who "belonged" to the people from whom they wished to escape. It was not available, in the same sense, to MacNeice, whose background was a mixture of Anglo-Irish and Ulster Protestant (C of I). Whatever his sympathies, he didn't, by class or religious background, "belong to the people" ' also clearly has relevance to Mahon himself. The mordant fastidiousness of his inverted commas here is less a register of disdain than an indication of his own outsider status in relation to these structures of feeling; although disdain is undoubtedly an element of it.

7   Edna Longley, *Poetry in the Wars* (Bloodaxe Books, 1986), 206.

8   Peter Fallon and Derek Mahon (eds.), *The Penguin Book of Contemporary Irish Poetry* (Penguin Books, 1990), xxii. This would undoubtedly seem to Michael Allen a retrospective redrawing of the transatlantic map, since, in an article on Seamus Heaney and America, he observes: 'Whatever pan-Irish notions [Michael Longley and Mahon] might have picked up as students in Dublin, they were excluded from the outset from a Hiberno-American rapport by their Northern Protestant cultural antecedents.' See Michael Allen, 'The Parish and the Dream: Heaney and America, 1969–1987', *Southern Review*, 31: 3 (1995), 727.

9   Haughton, ' "Even now . . ." ', 111–13.

10 T. S. Eliot, *Selected Essays* (1932; Faber & Faber, 1951), 293.

11 Christopher Ricks, *The Force of Poetry* (Clarendon Press, 1984), 34–59. It is relevant, of course, that Ricks believes that the sharing of this kind of image derives from the sharing too of 'an imagination of civil war'.

12 Allen, 'The Parish and the Dream', 732, makes a different, but possibly related, point about the use of the word in Seamus Heaney's 'Elegy' for Robert Lowell: 'The word "America" functions here with

the enigmatic, liturgical force it always carries in the literature of the [American] Dream (at the end of *The Adventures of Augie March*, for instance).'

13 Edward Snow, *A Study of Vermeer*, revised and enlarged edition (University of California Press, 1994), 163.

14 Ibid., 166.

15 I quote here the version published in *Lives* (1972), since that of the *Selected Poems* – 'I put out the light / on shadows of the encroaching night' – is such a disfigurement. It loses the literariness which is so strong a feature of these poems and is intensified in this version by the fact that the Mailer title is derived from Matthew Arnold's 'Dover Beach', which is also referred to in this stanza in its original form; and, in that loss of allusion, it also loses, it may be, a relatively oblique reference to the Robert Lowell to whom Mahon is, in part, indebted for his octosyllabics, since Lowell is prominently featured in Mailer's book, which deals with the march on Washington in 1967.

16 Deane, *Celtic Revivals*, 157.

17 Daisy's nightingale flies in from *The Great Gatsby*, and an acquaintance with its appearance there adds poignancy and depth to these lines. In this, it is a model of how allusions work in this poem: very specific, they also ramify with significance; but most individual readers will inevitable not pick up all (or perhaps even the majority) of them.

Notes to Chapter 9: To stop the bleeding: the poetry of botany in Michael Longley

1 See Arthur C. Danto, 'Playing with the Edge: The Photographic Achievement of Robert Mapplethorpe', in Mark Holborn and Dimitri Levas (eds.), *Mapplethorpe* (Jonathan Cape, 1992), 311–39.

2 Hugo Williams, 'Siren', *London Review of Books*, 15 Aug. 1991, 22.

3 Roland Barthes, *Camera Lucida: Reflections on Photography*, trs. Richard Howard (Jonathan Cape, 1982), 55–9.

4 'Male Nipples and Clitoral Ripples', in Stephen Jay Gould, *Bully for Brontosaurus* (1991; Penguin Books, 1992), 127.

5 Seamus Heaney, 'Place and Displacement: Reflections on Some Recent Poetry from Northern Ireland', in Elmer Andrews (ed.), *Contemporary Irish Poetry: A Collection of Critical Essays* (Macmillan, 1992), 142.

6 Rainer Maria Rilke, 'The Ninth Elegy', in *Duino Elegies*, trs. J. B. Leishman and Stephen Spender (1939; Chatto & Windus, 1981), 85.

7 Gerard Manley Hopkins, letter to A. W. M. Baillie, 10 Sept. 1864, in C. C. Abbott (ed.), *Further Letters of G. M. Hopkins*, 2nd ed., revised and enlarged (1938; Oxford University Press, 1956), 215–17.

8   Michael Longley, *Tuppenny Stung: Autobiographical Chapters*
    (Lagan Press, 1994).
9   Ibid., 29.
10 Ibid., 73, 74.
11 See Neil Corcoran, *English Poetry since 1940* (Longman, 1993), 187.
12 John Kerrigan, 'Ulster Ovids', in Neil Corcoran (ed.), *The Chosen
    Ground: Essays on the Contemporary Poetry of Northern Ireland*
    (Seren Books, 1992), 246.
13 Hugh MacDiarmid had, it should be said, already found such room
    in his beautiful poem 'Milk-Wort and Bog-Cotton', first published in
    Scots Unbound and Other Poems (Stirling, 1932). I am grateful to Dr
    Patrick Crotty for bringing this poem to my attention.
14 Heaney, 'Place and Displacement', 140.
15 Ibid., 141.
16 Peter McDonald, *Mistaken Identities: Poetry and Northern Ireland*
    (Clarendon Press, 1997), 130.

Notes to Chapter 10: *One step forward, two steps back: Ciaran Carson's* The Irish for No

1   Ciaran Carson, 'Escaped from the Massacre?', *The Honest
    Ulsterman*, 50 (Winter 1975), 183–6.
2   Cited in Neil Corcoran, *The Poetry of Seamus Heaney: A Critical
    Study* (Faber & Faber, 1998), 53. Terence Brown has written excel-
    lently on the fate of the 'well-made poem' in Northern Ireland in 'A
    Northern Renaissance: Poets from the North of Ireland 1965–1980',
    in *Ireland's Literature: Selected Essays* (Lilliput Press, 1988).
3   *The Irish for No* exists in three different editions: Gallery Press
    (1987); Wake Forest University Press (1987); Bloodaxe Books (1988).
4   T. S. Eliot, 'Ulysses, Order and Myth' (1923), reprinted in Richard
    Ellmann and Charles Feidelson Jr (eds.), *The Modern Tradition*
    (Oxford University Press, 1965), 679–81.
5   Fredric Jameson, introduction to Jean-François Lyotard, *The Post-
    modern Condition: A Report on Knowledge* (Manchester University
    Press, 1984), xxiv.
6   Ibid., 41.
7   Reviewing two books by Williams, he writes: 'I hereby acknowledge a
    debt.' See 'Against Oblivion', *Irish Review*, 6 (1989), 113–16. It is
    worth noting that, in addition to his experimentation with the long
    line, Williams also characteristically employs American urban work-
    ing-class material.
8   Quotations in these paragraphs are from Carson's letters to me of 5
    May and 19 Oct. 1989.
9   Ciaran Carson, *The Pocket Guide to Irish Traditional Music*

(Appletree Press, 1986), and *Last Night's Fun* (Jonathan Cape, 1996). The latter is in fact an outstanding example of a poet's prose (although it is not poetic prose) and a complement to the poems; described in a subtitle as 'a book about music, food and time', its exuberance and zest are also emphatically positioned as a gesture 'against oblivion'. That is to say, it is actually a book about music, food, time and death.

10   Cited in Harold Osborne, *The Oxford Companion to Twentieth-Century Art* (Oxford University Press, 1981), 130.

11   Ciaran Carson, 'Sweeneys Ancient and Modern', *Honest Ulsterman*, 76 (1984), 73–9. A revised and expanded version appears in Curtis (ed.), *The Art of Seamus Heaney*, op. cit.

12   The actual lines are: 'I, too, often shrivel the grey shreds, / Sniff them and think and sniff again and try / Once more to think what it is I am remembering, / Always in vain.'

13   Jacques Derrida, *Dissemination* (University of Chicago Press, 1981), 274.

14   Ibid., 202.

15   Jacques Derrida, *The Postcard: From Socrates to Freud and Beyond* (University of Chicago Press, 1987).

Bibliography of Secondary Material

Albright, Daniel (ed.), W.B. Yeats: The Poems (London: Dent, 1990)
Allen, Michael, 'The Parish and the Dream: Heaney and America, 1969–
1987', Southern Review, 31: 3 (1995)
Andrews, Elmer (ed.), Contemporary Irish Poetry (London and
Basingstoke: Macmillan, 1992)
Austin, J. L., How to Do Things with Words, ed. J. O. Urmson and Marina
Stisà (Oxford: Oxford University Press, 1975)
Barthes, Roland, Camera Lucida: Reflections on Photography, trs. Richard
Howard (London: Cape, 1982)
Benjamin, Walter, Illuminations (1970; London: Fontana, 1973)
Berryman, John, The Freedom of the Poet (New York: Farrar, Straus and
Giroux, 1976)
Bloom, Harold, The Anxiety of Influence (Oxford: Oxford University
Press, 1973)
— Yeats (Oxford: Oxford University Press, 1970)
Bowen, Elizabeth, The Mulberry Tree, ed. Hermione Lee (London: Virago,
1986)
Brown, Terence, Ireland's Literature: Selected Essays (Mullingar: Lilliput
Press, 1988)
Carey, John, 'The Stain of Words', Sunday Times, 21 June 1987
Carpenter, Humphrey, W. H. Auden: A Biography (London: Allen and
Unwin, 1981)
Carson, Ciaran, 'Against Oblivion', Irish Review, 6 (1989)
— 'Escaped from the Massacre?', Honest Ulsterman, 50 (Winter 1975)
— Last Night's Fun (London: Cape, 1996)
—The Pocket Guide to Irish Traditional Music (Belfast: Appletree Press,
1986)
— 'Sweeneys Ancient and Modern', The Honest Ulsterman, 76 (1984)
Clarke, Austin, 'The Gate', with a commentary by Dardis Clarke, in W. J.
McCormack (ed.), In the Prison of his Days: A Miscellany for Nelson
Mandela (Mullingar: Lilliput Press, 1988)
— Reviews and Essays, ed. Gregory A. Schirmer (Gerrards Cross: Colin
Smythe, 1995)
— 'Scalping the Muse', Irish Times, 30 Sept. 1950
— Twice Round the Black Church (London: Routledge & Kegan Paul,
1962)

Corcoran, Neil, *English Poetry since 1940* (Harlow: Longman, 1993)
— *The Poetry of Seamus Heaney: A Critical Study* (London: Faber & Faber, 1998)
Cullingford, Elizabeth Butler, *Gender and History in Yeats's Love Poetry* (Cambridge: Cambridge University Press, 1993)
Davie, Donald, 'Austin Clarke and Padraic Fallon', in Douglas Dunn (ed.), *Two Decades of Irish Writing* (Manchester: Carcanet, 1975)
Deane, Seamus, *Celtic Revivals: Essays in Modern Irish Literature 1880–1980* (Faber & Faber, 1985)
— *A Short History of Irish Literature* (London: Hutchinson, 1986)
— (ed.), *The Field Day Anthology of Irish Writing*, 3 vols. (Derry: Field Day Publications, 1991)
Denman, Peter, 'Know the One? Insolent Ontology and Mahon's Revisions', *Irish University Review*, 24: 1 (1994)
Derrida, Jacques, *Dissemination* (Chicago, Ill.: University of Chicago Press, 1981)
— *The Postcard: From Socrates to Freud and Beyond* (Chicago, Ill.: University of Chicago Press, 1987)
— 'Two Words for Joyce', in Derek Attridge and Daniel Ferrer (eds.), *Post-Structuralist Joyce: Essays from the French* (Cambridge: Cambridge University Press, 1984)
Donoghue, Denis, *We Irish: Essays on Irish Literature and Society* (Berkeley: University of California Press, 1986)
Eagleton, Terry, *Crazy John and the Bishop and Other Essays on Irish Culture* (Cork: Cork University Press, 1998)
Eliot, T. S., *On Poetry and Poets* (London: Faber & Faber, 1957)
— *Selected Essays* (1932; London: Faber & Faber, 1951)
— 'Ulysses, Order and Myth' (1923), reprinted in Richard Ellmann and Charles Feidelson Jr (eds.), *The Modern Tradition* (New York: Oxford University Press, 1965)
Fallon, Peter, and Derek Mahon (eds.), *The Penguin Book of Contemporary Irish Poetry* (Harmondsworth: Penguin, 1990)
Gardner, Helen, *The Composition of 'Four Quartets'* (London: Faber & Faber, 1978)
Garratt, Robert F., *Modern Irish Poetry: Tradition and Continuity from Yeats to Heaney* (Berkeley: University of California Press, 1986)
Gould, Stephen Jay, *Bully for Brontosaurus* (1991; Harmondsworth: Penguin, 1992)
Grohmann, Will, *Paul Klee* (New York: Harry N. Abrams, n.d.)
Haffenden, John, *Viewpoints: Poets in Conversation* (London: Faber & Faber, 1981)
Harris, Daniel A., *Yeats, Coole Park and Ballylee* (Baltimore, Md: Johns Hopkins University Press, 1974)
Haughton, Hugh, ' "Even now there are places where a thought might grow": Place and Displacement in the Poetry of Derek Mahon', in Neil

Corcoran (ed.), *The Chosen Ground: Essays on the Contemporary Poetry of Northern Ireland* (Bridgend: Seren Books, 1992)

Heaney, Seamus, 'A Tale of Two Islands: Reflections on the Irish Literary Revival', in P. J. Drudy (ed.), *Irish Studies 1* (Cambridge: Cambridge University Press, 1980)

— *Among Schoolchildren: A Lecture Dedicated to the Memory of John Malone* (Belfast: John Malone Memorial Committee, 1983)

— 'Anglo-Irish Occasions', *London Review of Books*, 5 May 1988

— 'Envies and Identifications: Dante and the Modern Poet', *Irish University Review*, 15: 1 (1985)

— 'Frontiers of Writing', *Bullaun: An Irish Studies Journal*, 1: 1 (1994)

— *The Government of the Tongue: The 1986 T.S. Eliot Memorial Lectures, and Other Critical Writings* (London: Faber & Faber, 1988)

— 'Introduction' to Padraic Fallon, *Collected Poems* (Loughcrew and Manchester: Carcanet/Gallery, 1990)

— [Interview], *Crane Bag* 1: 1 (1977)

— 'An Interview' [conducted by Rand Brandes], *Salmagundi*, 80 (1988)

— *Place and Displacement: Recent Poetry of Northern Ireland* (Grasmere: Trustees of Dove Cottage, 1985)

— 'Place and Displacement: Reflections on Some Recent Poetry from Northern Ireland', in Elmer Andrews (ed.), *Contemporary Irish Poetry: A Collection of Critical Essays* (London and Basingstoke: Macmillan, 1992)

— *The Place of Writing* (Atlanta: Scolars Press, n.d. [lectures delivered 1988])

— 'The Poet as a Christian', *Furrow*, 29: 10 (1978)

— *Preoccupations: Selected Prose 1968–1978* (London: Faber & Faber, 1980)

— *The Redress of Poetry: Oxford Lectures* (London: Faber & Faber, 1995)

— *Robert Lowell: A Memorial Address and an Elegy* (London: Faber & Faber, privately printed, 1978)

Heffernan, James A. W., *Museum of Words: The Poetics of Ekphrasis from Homer to Ashbery* (Chicago, Ill.: University of Chicago Press, 1993)

Innes, C. L., *Woman and Nation in Irish Literature and Society, 1880 – 1935* (Hemel Hempstead: Harvester Wheatsheaf, 1993)

Jameson, Fredric, 'Introduction' to Jean-François Lyotard, *The Postmodern Condition: A Report on Knowledge* (Manchester: Manchester University Press, 1984)

Jeffares, A. Norman, *A Commentary on the Collected Poems of W. B. Yeats* (London and Basingstoke: Macmillan, 1968)

Julius, Anthony, *T. S. Eliot, Anti-Semitism and Literary Form* (Cambridge: Cambridge University Press, 1995)

Keller, Lynn, 'An Interview with Paul Muldoon', *Contemporary Literature*, 35: 1 (1994)

Kendall, Tim, *Paul Muldoon* (Bridgend: Seren Books, 1996)

Kerrigan, John, 'Ulster Ovids', in Neil Corcoran (ed.), *The Chosen Ground: Essays on the Contemporary Poetry of Northern Ireland* (Bridgend: Seren Books, 1992)

Kiberd, Declan, *Inventing Ireland* (London: Cape, 1995)

Kinsella, Thomas, 'Introduction' to Austin Clarke, *Selected Poems*, ed. Thomas Kinsella (Dublin: Dolmen Press, 1976)

Longley, Edna, 'Derek Mahon: Extreme Religion of Art', in Michael Kenneally (ed.), *Poetry in Contemporary Irish Literature* (Gerrards Cross: Smythe, 1995)

—— ' "Inner Emigré" or "Artful Voyeur"? Seamus Heaney's *North*', in Tony Curtis (ed.), *The Art of Seamus Heaney* (Bridgend: Seren Books, 1982; third edn. 1994)

—— ' "It is time that I wrote my will": Anxieties of Influence and Succession', in Warwick Gould and Edna Longley (eds.), *Yeats Annual No. 12: That Accusing Eye: Yeats and his Irish Readers* (London and Basingstoke: Macmillan, 1996)

—— *The Living Stream: Literature and Revisionism in Ireland* (Newcastle upon Tyne: Bloodaxe, 1994)

—— *Poetry in the Wars* (Newcastle upon Tyne: Bloodaxe, 1986)

Longley, Michael, 'The Neolithic Night: A Note on the Irishness of Louis MacNeice', in Douglas Dunn (ed.), *Two Decades of Irish Writing* (Manchester: Carcanet, 1975)

—— *Tuppenny Stung: Autobiographical Chapters* (Belfast: Lagan Press, 1994)

—— (ed.), *Louis MacNeice: Selected Poems* (London: Faber & Faber, 1988)

Lowell, Robert, *Collected Prose* (London: Faber & Faber, 1987)

McCormack, W. J., 'Austin Clarke: The Poet as Scapegoat of Modernism', in Patricia Coughlan and Alex Davis (eds.), *Modernism and Ireland: The Poetry of the 1930s* (Cork: Cork University Press, 1995)

—— *From Burke to Beckett: Ascendancy, Tradition and Betrayal in Literary History* (Cork: Cork University Press, 1994)

McDonald, Peter, *Mistaken Identities: Poetry and Northern Ireland* (Oxford: Clarendon Press, 1997)

McGuckian, Medbh, and Nuala Ní Dhomhnaill, 'Comhrá, with a Foreword and Afterword by Laura O'Connor', *Southern Review*, 31: 3 (1995)

MacNeice, Louis, *The Poetry of W. B. Yeats*, with a foreword by Richard Ellmann (1941; London: Faber & Faber, 1967)

—— *Selected Literary Criticism*, ed. Alan Heuser (Oxford: Clarendon Press, 1987)

Mahon, Derek, *Journalism: Selected Prose 1970–1995*, ed. Terence Brown (Loughcrew: Gallery Press, 1996)

Muldoon, Paul, 'Sweaney Peregrine', *London Review of Books*, 1 Nov. 1984

—— *The Essential Byron* (New York: The Ecco Press, 1989)

—— (ed.), *Faber Book of Contemporary Irish Poetry* (London: Faber & Faber, 1986)

O'Donoghue, Bernard, *Seamus Heaney and the Language of Poetry* (Hemel Hempstead: Harvester Wheatsheaf, 1994)

Paulin, Tom, *Ireland and the English Crisis* (Newcastle upon Tyne: Bloodaxe, 1984)

— *Writing to the Moment: Selected Critical Essays 1980–1996* (London: Faber & Faber, 1996)

Richtarik, Marilynn J., *Acting between the Lines: The Field Day Theatre Company and Irish Cultural Politics 1980–1984* (Oxford: Clarendon Press, 1994)

Ricks, Christopher, *Beckett's Dying Words* (Oxford: Clarendon Press, 1993)

— *The Force of Poetry* (Oxford: Clarendon Press, 1984)

Sirr, Peter, 'Some Distinction: Padraic Fallon's Athenry', *Eire-Ireland* 20: 3(1985)

Smith, Stan, *The Origins of Modernism: Eliot, Pound, Yeats and the Rhetorics of Renewal* (Hemel Hempstead: Harvester Wheatsheaf, 1994)

Snow, Edward, *A Study of Vermeer*, revised and enlarged edition (Berkeley: University of California Press, 1994)

Steinberg, Leo, *The Sexuality of Christ in Renaissance Art and in Modern Oblivion* (London: Faber & Faber, 1983).

Yates, Frances, *Giordano Bruno and the Hermetic Tradition* (London: Routledge & Kegan Paul, 1964)

Index